Flying Flak Alley

FLYING FLAK ALLEY

*Personal Accounts
of World War II
Bomber Crew Combat*

Alan L. Griggs

McFarland & Company, Inc., Publishers
Jefferson, North Carolina, and London

Grateful acknowledgment is made for permission to quote from the following copyrighted works: *Flight of a Maverick,* by Robert H. Fesmire. Copyright 1995 Eggman Publishing, Inc. By permission of his son, Robert C. Fesmire. *From the Class of 41,* by Thomas M. French. Copyright 2003. By permission of the author/publisher. *One Chance in 37,000,* by R.M. Benson. Copyright 1986 J-Mar Printing. By permission of the author's brother, Bob Benson. *Remembrance of War: The Experiences of a B-29 Pilot in World War II,* by J. Ivan Potts, Jr. Copyright 1995 J. Ivan Potts and Associates, Inc. By permission of the author/publisher. "Splash One Dreamboat," by Arvid Shulenberger, and associated pictures are copyrighted by his son, Eric Shulenberger.

LIBRARY OF CONGRESS CATALOGUING-IN-PUBLICATION DATA

Flying flak alley : personal accounts of World War II bomber crew combat / [edited by] Alan L. Griggs.
p.   cm.
Includes bibliographical references and index.

ISBN 978-0-7864-3707-8
softcover : 50# alkaline paper ∞

1. World War, 1939–1945 — Aerial operations, American.
2. World War, 1939–1945 — Personal narratives, American.
   I. Griggs, Alan L., 1950–
D790.F56   2008   940.54'49730922 — dc22   2008001067

British Library cataloguing data are available

©2008 Alan L. Griggs. All rights reserved

No part of this book may be reproduced or transmitted in any form or by any means, electronic or mechanical, including photocopying or recording, or by any information storage and retrieval system, without permission in writing from the publisher.

On the cover: Flak bursts encountered by US planes over target in the European theater (courtesy John Kolemba); WWII Pilot wings pendant

Manufactured in the United States of America

*McFarland & Company, Inc., Publishers
Box 611, Jefferson, North Carolina 28640
www.mcfarlandpub.com*

In loving memory of Lee Griggs

In history, as in human life, regret does not bring back a lost moment, and a thousand years will not recover something lost in a single hour.
— Stefan Zweig

Hello again, everybody. It's a bee-yooo-tiful day for baseball.
—Harry Caray

The moral tests to which the crew of a bomber were subjected reached the limits of human valour and sacrifice. Here chance was carried to its most extreme and violent degree above all else.

— Winston Churchill

How incredible it is for a man today to look back and say he could load a plane up with gasoline, bombs, and nine other men and then go out and fly a mission, get shot at, come back, and do it again and again and again and again. Somehow we did it and it was amazing.

— B-24 copilot Jim White

I recall what a bomber looked like when it got a direct hit, especially when it was loaded with bombs and the tanks were almost full of gas. What you saw was something that looked like a vapor cloud. No debris. No parachuting airmen. Nothing. The only time we gave it deep thought was when we came back to base and we sat there on our cots for a while and said, "Damn, that didn't happen to me and I'm glad." Was it a risk flying one of those airplanes? You better believe it.

— B-17 waist gunner Leonard Mika

ACKNOWLEDGMENTS

This book represents a labor of love that eventually spanned five years, the death of a child, and quite a few starts and stops. Throughout, I was buoyed by the support of many: the men whose stories comprise this book as well as their wives and families, my friends and family, and practically everyone I told about the effort.

A debt of gratitude is owed to William A. Rooney, a published historian himself, for his expert editing and unfailing support, and to Michael Bess, Chancellor's Professor of History at Vanderbilt, for his sage advice, encouragement, and wonderfully written foreword.

To Wayne Campbell, Winston Evans, Kaye Evans, Tom Ridley (even if he was a top flight fighter pilot), Larry Smith, Yvonne Smith, Jonny Scruggs, Cathy Mumford, David Van Hooser, George Menzel, Samuel Hynes, Eric Shulenberger, Tom Gibson, David Barton, Steve Hall, Ken Tucker, Joe and Margaret McCluney, Ivan Potts, Jr., Barry Cross, Bill Roberts, Ron Russell, Robb Harvey, Dick Gardner, Sandra Harris, LeAnn Polk, Harry Williams, Jr., Steve Horton, Frank Loose, Ed Wyrick: my eternal thanks for your help and encouragement. To all others who know of this book and who offered their best wishes along the way: you will always be very special to me. Thank you.

To the men, their wives, and families who opened their hearts and homes to me, who willingly shared stories they rarely shared with others, even family, and who offered encouragement and hope through this long process: I am humbled by your generosity, your courage, and your sense of duty. All of us — future generations included — owe you much.

And now to my family: Sandra, Elizabeth, and William. We bear the hurt and pain of a tragic loss. Life changed forever on December 7, 2005, yet we survive, endure, and move forward, knowing there are better days ahead. For the many hours when my mind was on the book and not on more important matters at hand, when I was less than an adequate spouse and parent, and for the incredible patience you gave me when it seemed this book would never be completed, my gratefulness is beyond words. I love you more than you can imagine.

Lee, I know you were proud of your dad's book plans and I know you are even prouder today. We love you and will always be thankful for the blessing you were, and are, in our lives.

Table of Contents

Acknowledgments   ix
Foreword by Michael Bess   1
Preface   3

1. Captain R.M. Benson   5
2. Lieutenant Bill Jernigan   10
3. Lieutenant Mandell Cypress   16
4. Lieutenant Charles Jackson   19
5. Captain Beecher Bilbrey   25
6. Sergeant Bob Rourke   30
7. Lieutenant Jim White   34
8. Lieutenant Thomas French   39
9. Sergeant Jim DeMontbreun   44
10. Captain Bush Cole   48
11. Sergeant Leonard Mika   54
12. Captain Bob Gregg   59
13. Lieutenant Harry Williams, Jr.   62
14. Captain Bill Reeder   68
15. Lieutenant Tom Graves   72
16. Captain Bill Becker   77
17. Sergeant David Oldashi   79
18. Lieutenant Roy Buck   82
19. Sergeant Bud Reeder   85
20. Major Clarence Evans   90
21. Sergeant John Katz   99

22.	Lieutenant Bill Rickman	102
23.	Lieutenant John McGonagle	105
24.	Lieutenant Art Driscoll	110
25.	Lieutenant Myron King	114
26.	Lieutenant Don Peterson	120
27.	Captain Al Suedekum	123
28.	Lieutenant John Lechleiter	126
29.	Sergeant Bernard Sanderson	129
30.	Sergeant Charles Whitehead	132
31.	Lieutenant Arvid Shulenberger	136
32.	Sergeant Bill Roberts	142
33.	Lieutenant Bob Smartt	148
34.	Captain J.O. Grizzell	150
35.	Captain Robert Fesmire	153
36.	Sergeant Bill Jones	160
37.	Lieutenant Ben Ernst	162
38.	Captain J. Ivan Potts, Jr.	165
39.	Sergeant Bill Eastland	175
40.	Lieutenant Bob Chambers	180
41.	Lieutenant Jim Kirtland	185
42.	Sergeant John Cunningham	189
43.	Major John Kolemba	192
44.	Major Cooper Schley	200
45.	Lieutenant Jack Downey	206
46.	Sergeant Robert Howell, Jr.	209
47.	Sergeant Robert Sheehan	213
48.	Lieutenant Bob Cartwright	219
49.	Lieutenant Jerry Neal	224
50.	Lieutenant Bob Elliott	226
51.	Lieutenant Eino Latvala	229
52.	Sergeant George Shreeve	233
53.	Lieutenant Mark Osborne	239
54.	Lieutenant W.C. Gibson	244
55.	Major Calvin Fite	248
	Index	253

PREFACE

I am a storyteller, have been for over 30 years since I began my career in journalism. I've learned the power of stories well told, their relationship to all of us, and their resilience over generations. As a student of history, I also know that many stories are lost because little or no effort is made to preserve them. We are poorer for that, I believe.

Bill Roberts and I share a background in journalism, though the ink is still under his fingernails while my work is now what is called "video vapor" after years in television news. Bill served as a gunner, flying the B-24 as part of the 376th Bomb Group, the proud "Liberandos" who flew 451 missions and received three Distinguished Unit Citations during World War II. Then he went back to work as a newspaperman.

I believe it was a conversation with Bill that peaked my interest in a group of gentlemen who meet once a month to break bread, share stories, and renew friendships. They are members of the World War II Bomber Group of Middle Tennessee. While they live in and around Nashville, many are from other parts of the country. They are a wonderful cross section of the young men, many just out of their teens, who flew bombing missions during the war. While age has wrought its inevitable effects, their memories of wartime experiences are vivid.

It is out of admiration for them and their deeds as well as a sense that their stories must be shared that led me to this book. For most of these men, their first trips away from home involved service to their country and overseas combat. What a world it was. Often they were up and out before dawn, drawing missions that lasted up to 10 hours, sometimes longer. Once airborne, they faced a series of hazards that included flak, fighters, bad weather, collisions, and mechanical and human failure.

As civilians, they were largely young men not long out of high school who became wise veterans, seasoned in the unpredictable whims of flying complex, lethal machines in high altitude combat, many not to see their hometowns and families again. Some survived long odds as part of the U.S. strategic bombing campaign over Europe. Others faced certain death if shot down over the jungles and vast stretches of water in the central and south Pacific.

Still others were eyewitnesses to the storm of fire that rained down on Japanese cities near war's end. A few found themselves prisoners of war, when every moment meant an uncertain future.

Then, at war's end, they returned home and resumed their lives, almost as if nothing unusual happened. More than a few didn't tell their stories until decades later. Some didn't share their thoughts until asked by this author. These are their true stories, preserved now for future generations to respect and admire. That is the least we can do to try and ensure that nothing like this happens again.

Alan Griggs • Nashville, Tennessee

Foreword
by Michael Bess

The air war over Europe and Asia during World War II played a major part in securing Allied victory. Nazi Germany was forced to allocate tremendous resources to its air defenses, diverting precious materiel and manpower from its other pressing military needs. Especially after 1943, the steady pummeling from the air also began taking its toll on German industrial output, particularly when the Allies began systematically targeting enemy fuel and transportation resources. The bombers also performed an important political role by giving Roosevelt and Churchill a plausible answer to Stalin's urgent appeals for a second front: The bombers were already taking the war to the Nazi homeland as early as 1941 and 1942, even if the actual invasion of Western Europe would have to wait until 1944.

In the struggle against Japan, the air war proved even more decisive. By the spring of 1945, American bombers had severely damaged sixty-six of Japan's largest cities and had degraded Japan's industrial and transportation infrastructure so severely that a famine was beginning to take place. Japan's capability to wage war effectively was being methodically dismantled.

All this was not without a heavy price. Civilian casualties on the ground in Germany and Japan were very high, and the casualty rates among the bomber crews reached such levels that Allied leaders at several junctures seriously considered calling off the bombing campaign altogether. The odds for airmen gradually improved during 1944 and especially 1945, as the Allies achieved air superiority over their enemies' territories; but until the very end a bomber crewman could not help but know that every sortie was inevitably a rolling of the dice.

This is the backdrop for the magnificent first-hand accounts that Alan Griggs has assembled for this remarkable book. The power of these stories lies in their very straightforwardness: they are plain, unadorned descriptions of what happened, as these men experienced it. One feels as though one is sitting across a kitchen table, listening to these men as they think back across the years, reconstructing what it felt like to be a part of the greatest military conflict in human history. Some of the stories illustrate the mundane aspects of an airman's routine experiences; others narrate events so harrowing or remarkable that they leave the reader speechless, in awe. Either way, we are getting a perspective utterly different from that of most history books, where the focus tends to be on the bird's-eye view, the tides of battles and campaigns, the shifting policies and strategic objectives, the great turning points that shaped the war's course. Here, with these narratives, we come down to the concrete immediacy of a single person's experience. We see the war up close and personal, the way it played out for individual men. Both aspects — this historian's perspective and the participant's perspective — are crucial for understanding the whole.

Perhaps my favorite aspect of these stories lies in the details. Suddenly, across the years, the bomber crewman will remember what his last cup of coffee smelled like on the morning he was shot down, or the color of the horizon, or the shattering of a piece of fruit brought along at high altitude and frozen by the cold at 30,000 feet. It is these tiny, seemingly insignificant details that are unique to these narratives: They have the rich immediacy of first-hand memory, the power of a testimonial from someone who was there.

For a person who has not lived through such a war, it is hard to grasp how these men were able to do what they did. To fly mission after mission, going in through flak and enemy fighters, seeing other planes going down in flames, seeing the empty seat at briefings after their return. And then, the next day, to climb back into their planes and go through the whole thing again. And the day after that, again. This kind of courage, this level of loyalty and commitment to their country's cause, places these men in a special category of honor. They deserve our undying gratitude and respect.

Michael Bess is Chancellor's Professor of History at Vanderbilt University and author of *Choices Under Fire: Moral Dimensions of World War II* (Knopf, 2006).

1

Captain R.M. Benson

DOB: May 16, 1919
Where: Grand Island, Nebraska
Air Force: 8th
Bomb Group: 96th
Squadron: 337th
Station: Snetterton Heath, England
Decorations include: Distinguished Flying Cross, Air Medal with clusters. Royce Benson was drafted into the infantry but transferred to the army air corps after completing basic training. He flew 35 combat missions as a B-17 pilot. His first was on July 4, 1944, to northern France and his last on November 30, 1944, to Merseburg, Germany. After his twenty-fifth mission, Royce was awarded the DFC. Royce became active in the Civil Air Patrol after the war and retired from the National Cash Register Company after 42 years of service.

A Typical Mission

On a typical mission, we would be put on the alert list the night before. This meant we had to get to bed early because we had a busy day coming up. We usually were in bed by 9:00 or 9:30 and in England in June it was still very light outside. It's very hard to go to sleep that early. By the same token, it's just as hard to wake up at 1:30 A.M. for a 2:30 briefing. There were times when we were awakened as early as 11:00.

Getting up at 1:30 A.M. was bad enough but to take a cold shower and shave with cold water was the limit. We found out real soon that if you didn't shave, your oxygen mask would rub your face raw after about eight hours.

The one bright spot on flying a combat mission was breakfast. They served us fresh eggs which were quite a treat after eating powdered eggs. Some ground officers would stay up late at the club just so they could get in on the fresh egg breakfast. We, the flying officers, called all ground officers "paddle feet." I guess because they paddled around on the ground.

During briefing we were given all the information about the target such as where we would start the IP [initial point was the beginning of the bomb run], our altitude, and, of course, the weather. We were assigned the positions we were to fly in the formation. Radio codes were given and what color flares were to be used by our groups to form on. We were taken to the flight line in trucks. The pilot and copilot pre-flighted the aircraft, first by visually checking the outside of the airplane, making sure everything was in its right place and working. Then into the cockpit where, by using our checklist, we would finish the pre-flighting. The other crewmembers would install their .50 caliber machine guns in their mounts.

We would take off and head for our squadron leader who would be shooting flares. Once we had the squadron formed, we would home into the group the same way. All this time we would be flying in circles over England and gaining altitude. Finally, when the Eighth Air Force was assembled, we would head out across the English Channel to France or Germany. Depending on the size and the number of aircraft, this sometimes took as long as three hours. By the time we crossed the Channel, we could hear the new pilots calling in to the group leader. "I'm getting low on fuel and am going to abort." They had used most of their fuel in the main tanks doing all the climbing and circling over England. The group leader would assure them that they had plenty to get to the target. Once we dropped our bombs and headed for home it was downhill all the way. It was very surprising how little fuel it took when losing altitude coming down from 30,000 feet.

Full Flying Gear (Note patches on aircraft, flak holes)

The next eight days we flew four, ten-hour missions. Three of them were to the same target: Munich, Germany, tank factories. Not only did we hit the same target three days in a row, but we flew in at the same time and at the same altitude on all three missions. The Nazis got so they could set their watches by us; they didn't have to change their guns' settings because of our altitude which was the same every day. I didn't understand the air corps planning on this one. The other long mission we flew that week was called "Cadillac #3." We flew down to a valley in southern France and dropped

R. M. Benson (courtesy Bob Benson)

guns and ammunition to the Free French soldiers. We came in at a very low altitude and, after getting the proper signal from the Free French, we dropped our bags of guns and ammunition. It was unusual for us to fly at such a low altitude. We usually were up at about 30,000 feet.

After returning to our home base in England we would be debriefed and then head for the mess hall. After going 12 hours or more without eating we were tired and hungry. The only thing we ever got to eat on a mission was a Ping candy bar. Try eating a frozen candy bar at 30,000 feet with an oxygen mask on. The temperatures at that altitude would sometimes be 45 below zero. At times, some of the crew would bring fresh fruit on a mission. I have seen an orange freeze so hard that when dropped on the floor it would break into hundreds of pieces.

So went a typical mission.

In Between Missions

At certain times we would be stood down, unable to bomb because of bad weather over the target or because of just plain bad weather all over. During these times we would practice formation flying. You would think by now we would know how to fly formation. This practice was mainly for the new and unseasoned crews just over from the States.

One day we were flying a practice mission and with a P-47 pilot flying around the formation so the gunners could track him with their guns. This was considered good practice for the gunners because it prepared them for combat. The pilot of the P-47 decided that we were flying too far apart and he tried to dive between us. He misjudged the distance and tore off the tail gunner's compartment of the B-17 flying just above and ahead of our plane. The section of the compartment came down into my number two engine. I had to feather the prop right away or the vibration would have torn the wing off. The P-47 pilot crashed into the ground and was killed. The tail gunner was more fortunate; at the time of the crash he was up in the bomb bay using the relief tube.

About two weeks later my crew and I were all set to go to London on a 48-hour pass. Just as we were leaving I was called by the squadron commander for some special duty. I was to fly as instructor for a new crew.

We were up about 17,000 feet and I had no idea where we were flying. I had given the pilot his instructions on how and where to fly in the formation. I had settled back in the copilot's seat and was listening to some music on the BBC. I was still burned up that my crew was in London having a good time while I was flying on a stupid training mission.

We were gradually getting into some heavy clouds and the smart thing to do would have been to close the formation in tight. The closer you flew to the lead aircraft the better. Something went wrong. New crews in the formation started to panic. Instead of closing in tight, they started drifting apart. All of a sudden our number three engine started chewing up the tail of the B-17 that was under us. The natural thing for the pilot to do was to pull up which he did only to crash into another B-17 above us.

Things were happening so fast I wasn't sure what to do first. The pilot's eyes were bleeding badly from shattered Plexiglas, so I didn't want him to bail out because he couldn't see where he was landing. The bombardier and navigator had already bailed out and I didn't blame them because half the nose cone was torn off. I finally got the airplane to fly straight and level but we had lost 15,000 feet. The needle on the radio compass kept spinning around. I had to feather both inboard engines and I found out I didn't have any compasses to work with. The only radio I had was VHF and it was not working well.

I asked the radio operator to start sending QDM's (distress signals) back to the base. The base finally picked us up and gave us a heading to fly back. I had to use the magnetic compass which in England is 30 degrees off. If it had not been for the help I received from the radio operator and engineer, I would have never found my way back to the base. When we approached the landing runway, the base had already been cleared and set up for an emergency landing. I brought what was left of that B-17 in very cautiously and landed. When I pulled the column back to level off for the landing, the already partially-sheared cables to the elevators completely broke. I had only one chance for landing and I made it.

We taxied to our parking spot and I came down out of the airplane to survey the damage. I almost fainted. The nose cone was torn off, two engines were feathered, the radio compass was completely sheared off, and there were large holes in the aircraft big enough to crawl through. The base commander met me at the airplane and we went to his office in his jeep.

The first thing he did was to pour me a half a water glass of bourbon. He said I looked like I needed it. I explained what had happened and why I brought the airplane back to the base. I never did tell anyone that the real reason I did not bail out was because I didn't have a parachute on. It was down in the catwalk.

The bombardier broke his leg when he bailed out. The pilot's eyes were not damaged after they cleaned out the Plexiglas. The fate of the other airplanes was not good. The first aircraft that we hit, the tail of which we chewed up, lost all the crew except the pilot, who parachuted to safety. The airplane above us was completely broken in half and no one was able to get out. A total of 19 lives had been lost on one practice mission.

The results of the inquiry into who was to blame for this unfortunate accident were classified. My own opinion was that there were too many people involved to be able to pin the blame on one person.

Not So Typical Missions

On the way home from Magdeburg we were coming down the final approach about 50 feet off the ground when all hell broke loose. The operations tower started shooting red flares at us like it was the fourth of July. Not only were they shooting red flares, but they were also shouting on my radio for me to pull up and go around. Half the people in the tower were jumping off the balcony onto the ground. The cause of all the excitement was the airplane in front of me which had a bomb hung up in the bomb bay. When the plane landed the bomb came loose and slid down the runway. Here we were sitting 50 feet above a bomb that could go off at any minute. I pushed the throttles all the way forward, turned on the super chargers, retracted the landing gear, and prayed in those few seconds, which seemed to last forever, before we could get some altitude and fly away from that runway.

We found out later from the bomb dispersal crew that the safety propeller on the bomb had only two turns to go before that bomb became armed. We had good reason to be frightened.

A couple of days later we were to bomb another airport in France. We went in on the bomb run about 20,000 feet and, just as we approached the target, there was a loud bang in the cockpit. We thought we might have taken a direct hit because it made so much noise. It turned out that a small piece of flak about one and a half inches long had come through the floor and hit the inverter under my seat. For the size of the flak, it made quite a large hole in the floorboards. I hate to think of what it would have done to me if it hadn't been for the inverter. On our way home after we let down from high altitude the engineer came down from his gun turret and picked up the piece of flak. His remark was, "My God, Lieutenant, it's got your initial on it!" Sure enough, after examining it, we found the letter "B" on it. I just wished the German gunners weren't so personal with me.

We flew another ground support mission next. Those in charge decided that we were not carrying enough bombs in the bomb bay, so they rigged up some gadgets to enable us to carry two more 250-pounders, one under each wing.

Just as I was turning onto the takeoff runway, I blew a front tire. It sounded as if we had dropped one of the bombs from under the wing. I called the tower and asked for instructions. We were told to remove our guns and equipment and they would send a truck out for us. We were then taken to the spare airplane. All this took about one hour's time and I had serious doubts of our ever catching up with the formation.

Fortunately for us, they neglected to install bombs under the wings on the spare aircraft. Not only did we catch up with the formation, but all day I had to keep throttling back to avoid overrunning the lead aircraft. It's amazing how much drag you get on an airplane with two bombs hanging under the wings.

On the 25th of August, we started on a mission to southern Germany. It was a small town near Munich. We reached the IP when I lost two engines; one was hit by flak and the other just plain overheated. We had to feather both engines and I knew we couldn't keep up with the formation on two engines. We dropped our bombs in some vacant field to lighten the load. We were 60 miles from Switzerland and 300 from England. I asked the crew to take a vote on what they wanted to do but they had to decide in a hurry because we could not maintain altitude. All of them decided to try to make it back to England rather than go to Switzerland and be interned for the duration of the war.

My navigator gave me a heading of 308 degrees and we headed back toward our home base. We had a disabled B-24 flying ahead of us about five miles and every time we would see flak we would move to the right or left away from it.

We reached the English Channel and I made an SOS call to the Coast Guard. They maintained boats and crews to help aircraft that had to ditch in the Channel. By coaxing the one engine that had been overheating, I was able to get a little power out of it. I got enough so that we could make it to the English coast.

Even though we had flown for nine hours and thirty minutes, we were told that because we did not get to the target we would not get credit for a mission. The maintenance crews finally checked out the engines on our airplane. They found all four engines completely burned out. With this report we got credit for the mission. They replaced all four engines and we flew only one mission without our favorite airplane. We were glad to have her back and we named her *Sassy Susy*. My wife suggested the name and the crew went along with it.

My crew considered themselves very lucky to go 35 missions and not one of us ever got a scratch. I don't think it was all luck because I had an excellent crew who knew how to work together. It was a great responsibility for me as a pilot to fly in combat but without the help of the crewmembers working together I don't think we would have been so successful.

2

LIEUTENANT BILL JERNIGAN

DOB: August 11, 1921
Where: Nashville, Tennessee
Air Force: 13th
Bomb Group: 307th
Squadron: 414th
Station: Morotai
Decorations include: Air Medal with clusters. Bill flew 37 combat missions as a B-24 pilot, averaging 10 hours a mission. His longest mission was to Borneo: 14 hours round-trip. After leaving active service in 1945 Bill joined the air force reserve and was recalled to active duty in 1950. He flew C-119s out of Japan on supply missions to Korea. From 1962 to 1965 Bill was stationed on Okinawa, where he flew C-130s on supply missions to South Vietnam. He retired in 1970 as a lieutenant colonel after having served in the air force for 28 years.

Training Days

I wanted to be a marine. In fact, I attempted to enlist in the Corps with some close boyhood friends but was unable to pass the physical due to flat feet. I then talked with army air corps recruiters and filled out an application. During my physical exam, I squeezed my toes up enough to form an arch. Since the doctor was at my back, he didn't notice the squeezed toes and my flat feet or I would have been physically disqualified.

Many of us who signed up with the army air corps waited several weeks or months to be called to active duty as there were not enough airfields, airplanes, and instructors to start training. I signed up in September 1942. It wasn't until February 1943 that I received orders to board a train for basic military training at Miami Beach. For many on the train it was their first time away from home and a few cried like babies all the way to Florida.

The old sergeants were there to teach us how to keep the barracks clean, uniforms ready for inspection, how to march, shoot a rifle and a pistol, march and march, and obey the sergeants' verbal commands. We were just another bunch of buck privates that needed to be

Bill Jernigan, kneeling, center (courtesy Bill Jernigan)

shaped up. The drilling was nearly continuous: from dawn to dusk we were kept busy. We ate and collapsed in bunks only to wake up at revelry and begin again. We continued to march and learn about soldiering. Then, after about four weeks, some of us were shipped to Middle Tennessee State Teachers College and others to colleges all over the country for five months of classes, testing, and ground school training. After the college training, I was sent to the classification center in Nashville for more testing, general knowledge, graph and chart reading skills, principles of mechanics, reading maps and photographs, speed and accuracy of perception, and understanding of technical information. Other tests included motor coordination, steadiness under pressure, and ability to react quickly to constantly changing events.

The eye testing was critical: color perception, distance vision, near vision accommodation, and depth perception. Some 20 percent of the recruits failed depth perception tests and were washed out of pilot training. My parents received a form letter advising them that I had been selected for pilot training and outlining the program I would be going through. The last paragraph read, "A pilot occupies a position that requires sound judgment, a keen and alert mind and body in the flying of an airplane. It is imperative that the men who fly our military aircraft possess these qualifications, for upon their skills will depend in large measure the success of our war effort."

After classification, I was assigned to pre-flight training school at Maxwell Field, Alabama, to study Morse code, chemical warfare, aircraft and ship identification as well as the use of gas masks. We marched in formation to classes, mess hall, physical training, and the daily retreats.

The physical training and academic studies were tough. Many fellows washed out. Next, I was assigned to Orangeburg, South Carolina, for primary flight training in a PT-17 Stearman. It had two open cockpits with the student in front and the instructor, a civilian pilot, in the back. We wore goggles and leather helmets.

After primary training, it was on to Shaw Field, Sumter, South Carolina, for basic training in a BT-13, closed cockpit, two-seater. The training was more rigid than primary and the washout rate was high. After basic we moved on to Turner Field, Albany, Georgia, for advanced training.

After graduation and receiving my wings, I was assigned to Harlingen Field, Texas, for B-24 bomber training. The B-24 was a four-engine bomber with twin tails and a nose wheel. Armed with ten, .50 caliber machine guns, it could carry a major load of bombs. The B-24 was built like a Mack truck, big and cumbersome. It had an aluminum skin so thin that you could cut it with a knife. The plane was capable of carrying a heavy load far and fast but it had no refinements. Steering it was difficult and exhausting because there was no power except the pilot's muscles. Above 10,000 feet, breathing was possible by wearing an oxygen mask. There was no heat despite temperatures at 20,000 feet as low as 30 degrees below zero. The wind blew through the plane like fury, especially from the waist gunners' windows and when the bomb bay doors were open. There were no bathrooms so to urinate there were two small relief tubes, one forward and one aft but at high altitude they would freeze. Defecating could be done only in a receptacle lined with a wax bag and then the bags were dropped out of the waist windows or through the open bomb bay doors. To move forward and aft required walking through the bomb bay over an eight-inch wide catwalk beside the bombs. The seats were not padded, incapable of reclining, and were crammed into a very small space. Absolutely nothing was done to make it comfortable for the pilots or the other crewmembers.

Our final stage of training involved our actual combat crew. This took place at March Field, Riverside, California. During that time a very close friend of mine was taking off in front of me. He was an instructor pilot on a simulated bombing mission. All I saw was a ball of fire when his plane exploded. I had to fly right by him and then force myself to concentrate on the mission at hand.

The B-24 existed and was flown for one purpose: to carry 500 to 2,000-pound bombs and drop them over enemy targets. There were over 18,000 B-24s made, more than any other airplane built. It was not operational before World War II and not operational after the war, as far as the U.S. was concerned. The B-24 did not win the war but I do not believe the war could have been won without it.

Through training and into combat, the pilots and crews of the B-24s came from every state. They were young, fit, and eager. Some had good educations, including college, while others were just out of high school. They were all volunteers. Most were poor. If they were lucky enough to have a job they earned a dollar a day, sometimes less. Most had never been out of their home states nor up in an airplane but all wanted to fly. In fact, most of us had never heard of Pearl Harbor and did not know its location.

From San Francisco to Morotai

A stop on the way to my assigned base was Tarawa. I remember seeing newsreels at movies about the marine landing at Tarawa and the bloody fighting there. Many LST's and other vessels were sunk in the shallow waters. Tarawa was a scene of devastation with a small chapel surrounded by thousands of marine graves, many of them marked "unknown." We really didn't know what to expect when we got there, never having been in combat. It was shocking to us.

The entire island had been fortified with coconut tree logs and with pillboxes and gun positions hidden along the beach fortifications. There were two large pillboxes with large guns and portholes for firing from within. The walls were 10 feet thick reinforced concrete half buried in the coral sand. I was told that one of the pillboxes had been knocked out by a single tank using a flamethrower. Our ships with their heavy guns did no damage to these pillboxes. There were shoes with feet still in them, human skulls along the water's edge, and stumps where trees had been. The stench was awful even after several weeks. Tarawa was a horrible sight I will never forget. The tremendous loss of life there was a tragic mistake. It had no strategic value at all to the war effort. It was the result of egotistical navy admirals who defied General MacArthur, the Supreme Pacific Commander.

From Tarawa, we flew on a C-46 to Guadalcanal. There was much more destruction there: LST's rusting in the water, palm trees blown away, big concrete blockhouses the Japs had occupied. The marines burned them out with flamethrowers. We could see the burned areas where the Japs had stuck their guns out. A U.S. battleship had hit the blockhouses with big shells, causing very little damage. At one end of the island, army engineers used bulldozers to push up all the Jap remains — guns, tanks, and other war refuse — into large piles. It was an unbelievable sight. The next leg was to Nadzab, New Guinea, then on to Morotai.

The island of Morotai was where I was based for most of my missions. We had a wide, coral runway of about 10,000 feet. The strip farther south was just over a small knoll and used primarily as a fighter strip although we occasionally had to use it in emergencies. I've read that today they are all grown over. I would have enjoyed going back but haven't had the chance. When I was stationed on Okinawa I took a trip down to the area and I thought about flying over the island. I was flying a C-130 but I figured all I would see would be jungle.

Just across the Morotai Strait is the top of Halmahera Island, a long island extending southwest toward the equator. All this area was known as the Dutch East Indies. Somewhere up around Daruba was an infantry detachment that patrolled the perimeter to keep back what we thought might be some 20,000 Japs. Occasionally one or two would cross the perimeter among some native work crews because they were desperate for food. Once in a great while one would creep in at night and cut the throat of some sleeping GI but I only heard of a couple doing that. There were virtually no natives on the island because they could hardly make a living. Some drifted in from nearby islands.

After putting up our tents near the ocean's edge we had to dig our foxholes in the hard, coral sand. We couldn't go down very far so we used sand bags and pieces of coconut trees to build up shelters. They were used night after night since the Jap bombers rarely appeared during the day. Before dark we had to inspect our foxholes to make sure there were no land crabs or coral snakes in them. I often found land crabs in mine.

We were right in the middle of some tall coconut trees. I didn't know of anyone getting hit by one but we could certainly hear the coconuts bouncing off the tents. We would crack them open and drink the milk. That's what most crews would do when they reached the base. The coconut was hard to get into but the men would drink the milk and eat the meat. It was always too rich for them so few bothered with more of them during their time there. The other thing I remember about Morotai is that I would swim almost every day. The coral would tear your feet up if you weren't careful. The water was a beautiful blue, full of many beautiful fish with different colors. I was in a tropical paradise except for the war.

To keep me company and to have some fun, I had a little brown monkey named Cheetah. I had landed on another island with just two engines one time and had to stay there several days until maintenance folks were brought in to repair my plane. In the meantime, the guys stationed on this island had picked up a few things and we traded with each other. I was given this monkey. He was friendly with everybody and he kind of looked at me like I was his mother. While I wrote letters he would come in and nuzzle his head under my arm. He was a real joy to me. Cheetah stayed on a little platform attached to a nearby coconut tree but I would let him off at times because he was pretty good at keeping the lizards out of our tent. He would spot them pretty quickly and feast on them. During our missions Cheetah stayed on his platform and waited for our return. I had a little leash to keep him in place but guys were always coming by and turning him loose. They gave him chewing gum and he kept it in a little pouch in his mouth. When they turned him loose he made a beeline for me in the tent.

I was only one of two pilots in our outfit that could fly our C-47 so we would go to Australia to pick up fruits and vegetables and eggs and other staples. One time I took Cheetah with me and word got around that I had a monkey aboard the plane. The authorities came and took him for quarantine purposes while I was gone. I really don't remember saying goodbye to him. I was very upset about it but there was nothing I could do since the law was the law there. The authorities promised me they would let me have him back but they wouldn't release him.

Our "Jungle Air Force" was a wild group. We were never based in or near cities and had to survive in jungles. Prior to the recapture of the Philippines, our Morotai base was the most westerly-advanced Allied air base stationed in the Southwest Pacific.

Rough as Cobs Was Us

In the old, lumbering B-24 I really felt safe. That was a good thing since I flew 37 missions averaging ten hours per mission often over water. During each mission briefing, besides being informed of our primary, secondary, and tertiary targets, we were informed of various islands along the route that might be safe in the event of ditching or bailout. This included information about whether the natives were friendly, the number of Jap military thought to be there as well as the locations of Jap fighter bases, and whether we were likely to encounter the fighters (which we frequently did).

We were also informed of the amount of flak we could anticipate. Along with this, we were told of known Jap shipping and naval units en route. Fuel permitting, we had permission to strafe two-masted schooners and larger ships.

We concentrated on targets in the southern and central Philippines along with targets in Borneo. A primary target was the oil refineries at Balikpapan, on the east coast of Borneo. The trip to Balikpapan was a very long mission for us — about 14 hours — and always we were greeted with terrible anti aircraft fire and fighter planes. We had to fly right into it so it wasn't unusual to have lots of holes in the ship upon our return to base.

En route from one mission I determined that we had an extra 30 minutes of fuel so I decided to strafe some Jap shipping in a nearby harbor, even though my gunners were very poor marksmen. I thought it would be good practice for them. We made a pass and I told them to commence firing. The nose gunner, with two, .50 caliber guns, fired first then the belly turret to be followed at leveling out by the waist and then the tail gunner. Upon commencing to climb out of the strafing run the only tracers I could see from the cockpit were nowhere close to the target. After two passes with a goodly amount of machine gun fire from the ships I told the nose gunner to start firing on command and not to move the gun. I would aim by controlling the plane's nose. We were successful in setting several ships on fire. I realized that I didn't have the best shooters on board. I don't know what it was; maybe they never did learn like they should have. They were trying their best but they never had much luck. I talked with them about this problem and they weren't defensive. They really couldn't argue with me. The nose gunner was having a terrible time hitting anything but I remember on that strafing run watching the Japs jump off their boats. We had a lot of fun on that one.

Another B-24 also elected to strafe the same harbor in a pattern with us. He ended up having just a little too much fun by staying later than we did. As a result they ran out of fuel and had to bail out 60 miles south of Sidate. They identified their position and we tried to find them the next day with a search mission. We spotted some rafts but no signs of the crew: 10 guys, all gone. The pilot was not a hot shot, just a young, innocent guy trying to do his best but when you are going down and coming back up the plane uses lots of fuel. Some pilots were better at economizing their fuel than others and knew that you could lean the engines out until they almost stopped. I'm sure he knew how but he just used some bad judgment. He was the only one I knew who ever had to bail out because of lack of fuel but plenty of times crews would have their engines on cross flow. They would be running very low on fuel, so low in fact that their engines would be sputtering while coming back in.

On a mission over Brunei we had an engine hit by anti-aircraft fire and had to shut it down. Knowing we didn't have enough fuel to make it back to Morotai and since we had no knowledge of a safe landing zone, it was apparent we would have to bail out or attempt a beach landing on some small island. I had the radio operator contact Morotai headquarters and inform them of my decision. All of the islands were known to be occupied by the Japs but we had selected one which was believed to have only a few Jap soldiers on it. Fortunately, we received a message back in about 30 minutes with information about an airstrip in the southwest Philippines on Sangi Island. The strip had recently been taken by Philippine Moros, a fierce tribe of warriors who had killed and beheaded all the Japs because a bounty was offered by the U.S. for all Jap heads. A small group of U.S. soldiers had been there a few days before we arrived and we lived with them until another B-24 came in and took us back to Morotai. I still have a couple of crude knives that I got by trading with the Moros.

A crew piloted by a close friend bailed out of a B-24 called *Woody Woodpecker* over the Togian Islands after the plane had been severely damaged by Jap fighters. All 11 men landed safely though widely spread out. Six were rescued the next day by a Navy PBY Catalina but other rescue attempts, including ground patrols over the next several days, failed to locate the remaining five. Rescue efforts were called off after it was learned that after gathering at Tobili Village the missing men were betrayed to the Japs, taken elsewhere, and never seen again. After that, I led five B-24s on a bombing raid of Tobili Village. We completely wiped it out with bombs and machine guns. We also skip-bombed nearby caves that the Japs were known to inhabit. It's still amazing to think about how we got information out of those islands.

The 307th Bomb Group was the longest flying, hardest hitting bomber outfit in the world, the most traveled heavies in any theater. We gave the Japs hell and made the "Tokyo Rose" radio program on many occasions with our actions.

I had some near misses in many places during a lengthy military career spanning three wars and I've often wondered what allowed me to survive. Did God have something special in mind for me to perform? If indeed He did, then I often wondered, have I accomplished it?

3

LIEUTENANT MANDELL CYPRESS

DOB: April 30, 1918
Where: Tuscaloosa, Alabama
Air Force: 7th
Bomb Group: 307th
Station: Oahu
Decorations include: Air Medal with clusters. Originating in Hawaii and using intermediate staging areas such as Midway Island, the 307th conducted some of the first bombing missions against Japanese strongholds in the central Pacific. As a bombardier aboard a B-24, Mandell flew over 400 hours of combat missions over vast stretches of water into the middle of Japanese forces during late 1942. Once the war ended, he became a successful real estate developer. He loved to fish and even managed his own boat.

Stars, Gooney Birds, and Condoms

I graduated from Hume-Fogg High School in Nashville, Tennessee, just one year behind a young lady who would soon entertain the world with her beautiful voice, Dinah Shore. While in bombardier training at Victorville, California, stars were always coming through to entertain the troops. Dinah was part of one show so I went up to her, introduced myself, and asked her to dance. She seemed happy to see me and was very gracious. That was quite a thrill for me, especially since we never saw any girls at Victorville.

We had to do KP while there, peeling potatoes and the like. One of the guys stationed with us would always sing. I suppose he did so to pass the time and take his mind off the pile of potatoes before him. We didn't think he was particularly good but he did have a deep voice. A lot of folks disagreed with our amateur assessment. His name was Ernie Ford, "Tennessee" Ernie Ford. He and I enjoyed talking about our times back in Tennessee. As it happened, Roy Rogers had a ranch near Victorville. He and Ernie developed a friendship and Roy helped him with his career.

After graduation at Victorville, the Bank of America offered to loan every new officer $250 with the understanding that we would pay back $25 a month. Most of us took it and went to Los Angeles for a good time. I remember going to the Florentine Gardens and drinking quite a bit. There was a wonderful Follies show there with singing, dancing, and chorus girls. We quickly found out that with our new silver wings women would flock to us. We had no problem finding them.

During combat crew training near Boise, Idaho, I was part of a group sent to the Mayo Clinic to test improvements in fliers' oxygen mask systems. The oxygen mask used at the beginning of the war was called a constant flow mask. Anywhere above 10,000 feet fliers had to use the mask. The diaphragm mask was perfected later. When a flier inhaled, it allowed the oxygen in and when exhaling the mask closed. They put us in a tank and lowered the amount of oxygen. Then we had to write our name. The less oxygen we received, the crazier we would write.

In the PX's on the Pacific islands, we had three things: shoe polish, razor blades, and condoms. We didn't need any of them. There wasn't any place to take women even if we

Mandell Cypress (courtesy David Cypress)

had a chance. Along the beaches we would take mattress covers and wet them then take them out and try to do some very amateurish surfing. What a combination we had on those islands — a beautiful moon, the brightest of stars, a continuous, warm tropical breeze, and the bombs.

Some of Midway Island's most famous and pervasive residents were the gooney birds. They would always hatch at a certain time of the year but that didn't stop all the navy men from betting when the first gooney bird would hatch. They had a pool going and the stakes got pretty high. They would do anything for a little entertainment.

While Europe was getting most of the attention from our government and the public, we were flying lots of missions in the Pacific and losing lots of fliers. Most of our group didn't make it back home. That was because we didn't have much of a chance if we had to bail out. If we were lucky enough to get on a raft, no one knew how long we would be stuck on it and there was no guarantee we would be picked up by our own forces. If we were unfortunate enough to fall into the enemy's hands, let's just say that life, however short it might be, would be very difficult.

Wake Island

Right after Pearl Harbor, a buddy and I were some of the first to the recruiting depot. We were put on a train, given two sandwiches and an apple, and sent to Maxwell Field at Montgomery, Alabama. In January 1942, everyone wanted to be a pilot but everything depended on the results from a series of tests. In my case, I ended up at Victorville, California, in bombardier school. We were supposed to be there six months but we were rushed into deployment.

To the Pacific I went, assigned to the 307th Bomb Group, 7th Air Force. When I got to Oahu and saw all the destruction — the ships and the hangers — I was in awe. Here I was a little boy from Nashville and I was at a location that just a few months previous had held the attention of the world. This was all new to me; I couldn't believe that I was over there, especially with such little training. We all lived with the feeling that the Japs could return, that they were just around the corner. I guess I was too dumb or too young but I really wasn't frightened.

We flew search and destroy missions every other day out of Oahu for 700 miles or so, thinking we would find the enemy at any time but encountering only more water. Before long, though, we saw our share of action when we were sent farther out to different islands to bomb the Japs.

Wake Island is almost 1,200 miles from Oahu. Shortly before Christmas 1942, our ship was one of 26 B-24s that flew to Midway and refueled with the mission of attacking enemy-occupied Wake Island. Midway hadn't been in our hands very long and the runways were still rough but we made it out of there. Altogether we carried 10, 500-pound general purpose bombs over some of the most boring scenery that can be imagined: water, nothing but water. Our navigator was relatively green but he did a great job of getting us to target. Our attack took the Japanese by surprise, which meant less resistance. All we had to do was drop our bombs on some part of the island because all those islands were so small that supplies, ammo, and machines were stored all over the place. After unloading our bombs, we came back to strafe their runways.

We made it out and flew back to Midway where everyone was happy about what we had done. We felt like we had hit the Japs a good lick. Our mission was first among the air attacks on enemy bases in the central Pacific. I suppose because of that Admiral Nimitz decorated us all. Considering that we didn't have much experience, it was a wonder we did what we did.

Another mission took us out of Oahu to a refueling point at Canton Island and then on to hit Naru, the location of an important phosphate plant. We were greeted by intense anti-aircraft fire and fighter opposition. We came back to Funafuti that night and before we could get settled the Japs returned the favor. Bombing our small airfield, they tore up our planes and seemingly hit something with every bomb they dropped. I was in my tent at the time and barely had a chance to hit the latrine ditch before the bombs fell. The whole island was a supply point with lots of ammo and fuel. Quite a few folks were wounded and most of our planes were damaged. The next day we took the crews of the undamaged planes and went over to Tarawa to hit the Japs once again so that they wouldn't return to Funafuti. Then it was back to Canton for fuel and our return to Oahu. You really have no idea how bad our communications were back then. We had to keep radio silence most places and because of that we really didn't know what was happening on the other islands.

With all our missions in those early days of the war, the weather was just as much as challenge as anything else. Most of the time we conducted hit and run missions from about 5,000 feet because the targets were so small and the weather terrible. There were tropical rains all the time.

Looking back, I wonder now why other people got it and I didn't. I flew over 400 hours of combat and I certainly experienced the sadness of losing friends. It's hard to explain your feelings when you return from a mission and know that you're not going to see your friend again.

4

LIEUTENANT CHARLES JACKSON

DOB: February 9, 1920
Where: Nashville, Tennessee
Air Force: 10th
Bomb Group: 12th
Squadron: 82nd
Station: Feni, India
Decorations include : Distinguished Flying Cross (2), Air Medal with clusters. Charles earned his first DFC for missions over enemy-held Burma. His second came on May 26, 1945, when, despite monsoon conditions, he participated in an attack on a headquarters of the Japanese high command. In all, he flew 63 combat missions as the pilot of a B-25 medium bomber. After the war Charles worked in the electrical supply business for 40 years and pursued his love of golf.

Bananas Solved My Problem

My father was a wealthy man in the late 1920s so for a few years my family enjoyed the luxury of chauffeurs, maids, and nurses. My parents had five children in six years and I'm happy to say that we were a close family. But the Depression ended all of that. My father lost his business and all of his money and, for a time, my four sisters were placed in an orphanage and I went to live with a neighbor. My mother enrolled in secretarial school and went to work to hold the family together.

My father was a Texaco gasoline distributor and when Texaco brought an airplane to Nashville I flew in it. After that I knew I wanted to be in aviation in some way. I graduated from high school in 1938 and went into the electrical supply business. Shortly after the war started, in January 1942, I got my draft notice. I told my mother that the government would put me in the infantry if I wasn't careful so I wrote on my draft notice, "joined the air corps." The next morning when I joined the air corps I was in for a surprise. When I went for my physical, I was told I was too light, too skinny. They told me they couldn't use me. "Well," I thought, "I'll fix that." So I went home and the next morning I ate five or six bananas. I stuffed myself then I went back down to the Air Corps office and weighed again. This time I passed and they signed me up. I was 22 years old.

I got to see and experience many things during my years in the service. During basic training at Bakersfield, California, a student washed out. One morning after that this student goes out and gets into an airplane, a BT-13, takes off and calls the tower. He asks for the major and when the major answers the student tells him to watch him fly. He flew the airplane through the field's hanger, going in the front and coming out the back. Then he took the plane up to a thousand feet and plunged it straight down in the ground, killing himself. I was in the barracks listening to the whole episode and then heard the crash.

During primary training we had a group of Chinese pilots with us. They had grown up in the Chinese countryside. Most American boys growing up had bicycles, skates, and tricycles and had a pretty good idea what the rate of closure was; in other words, how to judge the distance between you and a stationary object. These Chinese boys never had any kind of informal training like that. They could not learn the rate of closure. As a result, they would take off and fly but when they got on the ground they would run into the wall. They had no sense of how fast the airplanes were going. Most of them washed out.

We left West Palm Beach, Florida, not knowing where overseas we were going. Following orders, we opened our envelope after one hour in flight and found out we were to take a course due south. Our destination was Calcutta, India. Eventually, I was assigned to the 10th Air Force, 12th Bomb Group, 82nd Squadron.

As we were flying over Africa on our way to India, I looked on the map and there was a lake about 50 miles north of our course, Lake Chad. I told the navigator that I had read about this place in *National Geographic* and I knew there were a whole bunch of animals there. So I left our three-plane formation and sure enough we were soon flying over thousands of zebras and antelopes and even giraffes, all kinds of animals. I got down on the deck and chased the animals around before heading to our scheduled stop of Khartoum. It was a lot of fun doing that but when we landed one of the other pilots chewed me out, saying he thought we had gone down. He said we should have let him know we were going to divert from our route but we were under radio silence. I'll always remember the beautiful, magnificent sight of all those animals running free. The crew had a good time that day.

Our final destination was Feni, India. We flew all our missions over Burma, crossing the Himalayas from Mandalay down to Rangoon and hitting cities, depots, trains, refineries, bridges, and other targets. Our missions were low level and involved both bombing and strafing.

Charles Jackson (courtesy Charles Jackson)

A bridge, wooden or not, was often an inviting target for low-level B-25 missions in the China-Burma-India Theater (courtesy Charles Jackson).

On our strafing runs I would start out at about one thousand feet, locate the target, fire tracers to lock on to the target, then hit the cannon button and fire the 75mm cannon located in the plane's nose. We couldn't fire the cannon more than three times on any run since the airplane would slow down by 15 miles per hour every time it was used. I loved the B-25. It was a very stable, easy airplane to fly. It could take a lot of punishment.

Some days we would fly two or three missions. On one mission, we flew over a schoolhouse. I didn't see it but one of the gunners said there was someone down there shooting at us. I went back to the base, told my commanding officer about it, and he suggested loading up some bombs and going back to do away with whoever was causing us problems. So we put four, 500-pound bombs aboard and went back. Sure enough, we were still taking fire from the schoolhouse. I flew down and dropped a bomb and missed it. Then I flew out, turned around and came back, dropping a second bomb and missed again. I did this four times and never hit that schoolhouse. I really didn't know what I was doing. I had some bomb training but not much.

I flew a plane called *Sunday Punch* six or seven times. It had a Tennessee connection because workers at the Oak Ridge Gaseous Diffusion Plant, called K-25, donated their Sunday overtime pay to buy one Mitchell medium bomber, B-25-J-27-NC. *Sunday Punch* got its name because the workers would report to their jobs but would not punch the clock. After the war, the workers invited me over to Oak Ridge to meet them and to be interviewed.

On some days we didn't fly so we went deer hunting and, on at least one day, tiger hunting. We knew there were a lot of tigers in the area where we were based. One day a friend

Top: B-25 pilot Charles Jackson standing in front of *Sunday Punch*. Workers at the Oak Ridge, Tennessee Gaseous Diffusion Plant donated their Sunday overtime pay to purchase the bomber (courtesy Charles Jackson). *Bottom:* The North American B-25 Mitchell medium bomber was used with devastating effectiveness for strafing and bombing missions (courtesy Charles Jackson).

and I got into a jeep and went looking for a tiger. We spotted one about one hundred yards away and shot it using an M-1 carbine. I still have its skin on the wall at home.

I was awarded two Distinguished Flying Crosses for my efforts. One was for reaching the 50-mission level. The other was for bringing a damaged plane back to base and landing it on one wheel. The gear had been shot out by anti-aircraft fire.

I've always felt that everything I did overseas, except being shot at in combat, was a marvelous adventure.

Gabriel

On January 7, 1942, I joined the United States army air corps and eventually was assigned to the 305th Bomb Group. Colonel Curtis LeMay was the commanding officer. I went to aerial gunnery school at a small desert town called Las Vegas and was assigned to a B-17 crew as a tail gunner. Weeks before the 305th departed for England the air corps asked for volunteers for glider pilot training. I entered the program and trained in Minnesota and New Mexico for a year. But because of a surplus of glider pilot trainees the glider program was suspended

Ground crew members get a rare chance to relax. Pilots will tell you they were only borrowing their ships for missions. The "owners" on a day-to-day basis were the crew chiefs (courtesy Charles Jackson).

and the remaining students were transferred into the air corp's regular aviation cadet program. I have always believed that if I had remained in the 305th as a tail gunner I would not have survived the war. The 305th suffered tremendous casualties during those early days of daylight bombing over Germany. Similarly, very high casualties were the fate of many glider pilots who were primarily deployed behind enemy lines in Normandy on D-Day.

Gabe is my guardian angel. Gabriel to those who call him by his formal name. I know he exists. Let me tell you why. One night during cadet training I was flying a Vultee BT-13 trainer at Bakersfield, California, when Gabriel appeared. BT-13s had a red light on the front of the wing. A few miles from our aerial training area was a tall radio tower with a red light on top. As an inexperienced pilot, the light in the sky appeared to me to be another BT-13 flying straight toward me. I pushed the stick forward, putting the plane into a dive to get out of "his" way. The tower saw me dive and instructed me to "Pull up! Pull up!" I responded immediately but came perilously close to the ground. After I landed, we pulled tree branches out of my plane's landing gear.

After I became a B-25 pilot we flew to Ascension Island, a small dot of land in the Atlantic Ocean, on our way overseas. The distance from Natal, Brazil, to Ascension Island nearly covers the maximum range of a B-25. On the day of our flight we encountered a persistent and strong wind from our right side. As a result, we missed the island by nearly a hundred miles. My navigator and I both agreed the island must have been on our right as we began to search for it. In just a few minutes the island appeared and we lined up our approach. In those days, the runway on Ascension Island sloped upward at a 15-degree grade. We landed without incident, glad to be on the ground after the many hours over water and having missed the island on our first try. As we taxied up the runway, the left engine kicked out — no gas. Gabriel had been watching again.

Our missions typically involved flying over the southern Hump (called the Chin Hills) in formation. Because of the buildup of cumulous nimbus clouds over the mountains we would have to fly back individually, each plane picking its course through the building afternoon thunderstorms. We were returning from a mission when we found ourselves landing amidst a flock of turkey vultures. One of the big birds hit the leading edge of our wing, missing the windshield and disaster by only a few feet. Gabe was working overtime for me.

I'm awfully lucky to be here. I just think about the 63 combat missions I flew and I'm just a great believer that God took care of me. I don't know why, but I believe that. Maybe it was because I never went on a mission without praying before, during, and after.

5

Captain Beecher Bilbrey

DOB: June 20, 1924
Where: Nashville, Tennessee
Air Force: 12th
Bomb Group: 320th
Squadron: 444th
Stationed: Dijon, France
Decorations include: Distinguished Flying Cross, Air Medal with clusters. Beecher served over 30 years in the army air corps, the air force, and the air force reserve, attaining the rank of lieutenant colonel before retiring in 1973. He flew the Martin B-26 on 33 combat missions during World War II and the F-84 fighter jet in England during the Korean War. As a civilian, Beecher worked in the wholesale drug business and then handled commercial real estate.

The Flying Prostitute

All my life I wanted to be in the air corps and fly. When I was young I made a collection of model planes. One day, years later, my young son took them and flew them across the room. That was the end of my collection.

My career in aviation got off to a very interesting start while in training at Greenville, Mississippi. I had an instructor, a short guy who hated tall people. He made life hell for me. I was scared of this guy and scared of what might happen to my short career. Well, he got in the backseat one day and we took off in a BT-13A. All of a sudden I heard his sweet voice call out, "Mr. Bilbrey, you've forgotten one thing. You son of a bitch, you didn't put your safety belt on!" He proceeded to jerk the joystick back and forth from his position in the back and beat my legs almost black and blue with it. The plane was swaying to and fro during this whole time. I have to admit that I came awfully close to resigning and going to gunnery school but my wife talked me out of that one.

A day or two later I went to the commandant of cadets and respectfully asked for a change of instructors. That was one of the major mistakes in my life. The commandant told

Beecher Bilbrey, second from left (courtesy Beecher Bilbrey)

me, "Yes, sir, Mr. Bilbrey, we'll take care of that. You report to your new instructor in the morning." Guess who they gave me? My old instructor's roommate. I got to count all the rivets in the left wing of another BT-13A. I had to walk around the entire field in a rainstorm with a parachute on my back. The washout train was steaming down the track. Then, miracle of all miracles, bad weather came along and we couldn't fly and somehow they forgot about me. They didn't wash me out. By then, I had learned how to respond to questions.

I graduated and got my wings on May 23, 1944, at George Field, Illinois. Before graduation, I sneaked around to find out where those of us who were moving on were going to be sent. We were ticketed to be copilots for heavy bombers. I didn't want that. Those long missions were not for me. Soon, though, our squadron was approached for volunteers to fly B-26s. Thirty of us stepped forward and my career took a different direction. The B-26 had a bad reputation at the time. It was known as the flying prostitute (no visible means of support). But that didn't make any difference with me. Just so long as I didn't have to go to B-17s or B-24s. I didn't like cold weather or long missions. I really didn't know anything about the B-26 other than its reputation and that it was a twin-engine plane. I was 20 years old at the time.

At Barksdale Field, Louisiana, I trained as a B-26 copilot and discovered that the Marauder, as it was called, was a great airplane. I still feel that way. It was fast, carried heavy armament, and a crew of six. You just didn't want to have a single engine on takeoff. After you got her in the air, the plane would take all kinds of punishment. But she had the gliding characteristics of a rock. On landing, we would come in at a severe angle and, just before crashing, haul back on the stick. It was an easy plane to fly once you got used to it.

I flew most of my missions as a copilot. Before takeoff, I would inspect the plane, making sure all safety pins were pulled. In the cockpit, I would read the checklist and the pilot would respond. Once the engines were started, I would check the gauges and look around us while taxiing. On takeoff the pilot had his hands full so I would wait for him to tell me to raise the landing gear with a thumbs up signal and then I would milk the flaps up. Our usual flying formation was in boxes of three, 12 to a box. Most of our missions were in the three to four hour range with the longest being about five hours. We usually started our bomb runs at 12,000 feet and dropped our four thousand pounds of bombs around 10,000 feet.

We would go up every morning and blow up bridges and the Germans would repair them overnight. Flying over, through, and around the Brenner Pass was always tough. If I had had a choice, I would have chosen to fly three missions over Germany rather than one mission through the Pass. The Germans had placed their accurate anti-aircraft guns halfway up the mountains and we were fat targets for them. We faced flak and, at least through the first of February 1945, we endured some nasty fighter opposition, mainly from Me 109s. Those guys would hit us either before or after our bomb runs, coming at us head on, from the rear, or doing a pursuit curve so that they would end up on our tail. In our briefings when they told us to expect jet opposition I thought I was in the middle of some Buck Rogers fantasy. Sure enough, we encountered some Me 262s. They would make head-on attacks and be through our formation before we could do anything about them. I can still see the red flashes coming from the guns of one jet. He was going after our wingman, not us, and got him.

I was never scared during all this time. I guess I was too dumb, too green, and too young. I thought I was bullet proof, thinking that the other guy's going to get it, not me.

I got to Alto airfield, Corsica, in October 1944. When I checked in, I told the sergeant that I wanted to get my bed and all the stuff that went with it. He said, "Yes, sir, lieutenant. Your tent is over there. Here's a hammer and some nails, now you can go build your bed." I was able to scrounge up some chicken wire to use for springs. As soon as we learned a crew was lost we made a beeline for that tent to get whatever the poor guys had — candy, booze, cots, blankets — and anything else that might ease our life. Nothing personal was taken. It sounds ghoulish but those people were either dead or POW's so they weren't going to need that stuff.

I viewed everything happening in my life at the time as an adventure. I was too green and too young to think otherwise.

A Pilot in the Infantry

After the invasion of France, my bomb group, the 320th, moved to Dijon, France. I discovered my new home would be the Chateau de Bessey. We made a club out of the first floor. Our living quarters were on the third floor, four to a room. Living in the chateau wasn't as fancy as you might think.

I didn't make many friends because you might go out on a mission and never see them again. My pilot for most of the missions, Tyler Wilson, was from Chattanooga. He had been a B-26 instructor which was good for me because he didn't spend much time telling me about the plane. We got along fine. One mission I was flying with a pilot named Johnson. I was doing my usual thing as a copilot — checking gauges and watching for action around us. Just before the bomb run Johnson froze and started to shake and moan. I had to take over the plane and finish the bomb run. After that, he got okay and took the controls back. He simply cracked up for an instant. I decided not to report him. How did I know that it wouldn't be me the next time? I didn't fly with Johnson again. If I had been scheduled to fly with him later I would have told them I was sick. I wasn't interested in flying with someone who might go to pieces on a bomb run.

We were enduring the worst winter Europe had seen in centuries. We didn't fly a mission from January 6 to the 19. To pass the time, a bunch of us got together to play poker. One day I was sitting in a poker game and drinking some fine French champagne out of a bottle like you would Coca-Cola. It was cheap and plentiful. Suddenly the adjutant entered, bellowing, "We need two volunteers to go the front with the infantry." Seemed that General Eisenhower had tired of the infantry and air corps fighting in the rear so he decided the thing to do was to "allow" the air corps to experience some of the infantry and the infantry to experience the air corps. The adjutant looked around at the officers in the room. Neither seeing nor hearing any volunteers the predictable happened. As a 2nd lieutenant I was outranked by the others, so he proclaimed, "Bilbrey, you're volunteered. Get your gear together and get on the truck in the morning at 0500."

The next morning bright and early I got on the truck, a six by six, and was taken up close to the front. We stopped at corps headquarters and proceeded to the basement of the building to get some sleep. Every now and then German artillery would lob some shells our way. After awakening, I was put on another truck and taken to the front. I had the choice of joining the 14th Armored Division or the 101st Airborne. I didn't want to end up in one of those cold tanks since the temperature was below zero so I said I would go to the 101st. The "Screaming Eagles" had just returned to the line after rest camp following their incredible experience at Bastogne. I found myself with the airborne boys in the village of Schweighausen on the Moder River. It was more like a big creek than a river.

I checked in and found out that the Germans were just across the Moder. They were peeping at us and we were peeping at them. I saw a bunch of dead Americans littering a nearby plaza. Their bodies had been untouched for a while. I asked a captain why somebody didn't remove them. "Are you kidding? They're all booby trapped." Across the river, there was a plaza and a group of buildings housing the Germans. I kidded the captain about not having any action. He said, "You want action? I'll show you action." He grabbed a field phone and called back to a mortar unit. Soon, mortar shells were lobbed over our heads and landed behind the buildings on the other side. I heard the Germans screaming. It wasn't long before they returned our fire. One shell blew up a wall near me. I had seen enough of combat but more was to come.

I slipped out of the building I was in and carefully made my way through a garden and into a nearby street. Unfortunately, some German gunner with a *Schmeisser* was having what he considered fun, shooting at anything that moved in my vicinity. That's when I found myself in a gutter with bullets whizzing by me. I tried to dig a hole in the cobblestone street. I had a chance to catch a ride with a jeep parked around the corner but the driver wasn't about to pick me up. I got the hell out of there the best way I could and soon ended up with another infantry outfit in a small village. They were housed in a barn. Before long, I heard a .50 caliber go off several times. Shortly afterward a G.I. with a southern drawl came in and said, "Lieutenant, we got a problem." "What is it, son?" a nearby infantry officer responded. "That German cow ended up between our lines and we had to shoot it." The lieutenant said, "That's a damn shame but you know what to do." So we had steak for dinner.

5. Captain Beecher Bilbrey

I spent about 11 days at the front going from one place to another. Along the way, I was issued a new M-1 with bayonet and two hand grenades which I hung on my flying suit. I also had my own .45 pistol with me. I never had to use any of them. During my time there I certainly ran into some interesting people. One was a P-47 pilot, a forward air controller. He was sent up close to the front with a jeep and a radio to call in fighters when needed. He told me about the time he made a run over a German village and about how he let go with his guns blazing down the middle of a main street just as people were coming out of church. "Baby buggies were going everywhere," he said. Personally, I was disgusted with the guy. I wasn't into that kind of thing. He was off his rocker.

I spent the night somewhere near the line and was taken to see a lieutenant colonel. He answered our knock on the door and invited us in. He reached under his cot and took out a jug of Schnapps. This old boy was about 50 years old and looked his age. Even though it was only 8 A.M., he was already drinking. I turned down the opportunity to do the same.

On my way back to my squadron, we took a captain out of the 14th Armored and let him fly a couple of missions with us. We put him in the nose on one mission to Heidelberg. It wasn't long before he was ready to get back to his unit.

6

SERGEANT BOB ROURKE

DOB: December 24, 1924
Where: New Orleans, Louisiana
Air Force: 15th
Bomb Group: 484th
Squadron: 826th
Station: Cerignola, Italy
Decorations include: Air Medal with clusters. After going down on his first mission and being rescued by Yugoslav partisans, Bob completed 35 combat missions as a B-24 radio operator/waist gunner. Once the war ended he returned to his native New Orleans, attended Tulane University, and worked in sales before joining a temporary employment agency.

A First Mission to Remember

I was 18 when drafted in August 1943. New Orleans was my home and I had hardly ever been away from there. I was employed by the American Telephone and Telegraph Company which earlier had asked me to agree to a 90-day deferment because of the importance of my job. Soon after being drafted I was assigned to the U.S. Air Corps at Keesler Field, Biloxi, Mississippi.

I knew a little about communications, having worked for the phone company. In fact, I was pretty good at Morse code. Part of my job involved operating different kinds of electronic equipment including teletypewriters.

Having lived in New Orleans, I had never seen snow until I was sent to radio school at Sioux Falls, South Dakota. We played in it like a bunch of kids. I also learned everything about radio communications. My time there was a lot easier than others'. They had to learn Morse code and, to pass, had to receive and interpret at least nine words a minute. It was very tough for most of them including a big old country boy from Wyoming who later became that state's governor, Stan Hathaway.

I didn't tell anyone I already knew how to receive Morse code at a rate of 22 words per minute. Some friends thought I was a genius. To be honest, I didn't operate a radio once

6. Sergeant Bob Rourke

Bob Rourke, kneeling, second from left (courtesy Bob Rourke)

during my time in B-24s. We were flying a deputy lead plane. It was our plane that radioed the "bombs away" report. I was really a radioman-gunner. Before a mission I usually got in the plane and checked the radio equipment but most of my time was spent in the left waist of a B-24 operating a .50 caliber machine gun.

The B-24 Liberator was a big, ugly bomber that I had a tough time getting used to. I would normally get air sick flying around in that thing while smelling the oil and gas and then, of course, I'd have to clean up the whole mess. But I stuck it out and overcame that problem. I'm glad I did because I had some very interesting experiences.

Nothing topped what happened on my very first mission in October 1944. We were part of the 15th Air Force, 282nd Squadron, 484th Bomb Group stationed at Cerignola, Italy. Five times we took to the air for our first combat mission but had to turn back because of weather or some other reason. We didn't get credit for any of those tries which didn't make us feel very good. Besides being a little nervous, we wanted to finish our tour of 35 missions and get back home. At the very least we wanted to get one mission under our belts.

The sixth time we tried turned out to be a real story in itself. Sure, we were nervous and anxious about flying over heavily defended targets and facing a certain wall of flak. We were awakened at 4 A.M. this day, had breakfast and a briefing, then hauled out to our plane. Vienna, Austria, was our primary target, a city usually protected by heavy anti-aircraft fire. On this mission, we turned away from our primary target, climbed to 28,000 feet, and proceeded to our secondary target. That's when the "fun" began.

We lost the number one engine due to engine fatigue. Then we lost the number two engine. By now we were lagging behind the rest of the formation. The pilot, Jim Kennedy from Corning, New York, called for us to jettison any excess equipment fast. So we threw what we could get out — guns, ammo — anything with weight. We also jettisoned the bombs. Where they landed, I don't know. This went on for a while and during that time we were still losing altitude. Kennedy ordered us to bail out, although he thought we were too low. It was bail or face a crash landing. A couple of guys up front near the pilot did jump. Tom Slattery, the top turret gunner, broke his back after jumping and ended up in a Yugoslav hospital.

The rest of us were scared to death, hoping everything would turn out okay. I remember that we were listening on the intercom when Kennedy told us we were going to crash land. On my very first mission! The terrain looked much like the Smoky Mountains but somehow Kennedy found an open field that might just accommodate our needs. We prepared for the crash the best way we could by following the proper crash procedure. We sat down and pulled our knees up to our chests, the next guy getting in front and doing the same thing, leaning on my knees. I tried to get some additional back support because I knew we were in for a bumpy ride. During a time like that, I found myself wondering whether the plane would topple over or even explode. We still were carrying quite a bit of fuel. Kennedy brought the ship in for a belly landing that seemed like an eternity with all the loud scraping and violent jolts our bodies absorbed but the landing probably lasted no more than 20 or 30 seconds. When we hit, everything moved forward. Stuff came loose and flew around. I had a half step supporting my back and without it I feel my back would have been broken. The pilot did a beautiful job of bringing our plane in.

I undid my heavy clothing and we all jumped out of the right waist window, an opening that was about six by four feet. Lonnie Cooper, our nose gunner from Vance, Alabama, was pinned in the crash by the top turret that had broken away. He cracked both ankles while pulling his feet out of his laced GI shoes. Still wearing our fleece-lined clothing, we immediately started running, thinking the plane was about to explode. It was then I remember looking in the distance and seeing a bunch of soldiers running toward us wearing hats with red stars. They were Tito's partisans, our allies in Yugoslavia. We were trained to hold up our arms in surrender and say "*Amerikanski!*" Little girls, women, and men seemed to suddenly appear around us like they had sprung from the ground. They came running up and shook our hands while pointing dramatically and yelling, "*Boche! Boche!*" meaning the Germans or the German allies, the Chetniks, were nearby. We didn't have time to destroy the plane. We had to get out of there fast or else face execution if captured by the enemy.

We started walking to a farmhouse with our rescuers showing us the way. Around this time they offered us goat's milk with black bread. I never thought I would drink goat's milk but I welcomed it then. We slept on the floor of the house and the next day began a three-day hike through the mountains to another safe house. There, we were met by an army captain officially assigned to the corps of engineers but who, in this capacity, worked with the OSS. His assistant was a navy radioman. This house was actually an old farmhouse in which the animals slept downstairs and we slept upstairs in one big room heated by a little, pot-bellied stove while using our parachutes as cover. Every morning a Yugoslav started a fire in the stove and at the same time picked up a hot coal to light his cigarette. Two peasant girls swept the dirt floor of our modest accommodation with tree branches.

Only one time during our stay did we really have a scare. The Germans fired a few mortar rounds which fell in our valley but no one was hurt. Early one morning I had to get up and go to the outdoor privy. I startled the captain so much that he pulled a German Luger on me. After that, I woke him up when I needed to answer nature's call. A 12-year-old girl also pulled guard duty around the house. She would challenge me at times until she got used to seeing me. The captain, who was from Virginia, stayed pretty busy during the day communicating over the shortwave radio, coordinating supply drops, and dealing with other secret matters such as troop movements. Our planes would fly over and drop tons of supplies in the valley — food, guns, ammo, and cigarettes. People would come out of nowhere, grab the stuff, and take off. It was impressive to watch.

We stayed 30 days at that house primarily because it snowed so much a rescue plane couldn't land. The navy radioman had been in touch with our base at Bari, Italy, to let them know of our whereabouts. Despite that, all of our parents and families had received telegrams telling them only that we were missing in action. Unfortunately, the telegram to my mother arrived on the anniversary of my dad's death.

One day we woke up to hear the captain tell us to get ready because the rescue plane was coming. We said our goodbyes, gave the folks there what we could, and thanked everyone. Because we were so confined, I think all of us were getting on each other's nerves by then. We couldn't even walk very far from the house to get fresh air. The DC-4 landed on a nearby farm field packed down with snow. The pilot never stopped his engines but simply landed, turned around, and quickly loaded us aboard. We were flown back to Bari where we were deloused with DDT, given new uniforms, and interrogated by intelligence. We discovered that another crew had reported seeing us receive a direct hit and that all of us were lost. Thank goodness that didn't happen. Eventually, our crash was chalked up to engine fatigue. We weren't hit at all.

I was just 19 at the time and so was Kennedy, the pilot. I believe the oldest member of our crew was 23. After a short rest back at our base, we were returned to action and participated in many bombing missions over Germany, northern Italy, and Yugoslavia. I particularly remember the missions over Dresden, Germany, and how severe the damage was there.

Most of the crew completed 30 plus missions before the German surrender. I completed a total of 35 missions due to extra flights with other crews. I operated a radio designed to jam German anti-aircraft. I was overseas only nine months but all this had been a real adventure for such a young guy.

7

Lieutenant Jim White

DOB: September 11, 1919
Where: Elmhurst, New York
Air Force: 15th
Bomb Group: 376th
Squadron: 514th
Station: San Pancrazio, Italy
Decorations include: Distinguished Flying Cross, Air Medal with clusters. Credited with 47 combat missions, Jim was awarded the DFC for nursing his B-24 back to a friendly base after losing two engines on a mission to an oil refinery at Vienna. Jim was trained as a fighter pilot so he was not in love with copiloting the B-24, something he felt was akin to flying a boxcar. Prior to the war, Jim was a CPA and taught at Fordham. Once the war ended he worked in finance for the Detroit *Times* and Cowles Communications. Later, he was director of finance for Newspaper Printing Corporation.

Budapest and the Brenner Pass

I wound up in Italy with the 15th Air Force and I'll never forget my first mission. I didn't want to talk about it for a long time and now it comes back to me. Talking is easier these days. The target was Budapest. Plenty of flak met us as well as Me 109s and Fw 190s. The group that I was flying with lost two planes on that mission and I saw one of them go down with the wing and two engines separated from the plane and no chutes go out. Another plane went down, spiraling down smoking. Five chutes came out and we reported that. That was a tough mission and I thought, "Lord, I'll never make it through 50 of these." Somehow I did.

How incredible it is for a man today to look back and say he could load a plane up with gasoline, bombs, and nine other men and then go out and fly a mission, get shot at, come back, and do it again and again and again and again.

One of our missions involved flying to Aviso Viaduct, a railroad viaduct near the Brenner Pass. I was copilot on this day. The pilot I was flying with was an excellent pilot — A.W.

Johnson. We went in lower than normal, at about 20 thousand feet. That meant there were only about 10 to 12 thousand feet between us and the anti-aircraft guns positioned on the surrounding mountains. We had some faulty information on where the flak was and our IP turned out to be right in the middle of a flak battery. We got the hell knocked out of us; the plane received over 200 holes in it. We made it back to the base thanks to our flight engineer, Ernie McWilliams, who had to go back into the bomb bay and repair some rudder cables that had come loose.

Ernie received the Distinguished Flying Cross for his actions, as did Johnson for getting our ship back. Johnson built a reputation for being able to bring ships back. I wanted badly to get my own crew so between missions I would slow time engines, breaking in new engines. I was still flying copilot on our B-24 at the time. Eventually, I was assigned to replace a new pilot that had gone down. Clyde Armstrong was killed and I got his crew.

I have to say that I didn't especially like flying the B-24. It was like flying a boxcar. You really had to muscle it. I wanted to be a fighter pilot but didn't make the grade. Bombers were certainly not as much fun as fighters. The only time you really flew a bomber was on take off and landing. The rest of the time was in formation.

Jim White (courtesy Tom White)

We went back to the Aviso Viaduct two more times but they weren't like our first mission because we had better information about where the flak was located.

A Close Call Over Vienna

My most memorable mission was to the Moosbierbaum oil refinery at Vienna, Austria. I had gone to Vienna five times, a target that was a double credit for the 15th Air Force so one sortie counted as two missions. The last time I went there, as I turned on the IP, I lost an engine. It vibrated excessively and I couldn't feather it so it ran away and put quite a drag on the plane. I couldn't keep up with the rest of the formation. I salvoed my bombs short of the target then latched on to another flight and stayed with them a little while but couldn't keep up with them. I finally got behind them and joined up with another cripple.

At that point, there were two cripples flying together but I couldn't even keep up with him for very long. Then, in trying to get over the Alps while maintaining air speed and altitude, I lost another engine. There was just too much pull on that thing but at least I could feather it. Unfortunately, both engines were on the same side. Number one went out first, then number two. The B-24 kept turning and, being a small guy, I had trouble reaching the rudder pedal. I had to lean back and put my shoulders on back of my seat and put both of my feet on one rudder. I couldn't see over the instrument panel so the copilot and navigator had to direct me as I flew the plane.

I was thinking about ditching in the Adriatic Sea and mentally reviewing ditching procedures all while trying to make it back as close as possible to our base at San Pancrazio. As we gradually descended, we threw all the guns and ammo overboard along with the oxygen equipment and flak suits. This went on for maybe a half hour to 45 minutes. Finally, we made it to an island called Vis off Yugoslavia. The landing strip was very close to the waterfront. Kids would fish tin cans out of the Adriatic, pound them flat, and then make stars out of them and paint them red. I believe the area is now part of Croatia.

We landed on an abandoned Italian fighter strip that had been prepared for emergency landings. I was the last one out of the plane, very happy to be on solid ground. The Yugoslav partisans pinned a red star on me, the symbol of their army, as recognition that I was a part of them. A British sergeant was in charge of the area. He had radio contact with the mainland and kept us all informed. He told us, "Tonight you do not go out because the Red partisans are going to go crazy. It's November 6, the eve of the Russian Revolution." We stayed indoors in the basement of a stone house, sharing a ten-gallon jug of wine while listening to the shooting going on. They were making a hell of a noise.

A C-47 arrived two days later and took us to a hospital in Rome. In all, 11 of us made it, including a photographer on board. I received the Distinguished Flying Cross for bringing crew and plane back in one piece. I flew three or four more missions before concluding my overseas service. I didn't get the Purple Heart, was never a POW, and I had no nightmares when I got home. I was very, very lucky.

Mission Notes

1. On 14 July, 1944, the 47th Wing dispatched 110 B-24s with an escort of 53 P-38s. Our target was the Budapest, Hungary, Ferencvaros marshalling yard. One hundred three of the bombers reached the target and dropped 262.5 tons of bombs. We also dropped 100 packages of leaflets in the target area. The target was obscured by smoke but the majority of the bombs were seen to drop in the target area, causing two large explosions, one large fire, and two small fires among tank cars.

Seventy-five to 100 Me 109s, Me 110s, Me 210s, Ju 88s, and Fw 190s were seen but only 30 to 40 of them pressed the attack. Two B-24s and five P-38s were lost. Eight Me 109s made two passes at us but missed. They hit another ship in our flight and set the #2 engine on fire. He started down and we saw six chutes. The escort knocked down five of the Me 109s. Over the target our electrical system went out and we received four holes in the fuselage. Another ship blew up over the target and disappeared with no chutes seen. The tail gunner of the ship ahead of us kept firing bursts over our heads at the enemy fighters.

2. On 15 July, 165 B-17s and 138 B-24s with 109 P-51s for escort were sent out to bomb the Romana Americana Oil Refinery at Ploesti, Rumania. Direct hits on the target caused huge fires and a large column of smoke rising 25,000 feet could be seen for 200 miles. Eight of fifteen Me 109s attacked the bombers while 30 Me 109s engaged seven of the escorting P-51s. We lost seven B-24s, one B-17, and one P-51.

We lost one supercharger about thirty minutes before the target and could not maintain our position in the formation. Shortly before turning at the IP the navigators salvoed the bombs through the bomb bay doors when he accidentally threw the wrong handle while testing the bomb bay doors. We lost another supercharger at the same time and turned on an intersection course to meet the formation. We missed them and returned to base alone.

Over Nis, Yugoslavia we were surprised at 16,500 feet by intense, accurate, and aimed flak. We rallied abruptly and got three or four scattered hits in the waist and tail. Guilinger received a cut over his left eye when the kick-out pressure forced the bomb salvo handle into the neutral position. This was the only injury any crewmember received except for Ostlin's frostbite.

9. On 31 July the 47th Wing dispatched 54 B-24s and 65 P-51s as escort to bomb oil storage tanks at Targoviste, Rumania. Our bombs hit to the right of the target. En route to the target we encountered moderate, accurate heavy flak that holed #1 gas tank, pierced the flight deck in several places, and holed the bomb bays, tail, and wings. *Flame McGoon*, the group's famous ship, received a direct shell burst. All four engines cut out and the ship went into a spin. When last seen at 10,000 feet no chutes had come out. Johnson and I had to use the one oxygen system by crossing the filler line and regular line because his system was shot out by a piece of flak that cut the line about eight inches from his knee. Another piece of flak came up between my rudder pedals, passed between my knees and went out through the top of the ship.

15. On 15 August 96 B-17s and 299 B-24s took off between the hours of 0200 and 0340, accomplishing the first heavy bomber mass night take off in Fifteenth Air Force history. The targets were the beaches in the Toulon-Cannes area and the occasion was the invasion of southern France. Two B-24s and no fighters were lost.

Our target was the beach area of the Gulf of St. Tropez but we returned the bombs to the base. Bombs couldn't be dropped after 0730 hours because of the invading troops. One flak position was firing and we saw P-38s dive on the gun position and silence it. In the air there were more planes of all descriptions than we had ever seen before and more than we have seen since. We saw every type of surface vessel in large numbers. Battleships and cruisers shelled gun positions on the shore and we saw explosions and repercussions rising thousands of feet in the air.

A ship behind us on take off flew back into the ground and exploded, killing all personnel. We observed at least five other such occurrences en route to the target. The exploding planes caused huge fires that lighted the night sky and filled our cockpit with light. Some of them blazed fiery paths a mile in length along the ground.

22. On 10 September 201 B-24s were dispatched with an escort of 61 P-38s to bomb the south ordnance depot and southeast industrial area of Vienna, Austria. The bombs of the 376th Group fell approximately 1,000 yards northeast of the target when they were dropped by PFF. The flak was intense, accurate, and heavy but no enemy aircraft were seen. Twelve B-24s and 2 P-38s were lost.

We received double mission credit for this mission. Ship #25 had an unexploded shell go right through the star in the left wing. A ship ahead of us had the right wing and numbers three and four engines shot off. Both parts of the plane spun down. Only two chutes were seen. Another ship went into a low, slow spiral and ten chutes came out. This was the most flak we had seen so far.

33. On 2 November we were flying #72 in the #5 position of the C box and carried eight, five hundred-pounders. The entire group turned back because of the weather. After a flight of three and one half hours we came in and landed. Number 73, flown by Lieutenants Cornay and Jones, landed behind us. Unknown to them they had a flat left main tire. They pulled off the runway into a ditch and the nose gear collapsed. The plane plowed into the ground and exploded. Debris and bodies were thrown hundreds of feet into the air. The explosion caught us in the side of the ship and caused severe pressure on our ship and bodies. A gun barrel landed in front of the plane. A bomb landed unexploded in the 515th squadron area. All personnel were killed. We received no mission credit.

37. Our bombs overshot the target, a railroad bridge in the Brenner Pass. We caught scant, inaccurate, heavy to intense, accurate, heavy flak four times from 1150 to 1210 hours. We saw flak bursting in red, white, and black puffs. We saw no enemy aircraft. A piece of flak came in through the astrodome, went through Guilinger's map, and on through the radio compass indicator in the nose by Guilinger's head. The glass sprinkled all over him but he was uninjured. We also had a hit in the life raft and twelve other holes throughout the plane. We saw #34 receive a hit in the bomb bay and go down burning. The pilot described over the radio how he was losing control and would have to abandon the plane. Then his bombs exploded and the ship disappeared. We saw no chutes.

8

LIEUTENANT THOMAS FRENCH

DOB: September 15, 1923
Where: Haskell, Texas
Air Force: 13th
Bomb Group: 307th
Squadron: 272nd
Station: Guadalcanal and Admiralty Islands
Decorations include: Distinguished Flying Cross, Air Medal with clusters. On June 15, 1944, Tom responded to the urging of a friend and volunteered to fly as co-pilot on perhaps the most exciting mission of the 42 he flew in the southwest Pacific. A 20mm shell blew out his windshield and instruments but Tom and his crew caught the enemy by surprise, sinking two ships and strafing an air base. Upon returning home, Tom graduated from Baylor University law school and began his career as an attorney before entering mortgage banking. He is a former national president of the Mortgage Bankers Association of America.

Snooper Mission Surprises

After the gut-wrenching mission attacking the main remaining Japanese fleet, we began a series of raids/missions on the central Philippines in an effort to assist our ground forces who were engaging in grim battles taking back the Philippine Islands, one by one. While these missions were certainly not "milk runs," (as easy missions were referred to), mostly we were hitting airfields and fuel concentrations as well as harbor installations. On some of these missions, we actually had some U.S. fighter protection from bases newly won over from the Japanese. For the *first* time (for us, at least), the power of U.S. forces was clearly greater than that of the entrenched enemy.

However, on December 15, 1944, something quite different happened. My friend John Poggi, who I had gone all the way through cadets with, had become the first pilot of his crew because his first pilot had been killed. He and the remaining officers lived in the tent next to us. On the 14th, Poggi (everybody went by his last name), who had no copilot, asked me if

I would fly a mission with him. He knew that I was one mission behind my crew. I said sure, without even knowing where we were going, hoping for a "milk run." We were all in for a rude surprise. This was easily the toughest mission ever!

We were to fly a single plane snooper mission to Jesselton, Borneo, which was near the northwest corner of Borneo, to see if this small town and harbor was being used as a staging area to send oil and gasoline to Japanese forces in the Philippines. Our mission was to enter the small harbor at low altitude, sink any shipping we found, and report back. The trip to the target took over six hours, but was uneventful with no Japanese interception. We certainly surprised the Japanese when we roared in at 200 feet.

John Poggi and his crew had been a lead crew and they were topnotch. We were ready with bomb bay doors open and guns manned, beginning with our first pass. This was a very busy harbor, with a number of oil freighters being loaded from rail cars parked at harbor side. Our bombardier hit one of the SDs (Sugar Dogs) on the first and again on the second pass. All gun positions were firing. As we pulled up from our first pass over the harbor, we came out over a Japanese fighter base that we didn't even know was there. After dropping four, 500 lb. bombs on the ships, the surprise was over. We were more than a thousand miles from base, and as a single, relatively slow heavy bomber, we had taken on a heavily defended harbor, railhead, and air base loaded with fighters — all by ourselves.

John Poggi was no better pilot than TMF (me), but he had always been much wilder. Did we make our discovery and immediately make a run for it? Hell, no! With Poggi, we took them on, in spades. Flying over the air base the first time we realized that their fighters were taxiing out to take off at the far end of the field. We also realized that if they got airborne we had no chance to get away. They were at least 100 mph faster than we were, so Poggi suggested, and I agreed, that we must pull up and go around and come back down the runway, downwind, at ground level, to see if our machine guns could immobilize their planes before they could take off. I remember seeing their landing gears collapse and the planes skidding out of control. The anti-aircraft guys at the base, and everywhere, were firing at us and we were firing back. We sustained many small hits but made it through, that time. Our gunners silenced one AA position with accurate fire. The bombardier was screaming for another harbor pass so he could try and sink another ship.

We wheeled around, ran down the harbor wharf, and dropped all our remaining bombs. We got some more direct hits on small ships. But that pass was one too many. The defenders were ready for us this time. We sustained heavy damage, particularly

Thomas French (courtesy Thomas French)

right in front of the copilot's position, fifteen inches from me. The minute we pulled up and got the bombs away, we knew we were hit bad. The hydraulic system was knocked out. All the engine instruments on the right side were gone. We had a two-foot hole right in from my windshield and hydraulic fluid all over the cockpit. With both pilots on the controls, we nursed the plane up to about 1,000 feet. It seemed like it was going to keep flying — at least for a while.

What to do next? We figured we had about five to ten minutes before the Japs cleared their runway and got other fighters in the air. The obvious route to our base was angling out to sea, away from the north coast of Borneo, where other fighter bases were located. But on that line at sea, the Jap fighters (knowing our base) were sure to find us. We didn't want to go down at sea with nobody to report to or to help. What other choices did we have? High mountains ran parallel to the coast and appeared impenetrable. We would never be able to get over them with the plane barely airborne. Then too, we had been told not to go down in the jungles of Borneo. The natives were said to be pro-Japanese and cannibals, to boot.

We had a conference on the flight deck and, with the navigator's help, came to a quick decision. Instead of going the obvious route out to sea, we decided to stay very low. We flew directly toward the mountains in the hope that the Japanese would not think we would ever even consider such a course. We HOPED we could find a pass, get through the mountains, fly and hide on the far side (if we made it), and finally turn toward our base.

Our airplane held together, we found a pass, and, even in our stricken condition, finally made it home. None of us really thought we would be able to overcome all the obstacles but somehow we did. Nobody was hit, though I got a little shrapnel scratch. Everybody kidded me, saying I ought to apply for a Purple Heart. I did not, of course.

As required, we sent a radio (still working) report to base telling what we had found. When we finally got the old bird on the ground, we had the whole group (307th) waiting for us. That week we had gotten a new commanding officer, Colonel Hinton. Hinton debriefed us himself. Everybody was very excited about our report and the fact that we had made it back to base, especially Colonel Hinton, who was new to combat. Colonel Hinton decided that he would fly another single plane mission the next day so he could see for himself and, presumably, become a hero. Sadly he did go, taking a blue chip crew with him. The Japanese, of course, were on alert and presumably shot him down. We never knew what happened.

The whole Poggi crew was recommended for decorations. Poggi received the Silver Star and I got the DFC. Because the medals were not actually awarded until much later, I'm not sure what the other crewmembers received. I hope the DFC at least, as it took all of us to pull it off.

I don't see how we made it through all the perils and dangers we faced, 42 times, and lived through them. Partly, we made it because of the skill of the crew. Partly it was just plain luck and partly, I believe, because the Lord had more for us to do. From that day forward, I have always thought that my remaining years were given to me in trust, and that I damn well should use them, not just to benefit me, but for all who looked to me for support and leadership. Though I have little to brag about, given the opportunities that came my way, and given a wonderful wife and loving children, I have tried hard to be worthy and responsible.

Even at 20, I was a dedicated patriot. I *never* for a minute thought that a great injustice was done because I was asked to serve my country and fight for her cause. The peril was on our "watch"— not some past patriot or future hero.

Sink the Yamato!

The B-24 had four engines—1250 HP each—radial design and twin tail. The 24 was not as handsome as the famous B-17, but it was strong and it had the first "Davis" wing that housed most of our precious gasoline. We flew at about 150 mph, sometimes a little faster or slower, but basically that was it. How fast you actually moved over the surface depended on the air mass movements, but since we had to go both ways, it evened itself out.

About our important missions, I remember:

- the long hours
- the massive size of the refineries
- the Japanese fighter and flak defense
- the clouds that forced us to attack alone
- that we did have some U.S. fighters on the scene helping us, including supposedly Charles Lindbergh, who was clandestinely actually flying the mission in a fighter
- that our squadron operations officer was shot down, was able to bail out, and landed on top of a U.S. sub that picked him up. Sadly, I think he was the only crewmember who was shot down that we ever got back.

The 307th suddenly got word to search the central Philippine waters to see if we could find and attack a major Japanese fleet. No one in the then 307th had ever seen a Japanese fleet, much less attacked one. We had no armor piercing bombs designed for attacking ships but we were going anyway. Our briefing was a joke. No one knew what to tell us to do if we found the enemy fleet. We did get one radar-equipped airplane (very primitive) to help us search. The novice operator kept having us close on small groups of islands. The effect was frustration and concern. It was critical that this naval armada be found! The extensive search vectors had seriously eroded our fuel supply for the journey home. Formation flying (the whole group, 24 airplanes) consumed much more fuel than single flight and we were, of necessity, in formation.

Our crew was leading the 372nd Squadron and right after Qualls, our navigator, and Mimms, our engineer, advised that it was essential that we start back to base, the radar plane advised that it had another sighting. The group leader decided that we would run down this last lead and if also false, we all break formation and head home. But the radar images soon turned into a massive fleet, led by the *Yamato*—the largest battleship in the world—with 18-inch rifles! So our squadrons were ordered to attack the battleships by squadron and we drew the *Yamato*! Some luck. In all, the Japanese armada included three battleships, four heavy cruisers and five destroyers, which immediately went into wild defensive gyrations and began to throw up massive color-coded anti-aircraft fire.

We circled, identified the *Yamato* (you couldn't miss that size) and began the longest bomb run in history. I think it was eight minutes. We held course, altitude and speed far longer than we should if we wished to survive the AA fire. Scotty, our bombardier, directed the other 372nd planes to drop their bombs when he signaled by radio, and he had to constantly change course directions to anticipate the evasive turns of the *Yamato*. The 13th Air Force story by Rust and Bell notes we scored only "near misses" but official accounts indicate several hits on the deck near the bridge. One admiral was hit and much topside damage was done. But, of course, we did not sink the *Yamato* as we had only runway-type bombs. However, we had found the Japanese fleet and thereafter the U.S. Navy began a chase that eventually destroyed the *Yamato* and virtually all the ships in the Japanese fleet. We (the 307th) lost three planes over the target, that I saw, and we collectively suffered many flak hits. We all went back to base "on a wing and a prayer."

One true story about this encounter is that the Japanese actually fired their 18-inch guns at us as we withdrew. Most naval people say that this is very unlikely, but our crew and others saw the guns fire the 2,000 lb. shells. A bomb run photo taken from our airplane was run in newspapers all over the world and is in every book about the 13th AAF. The 13th AAF was not important in size, but we were center stage on October 26, 1944.

9

SERGEANT JIM DEMONTBREUN

DOB: March 28, 1924
Where: Nashville, Tennessee
Air Force: 13th
Bomb Group: 42nd
Station: Mindanao
Decorations include: Airman's Medal (awarded 1945 but not presented until 2006). Toward the end of the war Jim served as a nose gunner on a B-24, seeing action on bomb runs and low level strafing. It was what he did before going overseas, on February 25, 1945, that illustrated Jim's courage under extreme conditions. Once the war concluded Jim graduated from Vanderbilt University and spent 44 years in the insurance business.

Alex

I always wanted to be a pilot and sure enough after all my tests I had qualified to train not only as a pilot but as a bombardier and navigator as well. I was advised to choose one of the last two but I was determined to be a pilot. I should have listened to the advice. During pilot training at Chickasha Field, Oklahoma, some of us were called into a theater and told that the pilot pipeline was full. "We don't need you," they said, and for "the convenience of the government" we were given the choice of other schools. Not knowing much about the choices, I asked someone which school was located in the biggest and most fun town. I was told armament school at Denver, Colorado, so armament school is where I headed. I studied all the armament on the B-24: the turret, machine guns, bomb bays, and bomb racks.

After additional training at gunnery school, I was assigned to a crew at Chatham Field, near Savannah, Georgia, as a B-24 nose gunner. Our crew completed all of our work except for one final mission. We were very close to going overseas and this being early 1945 we were sure to see some combat. We already had an assigned navigator but were told on this last training mission we would be carrying another navigator, a veteran of 50 missions over Germany, who would be teaching our man how to operate a sextant.

Around 4 o'clock in the morning we all climbed into our ship for a ride out over the ocean. On this February morning, we gunners weren't going to do anything. We were just going along for the ride to get in some flight hours. My friend Alex and I decided to get on the little deck in front of the ball turret. It was a small shelf where the oxygen bottles were stored. There we could just relax and let the others do the work. Alex's name was Kenneth Alexander, a waist gunner who had just become a proud father. He showed me pictures of his wife and even gave me a cigar to celebrate the birth of his daughter.

Soon our plane began its taxi to position prior to takeoff. The engines revved up and we started down the runway. For some reason it felt like the plane ran and ran and ran, taking forever to get off the ground. Something didn't seem right. All of a sudden we felt the plane leave the ground into what I thought was a climb that was too steep. It wasn't long before we suddenly felt the plane sway sideways and then I saw a big streak of fire go past the waist window. I felt my body being thrown around the

Jim DeMontbreun (courtesy Jim DeMontbreun)

plane and I was absolutely powerless to do anything about it. My head hit the bomb rack on the other side of the deck and I suffered a deep split across my scalp.

I remember the pilot struggling to keep climbing, pushing the engines to their full capacity. But we hit some trees and soon after that we hit the ground. That's when I believe the airplane broke in half at the bomb bay. I went flying through the air about 30 or 40 feet before landing in 8 to 10 inches of water. When I slowly raised off the ground, I first thought we had crashed in a field because everything was open. I looked around and saw that trees as big as telephone poles had been leveled and it was then I noticed we were actually in a swamp. Everything was on fire and my head was killing me. My head was bleeding badly.

I decided it was best for me to get the hell out of there but before I could move very far I heard moans. One of the guys had his head jammed in the water and was trying to breathe. I went over and pulled him out and dragged him next to a tree. He died right there. He was the navigator who had made all the missions over Europe. I heard the pilot screaming, "Mother, Mother, Mother!" I ran over to where he was. He was still strapped in his seat but had landed away from the plane. He was conscious but had a nasty slash across his forehead that revealed the white of his skull. I looked down and one of his legs was just bone, all the meat was gone. I managed to put my hands under his arms and tried to get him away from the fire.

Then I heard more screaming. The copilot was still in his seat. I took a hold of his arm and it was just mush, almost completely cut off. I dragged him away and then looked back and saw the tail gunner walking. He had come out of the back of the plane, an area that was still relatively intact. Other screams got my attention. Another one of the crew came out, a waist gunner. He was on fire. I managed to get him off to the side. I could tell I was getting weaker from the loss of blood. Soon I saw planes circling above. Then maybe half an hour later I heard noises coming into the swamp. The rescue people were arriving.

I hollered for Alex, calling his name. I heard him screaming but couldn't tell where he was. Oxygen bottles and ammunition were exploding but I looked and looked and still couldn't find him. He was next to me before the crash and we shared laughter and joy over the birth of his daughter. I tried to get into the plane but still couldn't locate him. The next day his body was found under a wing tip where he had either drowned or burned to death from the gasoline burning on the water. The chaplain showed up with the group of rescuers and he was feeling around my neck looking for my dog tags. I reached into my pocket and handed them to him. He wanted to know if I was Protestant or Catholic because he was going to give me last rites. As I was being loaded into the ambulance I asked the chaplain if he could put something under my head to help support it and ease the pain and I remember him pulling off his beautiful uniform jacket and putting it where it would make me feel a little more comfortable.

We were put in an ambulance, loaded in racks of three on each side, and taken back to Chatham Field. We were in bad shape. The navigator was already dead. Our crew chief had been in the nose of the plane working on the nose wheel when we went down. They found his body hanging in a tree. The radio operator injured his spinal cord and was never the same. As for the pilot and copilot, one lost his leg and the other lost an arm. One crewmember was burned so badly that when I saw him in the hospital he was so wrapped up all I could see were the holes for his mouth and eyes. The bombardier suffered serious internal injuries.

I found myself in a hospital at Hunter Field with a huge laceration down the top of my head, a burned ear and a bad cut on my leg. My parents were notified that I had been critically injured in a plane crash. I finally began to realize everything that had happened. I asked to make a phone call to my parents. It was late in the evening when I reached them and told them I was okay. Dad had already gone to the draft board to request gas ration coupons to drive down to see me.

I've asked myself and the good Lord many times and I even asked my minister why I was spared when the rest of my crew either died or suffered injuries that would affect them the rest of their lives. My minister simply said, "Jim, God had a plan for you. He had something for you to do." Why did he take Alex and not me? I lived and someone sitting next to me, a great guy, a good friend and a new father, died such a terrible death.

The official reason given for the crash was an engine loss on takeoff. The real problem I think was that the copilot pulled up the flaps instead of the wheels. That caused the plane to lose lift and fall to the ground. To this day, I don't remember hearing an engine sputter or backfire. That airplane was performing all right except we were losing altitude.

The copilot's parents came to the hospital to visit their son. His mother was a sweet lady and told me how her son wanted to fly since he was a young boy. He used to sit at the table and make airplane noises with his knife and fork, she said. He always wanted to be a single engine pilot and was training to be one when he buzzed someplace. As a result of that, he was put back into multiengine training. I could hear her boy screaming, "My arm! My arm!" A stick was attached to him so that when he woke up he would feel it, think his arm was still there, and not do anything extreme.

I stayed in the hospital for over a week and then went home on a 10-day leave. When I got back to Chatham Field all my personal items were gone. All the other crews had shipped overseas. I was put in the replacement barracks and continued training as a nose gunner but I had no crew. They didn't have a place to put me so I remained in the replacement pool. I soon got orders to go overseas. I went on to serve in the 13th Air Force, logging nine combat missions as a B-24 nose gunner in the southwest Pacific. I never heard anything about the guys in the hospital or the ones who were killed. No one interviewed me about the accident.

10

CAPTAIN BUSH COLE

DOB: September 26, 1922
Where: Livingston, Texas
Air Force: 15th
Bomb Group: 376th
Squadron: 512th
Station: San Pancrazio, Italy
Decorations include: Purple Heart, Distinguished Flying Cross, Air Medal with clusters. Because of health questions, Bush Cole had a hard time persuading a recruiter to accept him. Good thing that recruiter listened. Bush flew 52 combat missions as a bombardier aboard a B-24, making himself known to his superiors after the destruction of the docks and oil tanks at La Spezia, Italy. Initially criticized by his superiors for breaking formation, he was lauded for his actions after reconnaissance pictures revealed widespread damage. Bush saw additional active service during Berlin and Korea. In civilian life he sold industrial equipment, raised cattle, and farmed.

Breaking Formation

In the first place, it's a miracle I even got in the service. I was born crippled with two club feet. My youth, at least until I was 13, was marked by a series of operations to correct the problem. There were six of us kids in my family and I was the only one with something wrong. I was strong enough, but never fast enough, to play on the first team of any sport.

At the age of 16, I started working in the oil fields around Corpus Christi, Texas. As soon after Pearl Harbor as possible I went down and signed up for the air corps. That was December 8, 1941. It's a good thing I was toughened up by all that work in the oil fields because I went through a lot just to get in to the service. "We don't need a cripple," they told me but finally, in March 1942, they took me.

I grew up in a patriotic family. My daddy used to always tell me and my brothers that he would rather go bury his sons on the prairie than see them not serve their country. His World War I experience served as an example for all of us. That doesn't mean there weren't

10. Captain Bush Cole

Bush Cole (courtesy Bush Cole)

any conflicting feelings about what I did in the service. I remember after I returned an old friend, an evangelist, ran into me at Texas A&M and took me to his motel room nearby. He declared that I should get down on my knees and ask God for forgiveness for the people I killed during the war. I told him he was still my friend but he was wrong. I understood him, but he needed to understand my point of view. During my time overseas as a B-24 bombardier, I got down on my knees and asked God to help me do the best job I could do. I would have even been glad to drop the atomic bomb if called upon to do so. At the time I thought it was the greatest thing we did during the war and I still feel that way.

During my time overseas I covered a lot of territory in the air, striking targets in Italy, Romania, Austria, France, and Germany. One of my missions took us over the harbor at La Spezia, Italy, on May 19, 1944. There were three flights of us and my ship was in the third flight. The squadron commander was in the first flight as we made our way up the west coast of that beautiful country. Cloud cover hindered our view of the harbor and we were ordered to move on to the secondary target. As the first two flights turned, I looked over and told my pilot that I could see the original target. "Can you take it in?" he responded. "If you'll turn 90 degrees to the right I can." With that, he broke formation and turned 90 degrees to the right, following my directive. The rest of our flight followed. I quickly took over flying our ship with the bombsight, knowing I had about a 15 second shot at the target. Each plane would be dropping its bombs on my signal. I'm glad Captain Wood believed in me. Of course, it helped that I was one of the best bombardiers in the outfit. I had led the entire 15th Air Force on several missions. What followed was a part of my life I'll never forget.

Our actual target was a group of oil storage tanks near the harbor. This was around the time of the Anzio invasion so this harbor was crucial to the Axis forces for the delivery of ammo to the front. I carefully coordinated the dropping of our bombs, watched the black smoke rise from hits, and returned with our flight to base.

Mission debriefings were sometimes good but always a pain in the ass for me. The colonel on our trip just chewed us up one side and down the other for breaking formation. He jumped on the pilot, "Why did you do that?" with his brave answer being, "The bombardier said he could hit the target and he did." The colonel didn't seem to hear or understand because after he finished with the pilot he jumped the rest of us. He proceeded to embarrass us in front of the rest of the guys and at the next day's briefing. He spent most of his time dwelling on the fact that we had broken formation.

The next day a reconnaissance plane flew over the harbor and returned with some very

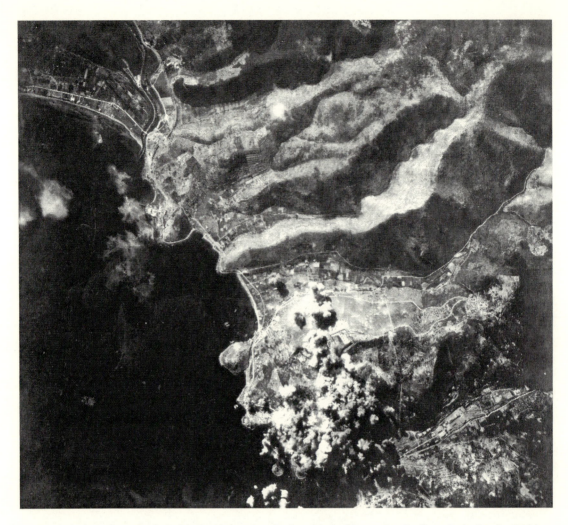

Aerial photo from Bush Cole's B-24 showing the bombing of Porto San Stefano, Italy, by the 376th Bomb Group on May 17, 1944 (courtesy Bush Cole).

interesting pictures. On the third day, after the mission and after the pictures had been carefully reviewed, the colonel told our crew to stand up at the briefing. I thought, "Now what? I don't have any more ass to be chewed." He said, "I want to apologize to Captain Wood and Lieutenant Cole. The mission over La Spezia harbor was one of the best we've had." Turned out the oil storage tanks were hit and set ablaze and ammo that had just been unloaded on the docks blew up, wrecking the docks themselves. A couple of ships were sunk as well. The general had even seen the mission report and wanted to know who led it and who was the bombardier.

A personal disaster had turned into something very sweet for the pilot and myself. As a result, each of us won the Distinguished Flying Cross for our work that day.

You Dead?

We had a navigator on our B-24 named Harry. Harry was a great guy but, to me, he was always scared. On every mission he wore a flak jacket and sat on another one. Our very first mission took us to the sub pens at Toulon, France. As the bombardier, I had three machine guns I could fire. I was standing up near them as we flew fairly close to the shoreline and had taken my steel helmet off and laid it down nearby.

Mushroom bursts from the flak were going off all around us. That sort of thing was still a novelty to me, of course. Maybe that explains why I looked out the window and said, "Harry, that's kind of pretty, ain't it?" Well, before I could hardly get the words out of my mouth a piece of flak exploded through my area, plowed a groove in that helmet of mine, and caused it to fly up and hit me, knocking me clear across the plane before it exited the plane on the other side. I looked around, tried to gather my senses, and didn't know whether to laugh, cry, or be scared.

Prior to going overseas, I had trained for a year for just this sort of combat but nothing could really prepare me for being shot at. Suddenly I thought, "Them sons of bitches are trying to kill Bush Cole." My first mission was the first time it really came to me that our enemies were really trying to kill me. It scared Harry to death.

Early the next month, we headed to Budapest, Hungary. We were flying one of the older B-24s with the glass nose. I liked flying those planes with the glass noses because I could look out and fire the guns around me. I guess I was a little crazier than most of the bombardiers because I shot at those German fighters coming at us. I shot down a couple of them, both 109's. Well, as our luck would have it on this mission, flak busted right through my area up in front and cut my face. I felt it hit me, sort of like falling on concrete and having my face scraped, but I didn't really think much about it. I had an important job to do and had to get it done. Harry, on the other hand, thought the worst. "Cole, Cole," he said, "are you dead?" I've always wished I would have turned to Harry and said, "Yea, Harry, I'm dead." I don't think I bled a lot, probably because it was too cold up there, but the wound was enough to earn the Purple Heart. Part of the accompanying citation noted the direct hits I made on the target that day.

Oklahoma Boy

Most of us gathered in the back of the B-24 as it began its takeoff for yet another mission over enemy territory. This trip counted as just one of my 52 combat sorties but it was the last scheduled mission for the boy from Oklahoma. He was a gunner from another crew and he wanted to fly with us so he could get back home and be with his wife who was expecting their first child. We were happy for him and probably a little envious as well.

Everything seemed normal as we picked up speed down the runway but that ended abruptly when our plane hit a hole, blowing a tire and throwing us all around the inside. Outside, the landing gear sheared off and as the plane cartwheeled off the side of the runway I hit my knee on the ball turret.

We were overloaded for this mission, carrying a double load of frag bombs to our unfortunate destination. Those bombs didn't get off the ground in this plane but one still performed its lethal duty. It broke loose from its shackle in the bomb bay and flew through the bulkhead, its fins hitting the boy from Oklahoma in the head.

The dust hadn't even settled when a six by six pulled up and some disembodied voice yelled out, "We need you guys to fly lead." So they took us off as quickly as they could and put us on another plane. All of us, except the boy from Oklahoma. "That guy in the back is hurt bad!" I said. "We'll get him, let's go!" came the reply.

We never knew who the boy was. I went to a bomb group reunion in Knoxville a few years ago when a stranger approached and acted like he wanted to talk. "You know me," he said, "I was flying copilot on your crew when that boy from Oklahoma was killed." Until then, I didn't know he had died.

You Won't Believe Me

This has nothing to do with my exploits during 52 combat missions as a B-24 bombardier or all the training leading up to my time overseas. All this happened when I was sent back to the states after combat for a little rest and then reassignment. In the fall of 1944, I arrived at Santa Monica, California, where I was to take it easy. Santa Monica and its area were a long way in distance and culture from the oil fields of south Texas where I grew up.

I was sitting in a restaurant one evening wearing my uniform, the only uniform I had worn overseas, when Dick Haymes, the singer and actor, walked over and introduced himself. He was making a movie at the time and invited me to visit him on the set. This was the beginning of an interesting friendship because not only did I visit on the set of *Diamond Horseshoe* but Dick also took me to dinner several times and even invited me to his home.

Through Dick, I danced with Ginger Rogers, met some beautiful women on the movie set, and acquired a brand new uniform. He took me down to wardrobe and told the folks there to fix me up with a new outfit. Betty Grable, the costar of the movie, was very nice to me and personalized an autographed picture which I still have.

It was Betty who set me up on a date with one of her gorgeous stand-ins. We went to the *Mocambo* nightclub, owned in part by movie star tough guy George Raft. The place was really crowded, with a deck for dining built above a lower floor for dining and dancing. Actually, the dance floor was so small there was hardly room to do anything but wiggle and hold on to each other. It was a glamorous place where Hollywood stars showed up to see and be seen.

My date and I were seated on the deck and had just ordered our meal. For me, it was the cheapest thing on the menu — chicken cooked in wine. I noticed the table below us on the main floor was vacant, but not for long. In came this fancy Hollywood-type blowhard, a big time movie producer, with a young blond on his arm. He was all over her, slobbering like a dog running after a "you know what" in heat. "Stick with me," he said for everybody to hear, "and I'll make you this and I'll make you that," he told her.

I have to admit that I didn't have a very good attitude in those days. My temper and my candidness had gotten me in trouble more than a few times. I admit it and I'm not very proud of it. Also, I guess I was still wound up from my combat missions and was still trying to relax. I had never been to rest camp while overseas. This guy was making me very nervous and my date noticed I was getting upset. The young woman below us started to order when "Mr. Big Shot" loudly proclaimed everyone knew him at the club and he would order. He then snapped his fingers and told the waiter to bring them two of his special steaks.

This was at a time during the war when a steak dinner was very hard to come by for most folks. He bragged to the girl about how people jumped when he hollered. Meantime, I was getting hotter and hotter. In a few minutes, their steaks arrived. She cut into hers and it was too rare. That's when the loudmouth jumped the poor waiter. "You take that back and get it right!" The waiter could only stammer a quick "Yes sir" and he was off to the kitchen. He soon brought the steak back and it was overcooked this time. Now all sorts of hell was raised.

I had reached the boiling point. I couldn't take it any longer. I got up, reached over the rail, and grabbed this hot shot by the scruff of the neck. I was as strong as a bull back in those days due to the years I had worked in the oil fields. "You son of a bitch," I said, "you eat that steak. I've been where men would kill each other for that meat. I'll ram it down your throat if you don't." I turned around at my table and my date was leaving, saying something about her reputation being damaged if she stayed any longer. As the headwaiter started toward me, I heard two guys behind say, "You tell him, lieutenant!" I looked and there were two marines standing there backing me up, one a gunny sergeant and the other a captain. I knew I could be thrown out but they weren't going to throw out the three of us.

I turned to the waiter and told him to bring me my check. "You don't have a check," he said. "Who says so?" I replied, "I certainly do." "No, Mr. Raft said you don't have one." I looked over to the side and I spotted George Raft standing with Rita Hayworth. He motioned for me to come to join them. When I reached them Raft said, "You don't have to pay the bill. You don't know how often I've wanted to do the same thing." The three of us made some small talk for a few minutes. Then, up walked this fellow who said he was the publicity man for Howard Hughes. He introduced himself as John Mayer and he offered to pay the bill, too. In fact, he argued with Raft about who would take care of the check. Raft won that argument.

Mr. Mayer ended up taking the three of us, the two marines and myself, to his fancy home in the Hollywood hills where we partied most of the night around his pool with some beautiful young ladies. I won't get into any of that but I can tell you it was a nice way to relax. In case you're wondering: "Mr. Big Shot" ate his steak.

11

SERGEANT LEONARD MIKA

DOB: March 22, 1924
Where: Detroit, Michigan
Air Force: 8th
Bomb Group: 385th
Squadron: 551st
Station: Great Ashfield, England
Decorations include: Air Medal with clusters. Leonard trained as a ball turret gunner on a B-17 but switched to the engineer/top turret position upon entering combat. He flew 30 missions as a 20-year-old on his first trip away from home, like many of the men in this book. Leonard returned home and graduated from the University of Michigan. He then began a 27-year career as an agent with the Bureau of Alcohol, Tobacco, and Firearms, U.S. Treasury, from which he retired in 1977.

A Carbine Aimed Right at Me

February 26, 1945, and Berlin was our target. I was flying engineer/top turret gunner on our B-17 that day. It was my seventeenth mission and very nearly my last. We dropped our bombs over Berlin and the group executed our standard dive to the right to get off the target. As the maneuver was being executed, the bombardier reported that the bomb bay doors would not move from the full open position.

Being the engineer, the pilot ordered me to get into the bomb bay and crank the door up. I disconnected my throat mike and oxygen hose and fastened a walk-around oxygen bottle to my jacket. I then stepped out into the bomb bay catwalk without a parachute. The catwalk was very narrow, so narrow that you couldn't place both feet side by side; one had to be in front of the other.

As I cranked those big doors against the drag, I would stop occasionally to get my breath. There was lots of resistance to my cranking. In fact, the crank would suddenly be jerked out of my hand and spring back around, hitting me on the shin, causing the doors to go back down. After this happened two or three times, the peculiar behavior stopped and I managed to get the doors closed. This was all taking place during the dive when I was fighting the drag of the doors.

After getting back into the cockpit area, I learned that the bombardier, for some reason, did not get the word that I was in the bomb bay fighting those doors. So he, being a dedicated bombardier, kept trying to close the doors by jiggling the switch. Each time he did that the crank would be jerked out of my hand.

During all this excitement, I found myself facing the business end of a rifle. The radio operator, upon learning what I was going to do, left his position at one of the waist guns, went into the radio room, got the carbine kept there, opened the radio room door to the bomb bay, and aimed it at me. He told me he was not going to let me fall from the bomb bay alive and without a chute. I can't say enough about the resolve of bomber crews to take care of one another.

Pitchforked

On a mission to Berlin, I was flying the left waist gunner position on our B-17. On the bomb run, the B-17 above us in the highest section took a direct hit in the bomb bay loaded with incendiaries. The ship was immediately engulfed in a ball of flame but, miraculously, all nine crewmembers got out safely. When they reached the ground, though, two crewmen were killed by civilians.

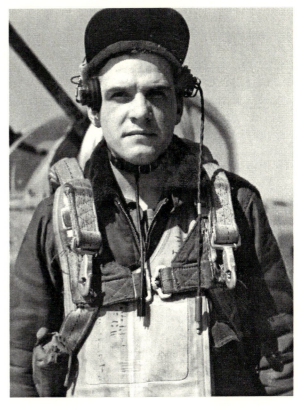

Leonard Mika (courtesy Leonard Mika)

The fate of the two crewmen, the ball turret gunner and the radio operator, began in the bomber when it was hit and the fire engulfed the bomb bay and the radio room. The procedure was, when enemy territory was reached, the radio operator left his position in the radio room and proceeded to the waist to man one of the guns there. So, at the time of the hit, the radio operator was at the waist position. He left his parachute in the radio room and it was consumed in the fire.

As the crew started bailing out, the radio operator faced a terrible death. The ball turret gunner was the last to leave the plane. Seeing the radio operator's dilemma, and thinking quickly, he embraced his fellow crewman in a bear hug and they both bailed out on one chute. They reached the ground safely, landing in a cultivated field among some farmers working there.

The radio operator was Jewish. When he took off his flying helmet, the farmers immediately recognized him as Jewish and pitchforked him to death. The ball turret gunner was of Spanish origin (his parents came from Spain). He was blue-eyed with an olive complexion and black hair that he wore rather long. The farmers took him for a Jew and pitchforked him to death as well. Such were the dangers that crewmen faced even after they made it out of their crippled planes.

The Green Scarf

The first time I saw a jet was toward the end of the war when our mission took us over an important German target. We had been told in our briefing that we could encounter jets and, sure enough, on our way back to base we got a close up view of this new kind of technology. We saw a plane coming toward us, first spotted by our tail gunner. I was in my normal position in the ball turret below our B-17 so when I heard the tail gunner's warning I turned the turret around and saw him, too. He was coming up to our level from the rear, climbing just as fast as he could. His airspeed was such that he had trouble lining up for a shot. Often, as I discovered, the jets were so fast they overshot our height. To prevent that they would suddenly drop their flaps which enabled them to level out and fire their guns.

When this guy dropped his flaps we recognized his plane as an Me 262, a lethal machine with a dangerous reputation for us and its pilots. We were trying our best to return safely when we got this jet on our tail. At least he was trying to get on our tail. When he dropped his flaps, the jet dropped below our ship and I picked him up and fired my guns into him. The last I saw of him he was going down to another level.

I remember seeing the pilot. He was that close. He had a full beard of red hair and was wearing a Kelly green scarf around his neck. I should have hit him. I thought I hit him but he kept flying. It appeared to me his jet engines were malfunctioning after being hit by the tail gunner prior to my shots. I just remember that it looked like he was trying hard to keep his plane under control. I've often wondered if he ever made it back safely.

Diary Entries

November 11, 1944: Made first flight of combat raids over enemy territory. First sight of the very publicized flak made an uneasy feeling, especially since two engines were ailing all the way. Flak intensity was low. On way home, dropped belt of .50 caliber rounds on farmhouse below due to a malfunction of turret. Returned home safely. (Koblenz raided)

November 14, 1944: Mission scrubbed at last minute. Bad weather all day, did nothing. About 8:30pm German buzz bomb went over at about 100 feet, directly over barracks.

November 21, 1944: Took off for Merseburg, Germany. Over Holland forced to abort due to low manifold pressure in two engines. Encountered light flak but damned close on return. P-51 escorted us all the way in. Right gun on turret would not fire. In flight 4 hrs. Sweating out the boys at this writing (1530), rough trip was predicted — 600 fighters and plenty flak. The boys returned o.k. except for one ship. (Mid-air collision destroyed plane and killed crew). Merseburg could not be hit due to overcast.

November 30, 1944: Merseburg raided today. 385 flak guns, no fighters. Saw 3 planes go down in flames, three chutes were seen to open from first ship. Flak very heavy, great number of ships lost, quite few wounded. Our ship full of flak holes. Miracles saved several of crew from very serious injury. 14 groups hit target. Trouble in ball turret again; lost all hydraulic fluid; rode raid soaked in oil. Never had been so scared in my life. Formation scattered, came home alone.

December 17, 1944: Bad weather, no mission, lying around. Foiled again — pilot struck by one of his brainstorms, decided to take our ship up for test hop at 4 o'clock. So, we spent Sunday afternoon flying. Phooey! In flight 1 hr. 35 min. Sat up till late singing hillbilly songs with Hill playing the guitar.

11. Sergeant Leonard Mika

December 24, 1944: Mission to Grossostheim airfield. Pretty good hits. Numerous fighters, enemy and our own. Quite a few went down, one B-17 lost from group. Flak all the way to target, none on way back. Largest number of ships ever seen in history were out today; 2,000 heavies plus mediums and fighters plus RAF. 385th sent up 62 ships. 100 lbs. G.P. bombs (38). All in all, good mission. In flight 7 hrs.

December 31, 1944: Mission to Wenzendorf airfield, by way of North Sea. 500 lb. bombs. Field totally and completely destroyed. Hit by enemy fighters again; several of ours went down, no heavies. Seen were jets, Ju 88, Me 210, Me 109. Plenty of excitement. In flight 8 hrs.

January 2, 1945: Mission to woods 10 miles from lines; troop and tank concentrations. Locality near Saarlautern and Metz. Target hit exceptionally well with fragmentation bombs; 100 lbs and 260 lbs. Got lost on take off due to ship change and joined another group. That group lost 4 ships because of direct hits from flak which was light but damned accurate. One ship blew up to our side; we had occupied that same spot earlier. God certainly watches over our crew. Saw only 3 chutes come out of another ship. In flight 5 hrs. 20 min.

January 5, 1945: Mission to Kaizerslauten marshalling yards. Bombed at 28,000 feet, extremely cold, 48 below. All equipment frozen stiff. Lack of gas forced us to land at a former Nazi air base in France. We were quartered at a chateau occupied by a combat engineer outfit. Officers and men slept on floors, benches, tables, etc. Engineer officers and men were very good to us. Flak was heavy, ship riddled.

January 11, 1945: Put on official spare gunner roster. Sweating out transfer.

January 12, 1945: Assigned to check out as flight engineer. Sweating out outcome.

March 2, 1945: Mission to Dresden, carrying 250 lb. bombs. Flew as engineer for Capt. Bash. A day memorable as Merseburg. Hit by fighters, Fw 190's; in one pass both wingmen were knocked down by fighters coming in from front and over our wing tips. Saw about 6 Forts go down in flames and broken up; about 15 fighters; no chutes, no flak. Ran out of gas, forced down in France. Time in flight before forced landing: 8 hrs and 30 min.

March 18, 1945: Mission to Berlin; terror raid. Medium flak, but accurate. Lost two ships from group; one crew, Bloom's, from our squadron. Very good friends of mine, especially Fink, the engineer.

March 20, 1945: Mission to Hamburg. Surprise 12:00 noon briefing. Flak, 300 guns; fighters, jet-jobs. Fired at enemy fighter and am positive of hitting him, others have claimed him, too. In flight 7 hrs., 30 min. Fighter knocked hell out of 17 on our right wing; he dropped back with two engines on one side feathered and wounded men on board. Jet came right below my turret. Me 262.

March 23, 1945: Mission to Holzwickede. Completely visual, 1000 pounders demolished marshalling yards and bursts of flame were seen all over. Target was near battle line; artillery could be seen bombarding towns and military objectives, starting fires all over the countryside. One B-17 was hit by flak barrage over target knocking off one wing, causing it to topple down on another 17. Both 17's went down, one in flames in a flat spin, the other in a nose spin, exploding in a great mass of flames on hitting a farmhouse and out buildings. No chutes were seen. Two bursts went off next to my turret causing the ship to lurch about 20 feet; no damage. Saw Cologne, or what was left of it, a cathedral amid the ruins. Saw Koblenz, Aachen, and Duren, also completely destroyed. Sweating out these last few.

April 4, 1945: Went to Kiel again. Same target (sub pens), this time visual. Moderate flak. Two planes from our group collided on way to target over North Sea. Tail section of one was imbedded in nose of other. Both ships went down and broke up. Saw bodies being thrown out. They didn't have a chance. On way back PBY VHF conversation reported only one body found still in chute, Mae West was not inflated. One crew had two more missions to go. One of the ships was 210-V, the ship our crew flew to Merseburg on Nov. 30, '44. Flew as waist gunner today — turret motor was burned out and could not draw any oxygen. In flight 7 hrs.

April 7, 1945: Mission to Gustrow, Germany, ordnance depot. Target completely demolished by 500 pound bombs. Visual. On way to target enemy fighters, Me 109's, hit the whole damn works. Each group was hit separately and at least one 17 was lost out of each. Our group was hit from the front and when one 109 cut down to the rear of the low squadron he tore off the left side of tail and sheared off left wing completely. Fighter and bomber went down in pieces. No one seen to bail out. Another 17 behind us was hit by a 109, too. The pilot set it on C-1 (automatic) and the crew bailed out, plane continued flying until it disappeared in haze. Miller, radar man, and good friend went down in the collision.

April 19, 1945: Started clearing the base.

12

Captain Bob Gregg

DOB: March 18, 1919
Where: Lancaster, Ohio
Air Force: 12th
Bomb Group: 320th
Squadron: 442nd
Station: Italy, France, Sardinia
Decorations include: Air Medal with clusters, Purple Heart, Croix de Guerre avec Palme. Bob flew 65 combat missions as the pilot of a Martin B-26, bailing out of his riddled ship as a German pilot saluted his efforts. Before the war ended he became a squadron leader. After the war he graduated from the University of Wisconsin and went into chemical sales, where he spent his professional career.

An "Honorable" Salute

I became very good at flying the B-26. I enjoyed it, even though it had a bad reputation because it killed a lot of people. It was such a hot plane with those two, big Pratt and Whitneys with almost two thousand horsepower each. I liked the fact that the B-26 could carry a nice-sized bomb load and still fly very fast. Yes, I liked it because I was really impressed with the speed. No doubt it was a challenge to fly since it was so fast. Because of that, the plane had a problem with high-speed stalls and that's what killed so many of our people. You had to have proper air speed on takeoffs and landings. Once you learned how to handle such power, got to know the plane's bad characteristics, and learned to compensate for them, it was a beauty. I loved that airplane. I could do everything with it that you could possibly imagine. There was just no other plane in the air force like it.

As part of the 320th Bomb Group, 442nd Squadron, I flew with the 12th Air Force out of Decimomannu, Sardinia. We called ourselves "The Boomerangs" because our planes kept coming back to base. It was claimed that we had the lowest loss-per-sortie in the entire wing. The runway at our base was really little more than a farmer's field. It was dirt with a little grass and plenty of bumps and potholes. During takeoffs my copilot's chief job was to keep his feet firmly planted against the dashboard to keep it from shaking so I could read the gauges. Our takeoffs were impressive, though. We would line up six abreast and leave the ground at the same time. That way, we wouldn't spend so much time and fuel flying around trying to form up.

My sixth mission took place on January 29, 1944. We carried four, one thousand pound bombs and were headed for the small Manziana railroad bridge near Rome. We got to be pretty good at low level bombing of bridges, railroads, and viaducts. Those viaducts the Italians used dated from hundreds of years ago and their arches were so beautiful. Our plane, aircraft number 39, was one of 35 Marauders ordered to plaster the bridge and its approaches on that day. But before we could reach the target we found ourselves in some serious trouble, buffeted by flak and hit by German fighters.

We were attacked by Me 109s and Fw 190s. They swarmed all around us and even though we were able to down a bunch of them with our .50 cals, we suffered extensive damage. I ordered the bombs jettisoned before we reached the target. Where they ended up falling I don't know but I did know we couldn't afford to carry their weight any farther. We were losing altitude and had been knocked out of formation. *Gunga Din,* flown by Lt. Elbert Stevenson, pulled out of formation to stay with us and give us some protection from the fighters but unfortunately it went down with the loss of seven lives.

As it turned out, cannon fire had severed some important wire controls in the cockpit. Our immediate concern was to get our plane under control because we were headed into a dive and, frankly, it didn't look good for us. The fighters were still working on us at that point. We had no elevator control but I remembered from training that I could do some tricks with the trim tabs. With the elevator controls out, the elevator trim worked in reverse of normal so after a roller coaster ride with the plane going like a yo-yo up and down the copilot and I were able to return to level flight.

At that point, I had the plane headed for Corsica where the British had a small base. I got up out of my seat and struggled back to the navigator's compartment to survey the situation. The bomb bay doors were stuck in the open position, there were no hydraulics, the right engine had no controls working and was stuck at a fixed rpm, and the waist gunner, Frank Marschke, was wounded, semi-conscious, and unable to help himself. I knew we couldn't land the plane. We were lucky to keep it in the air as it was.

The enemy fighters finally ran out of ammunition. Then something happened that I didn't see since I was away from the cockpit but my copilot told me about later. He said he would never forget the sight of a German Fw 190 coming along side our plane and the pilot saluting us as he peeled off for his return to base.

By now we were down to six to eight thousand feet and I was hoping hard that we would make the coastline of Corsica so we could jump and avoid the mountains that lay ahead. Our altitude continued to drop but

Bob Gregg (courtesy Bob Gregg)

we made it over land. It was time to bail out through the open bomb bay. I can remember Frank saying he wasn't going to jump. "Go ahead, boys, go ahead," he said. I was yelling at him, ordering him to jump but he wasn't listening to me. I was able to give Eugene Floto instructions how to bail out with Frank in his arms. With the help of Jerry Rogers they got out safely with Floto pulling Frank's ripcord and then his own as he fell free. Jerry then went out and somewhere during this time I got the bombardier out safely.

Copilot Cliff Conrad gave me a frantic cry and I waived him back. I was looking out through the bomb bay trying to see where the others had landed when Cliff gave me a quick shove and I found myself in a free fall. Cliff quickly followed. We had all made it out! I never really had any parachute training prior to going overseas so I didn't know how to manipulate my chute. I barely knew how to pull the ripcord. Despite that, everything was going smoothly with my descent until I got close to the ground and the winds started hitting me. I swung like a pendulum since I didn't know how to control my chute. My boots just scraped the tops of some small trees and I ended up falling on my back. I lay on the ground quickly wiggling my toes to check myself. I had never hit anything that hard in my life. It felt like I had broken every bone in my body but I guess the trees, while they cut me up, kept me from being hurt worse.

As I floated down, I could see the British in their American jeeps headed out to where they thought we would land. I dragged myself up and got my foot to work. I could still walk, however barely, so I gathered up my chute and crawled through the trees toward the British as we yelled back and forth trying to find each other.

I made it back to my base two days later. Some of the boys in my crew were taken to the hospital with wounds from flak and cannon fire. As for me, the damn doctor back at the base wasn't much help. "Bob, you OK?" he asked. I told him I would live but my leg, as it turned out, needed more medical care than it got. I was just glad to be alive. I did a hell of a lot of praying before I hit the ground. I believe strongly in the good Lord. To this day, I know I wouldn't be here without His help. When you're that close to being killed, the good Lord is nice to lean on and talk to.

I was told that our little escapade was the only time during the war when three Distinguished Flying Crosses were awarded to members of one crew for their courageous acts on a single mission. I was not one of the recipients. I was put in for the DFC in 2004 but you have to have folks who can verify what you did. Hell, they're all dead now.

I went on to fly 59 more missions, getting cut up a few times from shrapnel and enduring some single engine landings. Missions took me over the Anzio beachhead, the invasion of southern France, and Monte Cassino. The Germans were tough to get out of there.

I was nearly killed by the French when we tried to train them to fly the B-26. The bastards were horrible pilots. They didn't have the good sense needed to fly such an airplane.

13

LIEUTENANT HARRY WILLIAMS, JR.

DOB: October 23, 1924
Where: Macon, Georgia
Air Force: 8th
Bomb Group: 92nd
Squadron: 327th
Station: Poddington, England
Decorations include: Air Medal with clusters. The B-17 was a plane Harry says he was destined to fly. As he tells it, he wanted to fly the biggest plane available from the time he got airsick flying a small trainer. Shot down over Belgium, he was rescued by friendly forces, returned to base, and completed 35 combat missions in the pilot's seat. Harry said he was never scared, just terrified all the time. After the war he graduated from the University of Georgia and worked in the insurance field for 39 years.

Good Old American Ingenuity

At the 92nd Bomb Group's base near Poddington, England, crews that didn't fly on a particular day got up, had breakfast, and spent the day sitting in the barracks reading, walking around the base, sleeping, or doing just what they wanted to do. On days like that I might go to the officers' club, have drinks at 5 P.M., eat supper, and return to the barracks for a few games of cards or some interesting bull sessions.

Most of the time we would wait to go to bed until about 11pm or after. There was a pole located near squadron headquarters with a light on it. You waited to see if the light was white or red. If the white light was visible, it meant go to bed and get a good night's sleep because you weren't flying the next day. If the light was red you knew you were flying so you went to bed and slept the best that you could until someone, maybe a corporal or a sergeant, came around to wake you up very early the next morning.

When I was awakened for a mission, the first thing I would ask was, "How much gas?" If he said, "2,780" it meant the tanks were loaded. My plane would carry all the gas she could carry which meant a long mission deep into enemy territory. Anything less than the full amount and I would have a chance of flying a "milk run," a mission with less danger.

After getting out of bed, there was time to wash up and use the toilet, which was outside the barracks, of course, then get properly dressed and go to breakfast, usually around 4 A.M. Then a walk over to the briefing which usually started about an hour later in a room that reminded me of a grammar school auditorium. There was a stage at one end with chairs out front. On the stage was a huge map of England and Europe covered with a curtain. When the briefing officers were ready the curtain would be pulled and the crews informed about the day's mission.

This is the point where things got real interesting. There was a string that started from the base and went out to the buncher. The buncher was a radio beam that left the ground and went straight up. Our planes would take off every 30 seconds and join the formation by circling around the buncher. So the string snaked along from our base across the English Channel, zigging and zagging on our true route to the IP, or initial point. There, we turned and went straight in to our target as part of the bomb run.

The string on the briefing map would also show our return route once the bombing had been completed. One morning we were being briefed and everything appeared similar to previous times except coming back the string got halfway across

Harry Williams, Jr. (courtesy Harry Williams, Jr.)

the Channel and stopped. This was a new experience for us to see the string run out. So we asked, "What happened? Did you run out of string?" The briefing officer replied, "Nope, we've got plenty of string." "Why did you stop there?" we wondered aloud. I'll never forget his answer. "That's where you run out of gas," he told us in a sort of matter-or-fact way. Somebody spoke up and asked, "Well, what'll we do then?" "That's where you use good old American ingenuity," was the answer, one we didn't expect and, frankly, didn't take great comfort in hearing.

I don't remember where we went on that mission except that it was way up in northwest Germany. All of us faced the challenge not only of making a dangerous bomb run but conserving the gas we had by controlling the mixture that reached the engine, a process called leaning. Some of our crews had to land in friendly territory on the continent. Some of them ditched in the Channel and some made it back to England. I'll always remember that string running out on the map and the answer we got as to why.

Why Do the Good Ones Get It?

The flight engineer/top turret gunner on my B-17 crew was a young man, some would say he was still a boy, from Pittsburgh. He might have been 19 or 20 but he had the respect and confidence of everyone in the crew, me especially. When he told me he had checked our plane prior to a mission I knew there was no need for me to follow behind and review his work. I had complete trust in him.

There was just something about him, a kind of charisma. Maybe it was just a combination of his quiet, steady demeanor and his strong sense of responsibility as the crew chief of the enlisted men on our plane.

Prior to several missions, he had begged me to let him take off his flak jacket. Everyone knew the jacket was heavy and I guess it was especially so for him since he didn't do a lot of moving around once in position in the plane. So far, I had turned down his requests strictly from a safety standpoint. I made sure my crew followed regulations on our missions and, as much as possible, while on the ground. My personal belief was that I could always loosen up on some restrictions but it would be much harder to tighten the screws. When I look back I'm still pretty amazed that I practiced that philosophy since I was just 19 years old.

We had been through some pretty tough missions but so far the crew was all safe and sound when the young man came to me again and asked to be relieved of the flak jacket burden. "I just can't operate with it on," he told me. This time I relented and gave him permission to leave it off. We met the inevitable flak during our mission that day. I don't remember it being particularly heavy or effective. In fact, we only took two hits to our plane, one in the vertical stabilizer and the other through a small hole in the top turret.

Fatefully, that piece of jagged metal went through the back of that young man. Despite his position being just a few feet behind me, I didn't hear him yell but I have a feeling I felt him collapse. The bombardier, who was the designated medic aboard, rushed to him and made him as comfortable as possible before pulling him down below into the front section of the plane where he could stretch out. I remember looking down at him and seeing him with a weak smile on his face, still no sign of blood anywhere.

During the trip back to base I thought seriously about putting a chute on the young man and bailing him out near a sizeable town, somewhere that would offer more immediate medical attention. I know that sounds a little rough but all the flying crews knew that was an option if it meant possibly saving the life of one of our comrades. I still saw no blood so the decision was made to keep flying back home. Approaching Poddington, we fired two red flares to signal wounded aboard and brought the ship in next to an waiting ambulance.

The young man was still alive when we landed but died once he got to the hospital. As it turned out, he had been bleeding internally all along. The piece of flak that had entered his back had been kept from exiting by his flight suit. I attended his funeral at the U.S. cemetery near Cambridge. Around that time the CO wrote his family to inform them of his death and what a fine young man he was. I didn't. I felt sorrow but I didn't know what to say to his parents. I also regret allowing that young man to go on a mission without the protection of his flak jacket. I never made that mistake again but my decision was one that has troubled me all my life.

Bad Day Over Belgium

We were headed for an enemy airfield at Giessen, Germany, north of Frankfurt. It was December 24, 1944, Christmas Eve, and the Battle of the Bulge was underway. Our folks had been trying to get us off the ground for two weeks but the weather in Europe was just plain awful. On top of that, as B-17 crews we never flew a close-in mission like this one. Normally, as strategic bombers, we would fly deep into enemy-held territory but this day's mission was more like what our B-25 and B-26 crews flew. Our commanders were doing all they could to stop the Germans since they had broken through our lines.

13. Lieutenant Harry Williams, Jr.

The fog was thick that morning. In fact, when we took off from our base at Poddington, England, I couldn't see down the runway. I kept both hands on the wheel and let my copilot work the throttle. Normally I would keep one hand on the wheel and one on the throttle but today he did the throttle work while yelling out the air speed to me as we rolled down the runway. In the meantime, I looked out the left side of the plane to keep it on the runway. This whole time I couldn't see the end so when the plane got to what I thought was an adequate air speed I pushed the stick forward a little bit to lift the tail up and came back on the wheel to take off and the plane responded. Just as soon as we lifted off the ground someone shouted, "End of the runway!" We were that close. Then we had to make a quick left turn to avoid the planes taking off from a neighboring air base and entering our flight pattern. The plane behind me turned too much and let his wing drop so he hit the ground. We got off safely, though, and moved steadily across the Channel. I remember it being a beautiful, sunny day once we had crossed the water.

Soon we were flying across Belgium and we had either a 70 or 80 mile an hour headwind. So if we were flying at 150 miles an hour with a 70-mile an hour headwind we were making about 80 miles an hour across the ground. What saved us was the tailwind coming back.

I was flying just to the left of the lead ship when suddenly there were four bursts of flak. A shell burst just in front of the lead ship; he moved slightly to the right and the second burst got us underneath, causing a momentary lift of the plane. We immediately lost the number three, or right inboard, engine. I remember thinking that I couldn't possibly keep up with the rest of the formation and needed to break away for a return to base. I dropped my wheels as a sign of distress and the lead called, asking what happened. I told him we had lost an engine and were dropping out. "Okay," he said, "try to hit a target of opportunity with your bombs if you can." "We'll try," I responded.

I struggled with the plane at that point, trying to get it trimmed up, but I wasn't too worried. One engine was gone but there was no fire and no need to panic. Once the bombs were dropped we could jettison everything else we could and make it back to base on three engines. But before I could get the lost engine feathered properly another engine was shot out by a nearby flak burst. This time it was the number two engine, the left inboard engine. Now we had one working engine on each side but it actually made the plane easier to fly. That's when I told the crew we might have to bail out. Then they said they couldn't get the rear and front hatches open. At the same time, we were losing altitude and we were being shot at by a lot of different kinds of guns.

Then a third engine was lost, engine number one, the far left engine. We had a good chance of making it back on three engines; we knew we could make it back to our lines with just two working engines; now, with only one engine still running and two engines on fire, I knew we had a big problem. I opened the bomb bay doors because I didn't think the hatches weren't open but in the meantime the crew had managed to open both of them. When the last engine went out, I hit the bail out bell and told them to get out. During most of this time, I knew there was a fire behind me and the copilot was reaching around and patting my back. "Oh, Lord," I said, "as if I don't have enough troubles, my parachute is on fire." Throughout it all, I believe the thing that saved us was the tailwind coming back. It pushed our crippled plane enough to get us close to our lines. We really didn't know where our lines were because this was the Battle of the Bulge and the lines kept going back and forth every day. The navigator was on top of things and we thought we were over friendly territory but we didn't know. For sure, we didn't have a choice now. About this time, two Me 109s decided to pay us a visit. They were lining up to shoot us down when they were driven away by our fighters.

We were going down fast now so everyone exited as quickly as possible. I was still trying to get the plane settled down as I put it on automatic pilot and headed for the nose hatch which, by this time, was open. There sat the navigator just looking out the hatch. I grabbed his harness and told him to get out and we jumped together. I asked him later what he was doing just sitting there and he told me he had watched the copilot go out and delay his chute opening so that he wouldn't hang in the air too long and become a sitting duck for German ground fire. He thought the copilot's parachute hadn't opened so he decided as long as I was flying the plane he was going to stay in it. Once I got out, I remember the deathly quiet of floating in the air while looking over to watch our plane go down in a ball of fire. About that time I remembered thinking back to the day in Savannah when I had to sign a receipt for the B-17 and was told how much it cost. I wondered at the time whether Uncle Sam would make me reimburse the government $250,000 for my shot down plane.

I wasn't in the air very long. In fact, I wasn't finished figuring out what I was going to do when I hit the ground. I collected my chute and saw that there were splotches of snow on the ground and a double row barbed wire fence nearby so I stuck the chute in the fence. I knew the lines were ahead of me. I figured I was behind the Germans so instead of going straight to our lines I would turn around to go backwards toward Germany then work my way back toward our lines. About that time I heard somebody hollering. So I looked over at about two o'clock and there stood two men in American uniforms about 100 yards away. I thought, "Well, some of the crew's gotten together." But I realized they would be at six o'clock, not two o'clock. "Who are you?" I shouted to them. They said, "We're Americans." I said, "Prove it." So one of them took his left hand and hit his right arm with it. That wasn't the recognition signal. During the morning briefing we had been told the signal would be a tip of your hat. During this time the Germans had lots of their men wearing American uniforms so it was difficult to tell friend from foe.

I didn't think these guys were Americans so I started back the way I had planned when they yelled, "Stop! Wait!" They walked closer and I thought seriously about pulling my .45. However, the only thing between me and them was a bush about four feet tall with no leaves and they had rifles. I thought, "Boy, don't be foolish." I stuck my hands up in the air and left the gun alone. I walked toward them and they said, "Put your hands down, lieutenant." They *were* Americans, two infantrymen from a Tennessee outfit. They said, "We were trying to stop you because you were going to those hills back there and they're full of Germans." I said, "What? Why aren't they shooting at us?" "They shoot at us and we shoot back at them. They shoot and we shoot and we've got a war started. They stay where they are and we stay where we are until we're told to go up there. If you had gone up there they would have shot you or captured you." Then I had the funniest feeling. Up until then, at age 20, I had been in charge of a B-17. All of a sudden that plane was gone. I was on the ground with no responsibility. When they said, "Come over here," I went over there. When they said, "Move over here," I moved over there. I wasn't afraid. That wasn't the point. All of a sudden I wasn't in charge.

They told me to get my chute, saying my future wife might enjoy having it, so I grabbed it and soon a jeep arrived to take me to a first aid station. This captain started talking to me, then got a glass and a bottle of whiskey and poured about two to three inches of it into the glass for me. "Drink this," he said. "No, captain, it's hard for y'all to get whiskey over here. We can get it. And I don't want to drink up your whiskey." "That's an order, son," he said.

"Drink it." So, I drank it. It was just like drinking water. It didn't have an effect on me. So he poured about an inch and a half more and told me to drink that. Pretty soon my tail gunner appeared and they put us in an ambulance for the trip to division headquarters.

It's just amazing to me that we all got out of the airplane and no one was captured. Eventually, all of us made it back to our base to fly again on other missions.

14

CAPTAIN BILL REEDER

DOB: December 18, 1921
Where: Nashville, Tennessee
Air Force: 8th
Bomb Group: 306th
Squadron: 368th
Station: Thurleigh, England
Decorations include: Distinguished Flying Cross (4), Air Medal with clusters. Among his four DFCs, Bill earned two for bringing crippled ships back to base and one for his participation in a unique communications effort that resulted in saving a bomber crew on D-Day. He was a B-17 pilot who flew *Lady Winifred* for most of his 28 combat missions from 1943 to 1944. Bill retired from the air force in 1972 as a colonel.

A Long, Slow, Low Return to Berlin

There are good days and bad days in flying. Some days you don't miss a trick, other days you can't hit the ground with your hat. March 22, 1944, started out to be a good day. Later on we began to wonder.

We were to go into Germany over the North Sea, making landfall somewhere east of Bremen through a gap in the flak defenses. From there on into Berlin where there was to be a ground fog that would prevent the *Luftwaffe* from flying in defense. We were to bomb the railroad marshalling yards in the center of Berlin.

I was leading the second element, lead squadron, lead group of the lead wing of the First Division. We would be the first over the target before the Jerries got our range. So we thought.

In a cloudless sky we approached Berlin and drove in on our bomb run. Then it began! The first four bursts of flak were very accurate tracking fire. Burst one exploded to the right of the lead plane's wing. Burst two hit just under his plane and ahead of my nose. A stream of blue smoke emitted from one of his engines. Burst three exploded just ahead of my right wing and my number four engine quit while the number three shuddered and "roughed up" with gauges going wild. Number four burst to my left front and oil pressure on number two engine dropped to zero.

"Feather two before we lose oil!" Ease out to the left before we lose airspeed and disrupt the whole formation behind us, I thought. Suddenly we were alone at 25,000 feet over Berlin in the middle of the main flak patch wondering, "Where do we go from here?"

First, we size up the situation. Number four: oil pressure OK, no power. "That's funny. Number three shaking out of its mounts. Set it at its highest attainable power with minimum shaking and lock the throttles." Number two feathered. Number one: "Run it at the highest power and watch the cylinder head temp. Don't let the temp get in the red." What do we get? One hundred five MPH indicated and a S-L-O-W descent of 100–150 feet per minute.

We couldn't maintain flying speed and altitude given the performance of the remaining engine power. So we slid back under the stream, gradually slipping lower and lower. The we began to see the weather front ahead of us with towering clouds and occasional views of the ground.

Bill Reeder (courtesy Bill Reeder)

Figuring that the *Luftwaffe* would be getting up and we would be fresh bait, we went down to about 9,000 feet to hide in the cloudbanks as we gingerly made our way toward home base. Somehow we "stooged" across Hanover with hundreds of flak guns. Even the light 40mm flak began to wink like sparklers around us, interspersed with the threatening black bursts of 88mm and 155mm. Noting that the larger bursts seemed to be coming in fours, indicating tracking fire, we turned this way and that each going, going into decaying blasts. We reasoned that if they were tracking they wouldn't shoot in the same place twice. It worked. At least they didn't hit us.

Finally we came through the weather front west of Hanover and it was decision time again. "Fellas," I said, "I'm going down as low as I dare to get under the radar and perhaps escape the fighters. Slim (Brage, navigator), lay us a course over the Zuider Zee and in across the hook of Holland so that we pass the fewest flak sites and we'll see where we go. If any of you would rather take your chances walking out or going to PW camp maybe you better jump now for we'll be too low when I hit the deck. Best I can offer is a cold swim in the Channel or with luck hit the ground in England. From now on we won't be able to parachute."

Down we went, as low as we dared. We began to see little Dutch villages. Villagers could be seen waving to us as we passed. Along the way we encountered a flak tower and noted the crew running up the stairs toward the guns. Sgt. Harbud laid down a hail of fire on the tower with the top turret. Since every fifth bullet was a red tracer, the message was received on the ground. Soon the gun crew in the tower was seen retreating to lower levels.

Passing IJmuiden, 88's were "laid down" for horizontal fire over the water. A few bursts scattered here and there but there was not enough time for them to get our range and we went safely out to sea. We gained a little altitude over the water as we limped along at about 105 indicated, maintained contact with air-sea rescue, and prayed for land to appear. We headed south for Southwold then redirected to Leiston. There we went straight in firing red flares.

We didn't realize until we tried to use the brakes that we had neither main nor emergency air brakes. Reasoning that the grass beside the runway would be muddy and would stop us, I kicked hard right rudder before losing rudder control and angled off the runway across the grass. Mud flew everywhere, the nose tipped down a bit, and the tail settled back to the ground. We all got out, kissed the ground, and fervently murmured, "Thank you, Lord." Then we waited for someone to come pick us up.

Later we counted up the battle damage to our trusty B-17 with call sign "Springbok Peter" or, as we had named her, *Lady Winifred*. Every engine was damaged, ranging from cables badly mangled to cylinder problems to an oil tank ruptured. Number one engine had to be changed. We had made it home but with a lot of luck on our side.

A New Mission on D-Day

For most missions we generally followed the same routine. Up at 3 o'clock, take the trucks to our briefing, go to the drying room for our flying suits. Meanwhile the gunners would get their guns and other equipment. If we had breakfast, it was quick. Then back on the trucks for the trip to our hardstand. Takeoff would be around 7 o'clock on runway 2–3. Climb to 17,000 feet, join the formation, and run the division assembly line to the coast where we would slowly climb to altitude over the Channel. There, we would test our guns, keep our tight formation, and begin watching for fighters and flak.

After finishing my 28 missions in May 1944 I was asked to stay on until D-Day. I knew the invasion of Europe was about to happen and I wanted to be a part of it, to even see it if I could. My new mission was to fly a modified B-17 with a high-powered transmitter in the bomb bay. This VHF [very high frequency] transmitter was new at the time, something that would improve communication between our planes and our base.

The plan called for me to orbit my plane at 25,000 feet, which would enable me to relay information from lead aircraft back to headquarters. They would report control points—where turns were made—and I would report on their mission progress. With VHF, we could talk a hundred miles or more. Depending on where the mission penetrated was where I would go up and circle, sometimes off the coast of Belgium, sometimes off Holland. As the mission returned, I maintained a watch for emergency signals. Sometimes planes ran out of fuel or were so battle damaged they had to ditch in the Channel. Part of my responsibility was to do what I could to help.

We were stationed off the coast of Holland one day when a pilot made a distress call, stating that he was putting his plane down in the Channel. We told him to give us a good fix on his location, which he did, and we soon started a spiral search for him. About the third or fourth run over the area we saw him in the water. The Royal Air Force always had patrol boats ready to rescue downed fliers so we helped them reach the site of the crash landing. We watched as the rescue boat picked up the crew. That was a good feeling.

I flew the VHF relay from May 1944 till the end of July. During one of our morning briefings we were told what was to happen on June 6. That was the day everyone had been building up to. German targets that would support the defense of our invasion — marshalling yards, troop buildups — were bombed. I remember on June 6 looking at the mission map which, before our briefing, was hidden by a curtain. Once it was removed I could tell by length of the string signifying our route and the reaction of the all the folks there that this was the day we had all awaited. There was lots of joy in that room.

On D-Day I was up two times. I flew early in the morning about four o'clock, came back to refuel around noon at Southhampton, and went back up and flew almost till dark. My position was just off the invasion beach. I remember the weather was not good that day. There was a layer of clouds below us that came and went but at times we could see the ships below. What a thrilling sight! We clearly saw them firing their big guns toward shore and spotted what appeared to be big, rectangular boxes being pulled by tugboats. I didn't know what they were until we got back to base. That's when an intelligence officer told us about the artificial piers, or mulberries, that were being used by our forces.

I was awarded the Distinguished Flying Cross, my third, for saving that crew in the Channel. Just as important, every June 6 for years I heard from my copilot, George DeVac. He called from California to talk about that very special day and how we contributed in our own way to its eventual success.

15

LIEUTENANT TOM GRAVES

DOB: June 5, 1922
Where: Richmond, Virginia
Air Force: 10th
Bomb Group: 12th
Squadron: 81st
Station: Fini, India
Decorations include: Air Medal with clusters. Like most of the men in this book, Tom was a 20-year-old far away from home, fighting a relentless enemy. As the pilot of a B-25 medium bomber he flew as many as five missions a day. Often they would be low-level strafing runs on trains and troop concentrations as well as skip bombing against fixed targets. He came to love the B-25, a plane bristling with machine guns that was equally effective at treetop level or 10,000 feet. After the war Tom held positions in the insurance, real estate, printing, and engineering fields.

A Strange and Scary Start

December 7, 1941, that "infamous" Sunday when Japan attacked Pearl Harbor, I was a member of the youth department of Belmont Methodist Church. Six of us who were close buddies left church immediately that Sunday for an outing in Edwin Warner Park so we did not hear the news until late that afternoon. That event quickly turned our world upside down.

The sneaky attack at Pearl Harbor made some of us really mad. I was just out of high school and I was ready to go fight. That attitude was not shared by everyone. There had been a very vocal few in the Methodist Youth Fellowship espousing "conscientious objection" relative to military service. Some of them took that route but I went to the army air corps recruiting office. A fellow there said that I could earn a staff sergeant rating and flight wings in 90 days by going to the army glider pilots school. I was excited about that. I would be a flying sergeant in 3 months!

Some of my friends at church were very supportive. They gave me a going away party and they went down to Union Station to see me leave on the troop train. The train headed east and in about 45 minutes they put our group of glider pilot recruits off the train at Smyrna, Tennessee. It was a "replacement pool" waiting for the glider schools to become available. Eighteen miles from home in Smyrna! As soon as I could, I phoned home and told them not to tell the gang where I was. They thought I was out fighting the war. We spent more time in replacement pools than we did flight training, so the 90 days was more like a year. I did become a flying sergeant but right after that the glider program folded. Those who had gotten their wings were transferred into the regular flying cadet program.

The twin engine B-25, the aircraft I flew in combat, carried a crew of 5. My crew and three other crews flew our B-25s from the states halfway around the world to Feni, India [200 miles northeast of Calcutta]. From the Feni Air Base we flew missions into Burma and China supporting the British ground troops with medium and low level strafing and bombing. It took about a year to complete the 65 combat missions required at that time but I almost didn't make past my very first flight.

Tom Graves (courtesy Tom Graves)

This was September 1944. We were picking up speed moving down the runway on takeoff when the right tire, the tire on my side, blew. At the time, of course, we were fully loaded with bombs and fuel. We were halfway down the runway, seconds before lifting the B-25 into the air. The thought quickly flashed through my mind, "Is this it? This is my first combat mission. I have ten months of training behind me and have ferried my own B-25 over from the states and now we are going up in flames?" As a new replacement pilot from stateside training, I was flying copilot for the first five missions. When the right tire blew, the pilot had several options, all of which were quite undesirable when you are loaded with bombs. He chopped the power and applied the brakes, being careful not to ground loop because of the dragging right tire. It took exceptional skill. We ran out of runway but the soft overrun area let us down easy. It was unbelievable, but we all lived to do right for many more missions.

Low Level Excitement

In April 1945, six B-25 bombers, their pilots, and crews were assigned a 10-day tour of duty in central Burma at an airfield named Myitkyina. It had been retaken from the Japanese just 9 months earlier. These B-25s were part of the 12th Bomb Group, 10th Air Force which had been performing medium altitude bombing missions into Burma and China from Fini, India. The 12th Bomb Group had seen action in the Italian and African campaigns prior to entering the CBI. My B-25, *Booby Trap*, and crew were one of the six on this tour of duty which explains my interest in the following story about retaking the airstrip at Myitkyina.

Immediately after the attack on Pearl Harbor, using Thailand as a springboard, the Japs attacked the southern tip of Burma. By the end of May 1942, they had taken almost complete control of the country. The seizure of Burma cut the Allied supply line from India to China. To overcome this obstacle, General Stilwell ordered the construction of the Ledo Road which began in northern India at Ledo and was to join the old Burma Road at Mong Yu.

In early 1944, Merrill's Marauders crossed hundreds of miles of rugged mountain terrain to seize a hard-surfaced airfield held by the Japanese. Myitkyina, a small northern Burmese town, was the railway terminus from Rangoon and an important stop on the Ledo Road then under construction. Because it was positioned on the outskirts of the airfield, Myitkyina was destined to take on an importance out of all proportion to its size. Control of the airfield was critical to Stilwell's continued advance eastward to China. It was assumed that the town itself would soon fall, allowing engineers to continue their work on the Ledo Road through Myitkyina and onto Mong Yu to connect with the old Burma Road. However, it was a three-month siege, with many of the GI engineers fighting as infantry. Myitkyina was finally taken by the Allies on August 3, 1944.

Being one of the group at Myitkyina for a 10 day assignment was exciting. It was different flying low level and short missions against an enemy that was much more close-up and personal than we had been used to in medium altitude bombing. One mission I remember well was on April 24, 1945, a beautiful day in central Burma. We were flying loose formation in two B-25s (twin engine medium bombers). I was flying the lead aircraft with Captain Nerone as navigator. Task: bomb and destroy troops and stores at Ryecai and Chaung, Burma. My wing man was a lean, tall, good-looking, red-headed Texan, L.E. Jensen. He and I had been flying quite a bit that day and loving it. Three times before we had landed from short missions and had been assigned another. This was the last mission of the day.

Three years earlier, Lloyd Jensen and I were in the states as student pilots. Even then we realized how much pure fun flying had become. Being only two years beyond our teens, we liked the excitement of close formation and low level flying. We had been assigned to the 81st Squadron, 12th Bomb Group about a year earlier. Now we were doing some low level bombing and strafing and it was exhilarating! At a real quick briefing we were assigned another mission. We were to fly out to a village 65 miles east at 3,000 feet, circle the group of 75 grass huts of various sizes and shapes, drop down and destroy them. Watch for heavy enemy fire. Wow! We knew that would be great fun if we could avoid the enemy fire. We would take turns diving in steep with our forward guns blazing and pulling out fast.

Now, with Lloyd on my right wing, we were wasting no time because it was only two hours till sunset. I wondered as we approached the village, were the villagers gone? Was the enemy there? We took turns diving, strafing, and dropping bombs (4,000 rounds of .50 caliber ammunition and a load of fire bombs). Because of our 10, forward-firing .50 cal. guns the Japs kept their heads down. There was very little enemy action. The tremendous explosions from inside the straw huts proved (as intelligence said) the Japs had moved the villagers out and were using their village as an ammunition storage area. Pounding the village for the last time, we turned west toward our base at Myitkyina and into the most beautiful sunset you could imagine. Behind us the village was an inferno. Mission accomplished!

Irrawaddy Beachhead, Burma

We were used to some home base comforts at our airfield back in India such as our own beds in well-built bashas. So my April 1945, visit to the advancing front line ground troops in Burma was rough camping for eight days and nights. We were visiting the boys of the British

15. Lieutenant Tom Graves

Second Division who were just completing a temporary bridge across the Irrawaddy River. Five of us B-25 pilots from a U.S. base (Feni, India, 200 miles east of Calcutta) were on an exchange visit with British ground troops. A British liaison officer, Major F.L. Canadine, R.A., was leading our group. We had been bombing and strafing Jap troops for months in this area, destroying their roads and bridges. So it was quite a change to get a "worm's eye" view of ground troops doing a similar job and hearing what they thought of us and our work. The "Brits" were part of the 14th Army's drive on Mandalay. They were digging in to defend the river crossing there at Ngazun, Burma.

On the morning of our second day we visited some forward ground troops. There were too many snipers still around so we did not visit the very front lines. When we heard the scream of an incoming shell all five of us Yank pilots immediately dropped to the ground thinking that the shell had our names on it. The ground troops securing the river bridgehead were all still standing, going about their tasks. "That one was going to hit nowhere near us," they laughed. "Stick with us and you'll learn." We spent much time talking to the British over cups of tea. There was always tea no matter how close you got to the front lines.

One reason for our trip was to evaluate what was left of roads, bridges, gun positions, and ammo stores that we had bombed and helped destroy there the previous weeks. The Jap hideouts in Ngazun had been as good as ever but their troops' getaway was speedy. Many a Jap had left his precious rice bag behind with his kit. Some rice was cooked ready for eating and there was dried fish that looked like octopus.

While near the ground action, I was fascinated with the light planes, called "grasshoppers," that flew all kinds of combat support missions in World War II particularly in the China-Burma-India Theater. Staff Sergeant W. Howe, a pilot, gave me a low level, hedge-hopping ride near the front lines and explained the types of missions to which they were assigned. "They call us 'Maytag pilots' but I love it. We do everything from carrying the mail to evacuating the wounded," Billy said. "I sometimes do a little combat. The Japs left one of theirs tied up in a tree with rifle and ammo to harass us when they retreated. I circled that tree for a long time using my service pistol and hand grenades before I got him." That tree was one of the sights Billy pointed out on my hedge-hopping tour.

"In the early invasion of Burma, some of the strips on which we landed were carved out on mountain tops," Billy motioned as he swooped his hand down. "It was like settling onto an aircraft carrier. Once, by the time I stopped rolling, I was at the edge of a precipice. Overshooting meant a crash landing hundreds of feet below in dense jungle."

I knew what he meant. I flew Piper Cubs in my flight training back in the states. Before helicopters, light planes were used to do the dirty work. The L5, called the "flying jeep," Stinson with its 185 horsepower engine was the largest. The smaller L1 was more popular. They were also called "stretcher ships." Many wounded and sick soldiers would have died in the jungle had it not been for light plane outfits with meaningful names — "Jungle Angels," "Burma Cubs," "Burma Butterflies," and others.

Billy explained, "We light plane pilots do everything; helping unload supplies from railroad cars, cutting elephant grass, carrying grain for British mules, watching smudge pots at night on jungle strips to replenish them with oil or putting them out quickly in case hostile aircraft approach. We work on our own planes, too (no mechanics were assigned to them). We fly as many as twenty missions a day, often sitting in our planes eating midday chow while our gas tanks are filled." Reaching into his pocket, Billy continued. "If we have a forced landing in the jungle we are prepared to buy our way out. We use 'escape rupees' and opium to pay for help. We give only as much opium as can be scraped off this chunk with a thumbnail.

We know the Japs offer bounty for our capture, so we wouldn't dare turn our backs on these jungle guides." As long as the natives knew that the downed pilot still had opium and a gun, they would work for him.

We all learned much to take back to our bomber base. Later, some of the "Brit" ground troops flew with us and experienced our bombing missions. Meeting the L1 pilot and the British ground troops was rewarding. Our admiration for the British soldiers was unbounded. We were proud to be associated with them in obliterating the Japs in Burma.

16

CAPTAIN BILL BECKER

DOB: June 5, 1923
Where: Cincinnati, Ohio
Air Force: 13th
Bomb Group: 307th
Squadron: 381st
Station: Morotai
Decorations include: Purple Heart, Air Medal with clusters.
On April 19, 1945, Bill was the bombardier aboard one of eight B-24s sent to bomb an enemy troop ship in Saigon harbor. Japanese fighters attacked, severely damaging his plane and causing it to eventually crash-land at a temporary base on Palawan Island. Every member of his crew was wounded. It was Bill's thirty-third combat mission, one he flew only as a favor for a friend — a pilot flying his last mission. Bill went on to record 38 missions, part of which he flew as group bombardier. In civilian life Bill was a manufacturer's rep dealing in liquid measuring instruments.

One Bad Mission

We probably should have taken it as an omen when our first pilot, the guy we trained with, went out on his first combat mission to get broken in and didn't return. That is, he didn't return for about two months. Loren Corliss was from Wichita, Kansas, and he was doing what almost all pilots did when they first got into combat: riding with another crew just to acclimate himself and get checked out at the same time.

We were kidding him before he left. "What do you want to keep in your bag?" we asked him while playfully dividing up his property should he disappear. We felt bad when we learned he was shot down. Thankfully, Loren's story has a happy ending. He was one of the few to be saved by some missionaries in the Philippines. A native boy found him and he was hidden and protected until he returned to our base on Morotai. Any idea Loren had that his wishes would be instantly granted because of his outstanding luck was quickly dashed when he asked to be reinstated with us, his original crew. He was turned down because we were way ahead of him in missions completed.

I suppose my worst mission occurred on April 19, 1945. Captain Briggs, the pilot, asked me if I would fly his last mission with him as the bombardier on his B-24. At the briefing we found out our target was a Japanese transport supposedly loaded with troops and sitting in Saigon harbor. We took off at 1:00 A.M. and headed to Palawan Island for refueling. There were only 12 airplanes on this mission. Four had mechanical problems so we finally got over the target with eight aircraft.

As a bombardier, I had come to love the Norden bombsight. It was a near perfect machine. Once its gyro was leveled up as the bomb run started I would get ready to sight the target using two knobs, one for drift and one for airspeed. Then I would engage the airplane and fly it myself to the target. I would look into the bombsight and see crosshairs, making any corrections throughout the bomb run. We never dropped bombs straight down on a target as many folks might think after watching movies or documentaries. We had airspeed, wind direction and strength, and other factors to consider all before our load was dropped. Also, the spacing of the bombs was preset by us, depending on the kind of target and the weight of the bombs. For example, if we carried 100-pound fragmentation bombs they would scatter everywhere whereas 500-pound bombs didn't drift.

When I looked into the sight on this mission I saw Jap planes rising to meet us from a nearby airfield. They looked like a bunch of angry bees as I lay on my stomach, calling them out to whoever would listen. They threw everything they had at us since there weren't many of us. Shells were flying everywhere, ripping our plane and leaving holes from nose to tail.

One or two Japs even dived directly in front of our planes, causing considerable prop wash and quite a bit of herky-jerky movement by us. By then, though, we had already dropped our bombs and as we left the target the transport was seen lying on its side. But the damage to us had been done. Two engines had caught fire, our oxygen system had been hit, and the upper turret had come loose and hit me in the back. My earphone cable had been cut by a piece of shrapnel that flew perilously close to my head. I thought I was going to die. In fact, every crewmember on my ship was wounded in some way but we finally managed to crash land on Palawan Island. The other planes fared little better. Of the eight that made it over the target that day, five never flew again.

Everyone kept their cool and did their job on that mission; that's where our superior training really paid off. The only things we could think of afterward were how lucky we had been to survive and how we had to make the Japs pay for their actions.

Bill Becker (courtesy Bill Becker)

17

Sergeant David Oldashi

DOB: June 15, 1922
Where: Greenville, Tennessee
Air Force: 5th
Bomb Group: 38th
Squadron: 822nd
Station: Nadzab, New Guinea, among others
Decorations include: Air Medal with clusters. David flew 35 combat missions as a radio operator/waist gunner on a B-25. As American forces advanced in the Pacific, his base moved with them. David returned from the war, graduated from the University of Kentucky, and worked in retail merchandising for nearly 40 years. He dedicated considerable time and effort as a scoutmaster with the Boy Scouts.

An SOS at OSS

I was nearing graduation at radio operator's school, Scott Field, Illinois, when one day this guy came by and said he wanted to speak to the top 12 people in our class. I was one of the 12 picked to listen to him talk about the OSS, or Office of Strategic Services. Until then I had never heard of the OSS. "You'll have a great opportunity to become an officer," he said as he buttered us up. "Oh, and by the way, you will be staying at the Congressional Country Club." He didn't mention anything about living in the wilderness; he just wanted to get some people to sign up.

All of us were radio operators, proficient in Morse code, and to most of us his sales pitch sounded great. He didn't talk about going behind enemy lines, only that we would be taken to the Congressional Country Club. He kept talking about that beautiful club. Boy, we thought that was great. Sure enough when we got there we were impressed with how lavish it was. We lived in nice accommodations and we weren't marching, just sort of hanging around. We could even go to Washington if we wanted.

Our relaxing interlude lasted about a week. Then we were told to pack our barracks bags. We should have figured something out then. A truck came late at night when no one was around and soon an officer made his presence known by telling us to load up. "Where are we going?" we all asked. Nobody knew and the officer wasn't talking so they loaded us up and took us to the deepest, darkest part of what I thought was Quantico, the vast Marine training ground in suburban Virginia. We passed a series of security gates at which each guard took the truck driver's credentials, carefully checked them, and then moved us on.

We ended up several miles into the woods at a big, rustic building. "Here's your cabin and this is who you are with," came the announcement. As it turned out, the housing and food were good but we still didn't know what was going on or why we were there. Then the call came out over the loudspeaker nearby that we were to assemble by groups: A, B, C, etc. Following that, we proceeded to different parts of the camp for different kinds of instruction: hand to hand combat, climbing nets (I couldn't climb a net if I had to), parachute drops, and different arms training.

I knew it was time for me to go when we met Major Fairburn, a gentleman with a well-known reputation for fearless hand-to-hand combat. Soon after that each of us was paired with an American who could speak a foreign language. Mine was some sort of east European language, Czech, I believe. Now, why would our leaders have these foreign speaking folks here for us? That's when I decided I needed to leave. I told my buddies that I wasn't staying and they just laughed. "Nobody gets out of here," they said.

Then I thought of my friend from college days at the University of Kentucky. He was the son of a major general and maybe, just maybe, his father could be my ticket out. I went to the appropriate OSS guy and told him I really didn't want to be in for the duration. To his credit he allowed me to call the general who knew me through his son. Soon after that transfer orders came in and I got reclassified to gunnery school. Eventually I ended up as a radio operator/waist gunner in a B-25, stationed in the South Pacific.

I never saw or heard from any of my OSS buddies again. I was afraid to inquire about them. God only knows where they ended up and what kind of experiences they had. I never regretted not staying in since I shouldn't have been involved in the first place. I can still see those cabins deep in the Virginia woods and smell the smells and see that big net going up. I can hear the loud voices of those tough instructors and feel the pressure when they threw us in the hand-to-hand combat.

When I left the OSS training area I had to swear that I would never talk or write about my experiences there. I've told more in this story than I have ever told before.

Hidden Carrier Attack

When we went into Wewak and Nadzab we were more or less rear guard workers, cleaning

David Oldashi (courtesy David Oldashi)

up Japs up and down the coast of New Guinea. Pockets of enemy troops remained but we were after shipping. Most of the Jap ships we encountered were wooden supply vessels that, if caught, would suffer the consequences of our powerful guns.

We had moved to Okinawa in July 1945, when intelligence told us that a Japanese escort carrier, *Kaiyo*, was in Beppu Bay, Japan. There were pictures of her sitting there covered with netting to keep our planes from spotting her. She was in the bay to undergo repairs after some bruising encounters with attack aircraft.

Our B-25 was picked as one of the planes from the 38th Bomb Group, 5th Air Force, to sink it. Lt. Colonel Ed Hawes, commanding officer of the 38th, would lead the attack. During our briefing when the pictures were shown, Hawes couldn't hide his exuberance. "Boys, we don't want to come back empty handed," he told us. That meant we were going down on the deck. He was so gung ho about this operation I figured a success would mean a big feather in his officer's cap. Well, his excitement got us all fired up. Everybody was hitting each other and pumping each other up. I really wanted to go on this mission since we would probably talk about it the rest of our lives.

Colonel Hawes needed a crew and as it turned out my name was on the board to fly with him as radio operator/waist gunner. I had only flown with him once before on a mission that wasn't very exciting, in fact it seemed more like training than combat. I really wanted to go with my regular crew so when I saw that my name had been struck from his crew list I was really happy. That meant I could stay with the boys I knew the best.

Sixteen planes would take part in this special mission which was scheduled to begin with an early morning takeoff although we were only about an hour and a half away from target. The flight plan called for us to fly at about 5,000 feet, then dive to 500 feet after we cleared some mountains. We would then fly through a valley populated by a small town before flying over water and hitting the carrier. We were to be spaced out so that two of us would go in at a time.

As we entered the valley on our run, I started firing away with my .50 caliber guns from the waist position. This was an opportunity to shoot and shoot some more and that's what I did. We shot up everything we saw in the valley as we flew by at maximum speed. Colonel Hawes was on the left and our plane was on the right as we dropped our bombs and fired our rockets on that ship in the face of heavy ground fire. As we pulled up and away in opposite directions, I looked out my left window to suddenly see Colonel Hawes' plane shudder after getting hit. The plan called for all planes to veer off after their runs to avoid our own bomb damage and circle the ship. Instead, it looked to me as if his plane simply turned over and went down into the sea. There was no explosion and I never saw him get hit. I radioed back to headquarters at Okinawa that the colonel's plane had gone down and gave them the position where he went in. They badly wanted all the information I could provide.

Soon we headed back to base, watching the explosions continue to rock the carrier. I told Al Dallinger, our bombardier, if he missed that blooming ship he ought to have his backside kicked. We were happy to discover later that we put the carrier out of commission. Unfortunately Colonel Hawes and most, if not all, of his crew were never found.

That night I went to a movie on the base. Somebody in front of me turned around after hearing my voice. "How can you be here? You're missing in action! They had you flying with Colonel Hawes." My friend didn't realize I had been bumped from the colonel's crew, thus saving my life. His was the only plane we lost in that action.

18

LIEUTENANT ROY BUCK

DOB: July 5, 1917
Where: Nashville, Tennessee
Air Force: 8th
Bomb Group: 85th
Squadron: 548th
Station: Stowmarket, England
Decorations include: Distinguished Flying Cross, Air Medal with clusters. Roy's opinion about the weather while flying over the English Channel proved to be fateful on one of his 35 combat missions as a B-17 bombardier. For him and his plane *Heavenly Body* it was the last mission of the war. After returning home Roy worked 34 years for South Central Bell, retiring in 1980.

What A Day to Ditch!

Like a lot of other young men during the war, I started out to be a pilot. My plans came to a sudden end one day during a storm when I plowed the ground in my PT-19 upon landing. So I had my choice of being a navigator or bombardier and I chose what I thought would be the easiest job — hitting a target at 25,000 feet. Before long I was packed off to bombardier school at Midland, Texas, where just about the most notable thing to happen to me was saving the life of our ball turret gunner. He was 39 years old and had a son flying in the navy. He always said he wasn't going to let his son get ahead of him. Anyway, during a routine oxygen check on one of our flights he didn't respond the right way so I checked on him. That's when I found that his oxygen mask had frozen. We got his oxygen flowing again and he thanked me for saving his life. I was 26 at the time and the pilot was about that age. We were a bunch of old folks compared to most crews we knew.

I was assigned to the 385th Bomb Group of the 8th Air Force as a B-17 bombardier. I always thought the B-17 was a good airplane. It could fly on two of its four engines. That was just fine with me because we had some close calls with flak. One time a nose window was shot out and we lost our hydraulics. Another time we got the signal to bail out because we couldn't get the number three engine under control but it finally just chewed up its gears and ran smoothly. A little piece of flak no bigger than your thumb fouled it up. I'd rather have enemy fighters to battle than the flak we faced everyday.

On our last mission, in September 1944, we were going to Bremen aboard *Heavenly Body*. I think it was an oil refinery we were ordered to hit. We were breaking in a new pilot, who was normally our copilot, because our regular pilot, Charlie Woodward, was wounded by flak on our 33rd mission. I remember looking down at the North Sea while we were headed toward our target, seeing lots of white caps on the water, and thinking what a day it would be to ditch in that.

We had just crossed the German coast when all of a sudden an engine on the right side acted up. It might have been from flak. The pilot had to let it windmill because it wouldn't feather at first. Later it did. The group leader told us to turn back since we had no chance of keeping up with the rest of the formation. We had quickly become a sitting duck for fighters.

Roy Buck (courtesy Roy Buck)

We turned around and dropped our bombs over the North Sea. At that point I was still pretty calm. We were busy throwing things out of the plane to make it lighter but after 20 minutes or so two other engines died. I'm not sure why they went out. Perhaps they were under too much strain. The B-17 was a wonderful aircraft but it wasn't going to fly on just one engine. We were also fighting a nasty headwind. The pilot ordered all of us into the radio room, the pre-selected place to go when ditching looked likely. I sat with my back against the fuselage with my legs out and someone sat in front of me the same way and someone in front of him in a similar position designed to provide us with adequate bracing for any violent contact. As the radio operator kept in touch with the guys up front, we all shook hands and kept quiet. I remember thinking how I always said my prayers before going on any mission.

We were losing altitude pretty quickly so we put our hands behind our heads to support our necks. The plane soon hit the water with a series of bumps, sort of like traveling on a rough road. The bracing really helped protect us but we actually weren't thrown around much at all even though we were a little stunned. Soon we found ourselves sitting in water and all of us knew how important it was to make a timely exit from our plane. It wouldn't take long for *Heavenly Body* to sink. The nose had broken off and the plane was split wide open. I just walked out on the wing and hollered back at the others, "Fellas, come out this way." "No," they said, "we're going to follow the proper ditching procedures." That meant they would get out through a hatch up top even though they saw how easy it was for me to get out. They wanted to make sure they got one of the two rafts that had popped out after impact.

The navigator joined me on the wing. His life jacket opened when he pulled the cord but mine didn't work. I had to blow it up. The rest of the crew was in a raft on the other side from us. Lucky for me I knew how to swim. I got up to the cockpit, looked in, and saw the pilot and copilot hunched over. I knocked on the window but got no response and no movement out of either one of them. About that time I got washed away. They could have died some other way but I'm thinking they probably had their spines snapped by the violence of the crash.

I kept thinking that I was *not* going to die on my very last mission. As I treaded water, I watched the plane sink. All kinds of things floated by me so I grabbed hold of an oxygen bottle and hung on. I tried to swim to the crewmembers in the lifeboat and they tried to row over to me but the more we tried the farther we were pulled apart by the waves.

We were in the water a good 30 minutes before I noticed some P-47s flying above, fixing our position. You could have just about hidden a house in those waves that day. We would ride the crest way to the top and then sink very low as we bottomed out. It was on one of those rides to the top that I looked out and saw a little boat approaching. Turned out to be British Air-Sea Rescue. Not long after that, I heard a fellow yell, "Hold on, mate, we see you." I was real happy when I saw them. They threw me a life preserver and their aim was so good it went right across my lip, leaving me with a nice burn. After that, they pulled me in and got me on deck. I was so cold. I shook so hard I think I shook the whole boat. They took a big towel and rubbed me down, then gave me a big shot of Scotch to warm me up a little followed by some hot broth. I got up after awhile to see about the rest of my crew. They were all lying down because most of them were seasick. I was still so happy I made some wisecrack about the fact that they could fly over 30 combat missions without any problems and then they travel on a little boat and get seasick. They told me where to go.

We lost our pilot and copilot but the rest of the crew made it out ok. We left the boat at the British naval base at Great Yarmouth. A nurse looked me over and pronounced me relatively healthy. I didn't even get a cut. That night they brought me a fish supper and I told them to take that stuff back. I didn't want to see any fish so they brought me some hot soup. Before we left for the base the next day, I went back to the boat and thanked the captain for saving us. He was glad to see me and said, "Yank, have a drink." So we had a small farewell party before saying our good-byes. He looked at my Bausch and Lomb sunglasses in a way that told me they would be a nice gift for plucking me out of the water. I gave them to him.

I also thanked my Maker. Our navigator was known to be an atheist so I asked him, "Herb, what were you thinking out there?" He said, "I hated to die a virgin." He made up for it later. I think I was left for a reason, a purpose. I don't know what it was. I was pretty upset to think about all that happening on my last mission. I was glad I did what I did but I wouldn't do it again. You go up 35 times on combat missions and if you get out of it with your life you're lucky, just lucky. I know I had a guardian angel watching over me.

19

SERGEANT BUD REEDER

DOB: November 30, 1922
Where: Poughkeepsie, New York
Air Force: 15th
Bomb Group: 97th
Squadron: 340th
Station: Foggia, Italy
Decorations include: Soldiers Medal, Air Medal with clusters. What were the chances of running into your brother overseas during the war? Pretty slim, for sure. But that's what happened to Bud while stationed in Italy. He flew 39 sorties and was credited with 51 missions (some missions received double credit) during his time as an engineer/top turret gunner in a B-17. He received the Soldiers Medal for his actions aboard a burning plane on one of those trips. Postwar, Bud worked in law enforcement for 30 years.

That's My Brother!

My job as a top turret gunner in a B-17 landed me in Italy for the duration of my combat experience, flying out of a two-runway field at Amendola, north of Foggia. I knew my brother was in Italy but I didn't know exactly where. Charlie was in an army anti-aircraft unit and then attached to the infantry because, at the time, the Germans were not much of a threat in the air.

The first big break I had finding Charlie came one evening when a movie was showing in an old barn on base. I was strolling over to see it when I looked down at a truck's bumper and saw his unit's number stenciled there. It was standard procedure for such designations to be placed on vehicles. Once I saw the number I just decided to sit at the truck and wait for the driver to return. Eventually he did and he told me where the unit was when he left. Turns out the unit headquarters was located north of Naples, up in the mountains south of Monte Cassino, not extremely far away but far enough to pose a challenge for me getting there.

At first I was told I couldn't go up there. "Are you crazy?" they told me, "you don't want to go up there." "You're not supposed to go up there and I can't give you permission," an

Bud Reeder (courtesy Bud Reeder)

officer informed me, adding "but you do what you want." With that double-edged permission, I took off with a two-day pass in hand and hitchhiked all the way. I got a ride with a lieutenant heading toward the lines in that area. He understood my mission.

As we got closer to my brother's area, the danger grew. The Germans were lobbing artillery shells all around us. Some of the shells left gaping holes in the road ahead of us so an MP stopped traffic long enough for our bulldozers to fill them in. We were out in the open the whole time and subject to continuous shelling but we stuck with our position until the bulldozers had done their work and the MP signaled us through. That's when the miracle happened.

The driver of the very first truck we encountered coming from the other direction was none other than my brother. I couldn't believe my eyes! I knew him the moment I spotted him and quickly jumped out of the jeep, not saying goodbye or thanking the lieutenant. I was pretty easy to spot myself because I was wearing my old air force sheep jacket. I couldn't believe my luck to spot Charlie so easily and so quickly. I jumped in the truck with him, explained that I had a two day pass just to see him, and off we went on his mission to load up on supplies for the troops in the lines. Heading north in the jeep I kept thinking, "How in the world am I going to find my brother in such a short time?" but I did and I knew it was a miracle.

When we returned to his unit, the men were all dug in on the sheltered side of a mountain with pup tents over the foxholes. I got to meet some of Charlie's friends and we had a great time together. The next day we crawled up to the top of the mountain and looked over the edge. There, we had a ringside seat for the bombing and strafing of the town of Cassino and the monastery above it. We were safe for the most part and we did that for the better part of two days. After saying our goodbyes, I hitchhiked back to my base with British truck drivers, one of whom took me all the way back to Foggia and another to my base from there.

The very next mission I flew was to — you guessed it — Cassino. I couldn't believe it. When we arrived over the target there were large clouds of dust so we just dropped our bombs on the dust and eventually wiped that city off the map. The mission was a little strange in that it was very short. In fact, we used our own base as the IP for the trip meaning the bomb run actually started at our base. It was low level bombing all the way and, at least over the target, things went well.

As a way of poking fun at me, my brother told me later he saw the planes flying over and then flying away, thinking that we had such an easy job because after that we returned home and to our own tents and beds. He didn't know that after we left Cassino and before we could get out over the sea, German batteries that stretched all along the Italian coast opened up on us. We lost two planes before we could reach safety.

While I was gone on this two day leave, my crew took the colonel's plane up to test fly its four new engines. Everything went well until the landing when the copilot threw the wrong switch and the landing gear actually came up while the plane was about to set down on the runway. The pilot had no time to do anything but land it the best way he could. They were never criticized for that landing even though there was lots of undercarriage damage and the props were torn up. It was just an honest mistake. Fortunately, no one was hurt.

Fire Over Ferrara

Someone at headquarters thought it would be good if we were to take out the railroad yards at Ferrara, Italy, up north, so on May 14, 1944, we headed that way. This time on our bomb run we encountered only flak, no fighters, thankfully, but the flak was bad. I was standing in my normal position, the top turret of our B-17, when suddenly I heard a bang and saw smoke pouring out from underneath the circular, raised platform I was standing on. Much to my horror and that of the crew, flames started spewing from below. Bomber crews will tell you that the worst possible event that can happen aboard your ship, short of a direct hit, is a fire, especially when the bombs haven't been dropped.

There's a difference of opinion about what happened next. I believe we were coming off our bomb run and had dropped our load when the fire occurred. Others say our pilot immediately pulled out of formation, salvoed the bombs, and turned for home.

Either way, we had a mess on our hands. The fire had already singed my trousers when I jumped down, doused my head with water from my canteen to get the smoke out of my eyes, and grabbed two extinguishers nearby. I quickly used them up, which wasn't hard considering the blaze was being fed by oxygen. As we later learned, it consumed a bunch of wires, electrical components, oxygen lines, and oil lines. At this point, though, I was still trying to fight the stubborn fire by myself. Moving as fast as I could through the open bomb bay to the rear, I grabbed two more extinguishers from the radio room, returned to my position, and used them to control and put out the flames.

The boys in the back told me later they all had on their chutes and were lined up to jump. They were pretty sure they were going to have to exit the ship but they waited until the very last minute. Good thing they did. The pilot, once he saw the fire just a few feet away from the cockpit, jumped out of his seat and slid down to the nose hatch looking for a chute. He was ready to jump. And he would have had the bombardier and navigator not stopped him and pushed him back up top where the copilot, who was flying the plane, pushed him back into his seat. I'm sure it was a quick, emotional decision he made because he was scared. We all were scared! I never was really mad at him but if he had jumped I would have been. He was not our regular pilot but was filling in for the day. Later, we found three of the four parachutes kept in the front compartment were burned so they would have been useless anyway.

We got back down on the ground and everybody was happy to be safe. My feet and ankles were burned but otherwise I was fine. I think I just went back to my tent and lay down but I didn't fly for four days after that. Now, here's the rest of the story. After I completed my combat missions and returned to the states, I was stationed at Dyersburg Army Air Field in Tennessee as a gunnery instructor. One day a guy from the orderly room came up to me and said, "Hey, you got awarded the Soldiers Medal." The Soldiers Medal, as I learned, was awarded, and still is, for heroism not involving actual conflict with the enemy. He had the paperwork and the box with the medal in his hand. "You want it now or do you want a parade?" I told him I certainly didn't want a parade so he just handed me the box with the medal and the citation that went with it. I didn't need a ceremony, I was proud someone thought enough of my actions to recommend me for a medal that few folks received.

Colonel Jacob Smart— Alive or Dead?

Our CO of the 97th Bomb Group was Colonel Jacob Smart, a man loved and respected by those who served under him. He was a regular guy, not too high up to speak to us common guys even though he was a West Point graduate and an officer with lots of responsibilities. Colonel Smart was special for a lot of reasons but one of them was the fact that he was picked by General Hap Arnold to organize, plan, and pull off the first Ploesti raid, a low-level raid over the vast oil fields using B-24 bombers. He did his job and he did it well in everything that he undertook.

That included leading his men into battle. On May 10, 1944, our mission called for us to hit an aircraft factory at Weiner-Neustadt, Austria. It was another long flight, lasting seven and a half hours, and I think it was the worst target we had. There was lots of flak and there were lots of fighters on this particular day. As a top turret gunner on a B-17, I often had a good view of everything going on around us. On this day I had a view but I was also very, very busy trying to keep the fighters off of us.

Colonel Smart was leading our group, flying in a plane in front and above. Behind him stretched the rest of us. The flak was hot and heavy on the bomb run and I remember seeing the colonel's plane take a direct hit. The whole front of his plane just blew off and shortly afterward I saw two chutes, but only two. I had seen, and was to see, lots of planes hit and go down but this was startling. Colonel Jacob Smart, commanding officer of our 97th Bomb Group, lost over enemy territory.

We found out several days later that the colonel was killed. While it saddened all of us, it didn't particularly come as a surprise because none of us thought anyone could have lived through that explosion. We tried to take his loss in stride because we were losing so many people on our daylight missions. I had flown with Colonel Smart as part of his crew several times and each time found him easy to get along. His absence was tough to take.

After I returned to my home in New Jersey, I noticed that there was to be a war bond rally in a nearby city. The guest speaker was a Colonel Jacob Smart from the Pentagon in Washington, D.C. I couldn't believe what I had read. I gathered some papers from the 97th that concerned him, some information that I thought he might like to have such as papers relating to the celebration of the group's milestone of reaching 300 missions. I packaged those things and took them with me to the rally. I got there a little early and went down to the stage area and there he was. I was able to talk with him for about five minutes, even after he had been introduced to the large crowd. I explained to him that I was on the raid when his plane went down and that I actually saw it explode. That was the first time he had heard a personal account of what happened. I gave him the papers I had. He moved on to make his speech before the large crowd and I returned home. During our brief conversation, he told me that all he knew was that there had been an explosion and he ended up floating down in a chute. He had been badly injured but landed safely and eventually taken to a POW camp.

I didn't see Colonel Smart until years later but I kept track of him. He became a general, reaching four-star rank before retiring. In fact, he was wounded again during the Korean War. I've met him a few times at our reunions and we always talk about the mission that day and how fate protected both of us during the war.

20

MAJOR CLARENCE EVANS

DOB: June 30, 1916
Where: Epps, Alabama
Air Force: 8th
Bomb Group: 445th
Squadron: 702nd
Station: Tibenham, England
Decorations include: Purple Heart, Distinguished Flying Cross. A graduate of the United States Military Academy (1939), Clarence entered Harvard Law School but his studies were interrupted by the war. He was recalled to active duty in 1941, eventually serving as a squadron commander in Europe. Clarence was shot down on his fifth mission and became a prisoner of war in February 1944. Upon war's end, he resumed his studies and graduated from Harvard Law School (1946). He has been an active lawyer since then. Among other notable achievements, he organized the original Kentucky Fried Chicken Corporation and served on its board of directors. He retired as a colonel in the air force reserve.

Jimmy

During training there was a fellow squadron commander in the 445th Bomb Group who just didn't perform. His outfit just wasn't up to snuff. Their bombing wasn't any good and as far as aircraft maintenance, they had too many planes out of commission. We kept very careful records on time back in those days; things such as ready time and flyable hours, how much time each plane was in the shop, and this guy was just "tail end Charlie" on everything.

Soon the under performing squadron commander was replaced by a new guy who just happened to be the movie actor Jimmy Stewart. We quickly found out that Jimmy was a doggone good fellow. He was single and he mixed well with all the boys, playing the piano at the officers club, for example. He was also very efficient. I had the top squadron as far as bombing records, maintenance, and performance were concerned but it wasn't long until Jimmy was giving me a run for the money. He was just as nice a fellow as you would ever want to meet. It ended up that Jimmy and I took our squadrons to England where we were based at Tibenham in East Anglia, northeast of London. Our squadrons flew several training missions around England and then we started flying combat missions over Europe.

We found ourselves working together quite a bit. As squadron commanders we not only flew but also found ourselves on the ground some days putting together the briefings, beginning with a 2 A.M. field order, and then conducting the briefings. Other times, about every fourth mission or so, we would act as controllers of the airfield. That reminds me of a special memory I have about Jimmy. You see it was a very emotional time waiting for our planes to come back from a mission. These were boys we had trained with for six months or so, so we were close to each one. Those beat up and damaged planes returning from their missions would always include plenty of cripples. We had to get those ships down and on the ground safely before we could land the others. Pilots would hit the runway with no gear down and sparks flew but we had to get those planes out of the way to make room for the others to land as quickly as possible. We tried to time it so a plane landed every 30 seconds.

Clarence Evans (courtesy Clarence Evans)

A lot has been written about how good a pilot Jimmy was but I haven't seen much about how he cared so deeply for his boys. He was a very conscientious fellow whose squadron suffered the first loss of a ship shot down. I'll never forget seeing him on top of that control tower, a two story building with a concrete roof. He was up there, I guess, for two hours or more even after the rest of us knew that plane was down somewhere or gone because it simply didn't have enough gas to stay up that long. I still get emotional when I think about Jimmy being there, hoping against hope that he would spot that ship in the distance and guide it in. I felt so sorry for him. He stayed up on that tower until 9 P.M. that night, knowing damn well that plane was gone. There really wasn't anything we could say to him at the time but that night demonstrated to me and the others just how much he cared for his men. That image of Jimmy has stayed with me. Yes, Jimmy flew his missions and got his crew back safely.

After the war, Jimmy and I remained friends. Whenever he came through Nashville he would always call. One year I was helping with a Community Chest drive. We were to have a big banquet and we needed a guest speaker. "Who could we get?" they asked me. I stuck my neck out and said, "Well, let me see if I can get Jimmy Stewart." Of course, there were plenty of horse laughs as a response to that idea but I called him. Turned out he had a conflict but he sent the well-known and popular comedian Joe E. Brown in his place. That was a very nice gesture on his part.

Jimmy Stewart and I not only commanded two of the best squadrons in the whole bomb group, but we were mutually respected, good friends.

The Gotha Raid

I flew as group commander in the lead ship on that day, February 24, 1944. The target was a Messerschmitt factory at Gotha, in central Germany. The whole 8th Air Force was going after various targets related in some way to Germany's aircraft industry. Our intent was to drive the *Luftwaffe* out of the air as part of what was called the "Big Week." Our bombers and fighters were to work together to deal a deathblow to Germany's efforts, or at least that was the plan.

Even though I was squadron commander (the 702nd of the 445th Bomb Group), I flew as group commander that day, in charge of 24 planes. I remember taking off in the dark, fully loaded with gas and bombs, and assembling on what we called the "zebra". That was the assembly ship. It was an old B-24 that carried lots of radio equipment and was very conspicuous by its appearance so that our many ships could form up on it as daylight broke over the East Anglia area of England.

Our air bases with B-17s and B-24s on them were located within 15 or 20 miles of each other so whenever we took off we had a very carefully defined area in which to assemble or else we would find ourselves over in the next man's territory and, first thing you know, you would fly straight into somebody. In all, the assembly procedure took about an hour and was a magnificent piece of teamwork and precision flying, often instrument flying until reaching the seven or eight thousand foot level when, usually, the clouds broke and the weather cleared.

The route of our mission took us over the North Sea, eastward across the Zuider Zee, roughly over Brussels, Belgium, and on into the heart of Germany. Then, we were to turn south, turn east, and then turn back to the north to what was called the initial point, or IP, Eisenach. The IP was the point at which the bombardier took over and flew the airplane, using his bombsight, over the target. He sat down in a cramped compartment below the pilot's cockpit, bending over his lenses with his hands on a bunch of knobs while controlling the plane and adjusting the crosshairs just right to drop the bombs.

We almost always had fighter support for most of the way. But to have such fighter support the fighters and bombers had to arrive at the correct meeting point at the correct moment. It didn't do any good for them to be there ten minutes late or for us to show up late. Our lives and our efforts depended a great deal on this important synchronization of efforts.

The fighters on this particular mission, from all I have ever heard and read since, were on time. And they discovered when they got to the rendezvous point that they were looking for our B-24s and couldn't find them, except that they saw some down on the ground burning. That's because as we proceeded with our mission we got ahead of schedule. Over the Zuider Zee we were one up. Recognizing this, I called the wing leader and told him, "one up." Back came the curt directive to "shut up and get off the air." We were discovering that the tailwinds were stronger than they had been forecast. A little farther into the trip and we were two up. Again, I broke radio silence and said, "two up." I thought we could make a dogleg out in order to lengthen the pattern a little bit and make up the time. I got the same nasty reply so I didn't say anything else. By then, we were a dangerous two minutes ahead of schedule.

We passed over Brussels two minutes before our fighter protection was supposed to be there to meet us. And that was just long enough to give the Jerries a good shot at us before our fighters got there. When the fighters eventually got to our rendezvous point, in two minutes, at 180 to 220 miles an hour, we were way down the road.

So, on the way in to the target we had very little fighter support, not because of the fighters but because of our own wing's fault. We flew on the wing lead [from the 389th Bomb Group] which eventually turned north, headed for Eisenach. From there, it was a straight line for, I guess, 15 miles. At Eisenach, the IP, the lead was to turn to the right, to the east, toward Gotha. As we flew over Eisenach, I watched the wing lead because I had my group flying on it. At that point I was slightly to his left and up behind him, watching for him to drop his bombs at Gotha so that we would follow.

As it turned out, I was making a decision not to follow the 389th because the wing lead, surprisingly and unexpectedly, dropped his bombs at that point. His planes started their turn back out to the right to make a big circle and head back west toward home. I knew we were going to make a split there but I had no choice. We had come that far and I wasn't going to give up without getting to the original target. So I quickly got on the radio and said, "Winston Red, hold your bombs. Hold your bombs. Not the target."

So we held our bombs and I led the group straight on into Gotha. We got to the target and destroyed it. I wondered from that day until much later whether I would be commended or catch hell for what I did. As it turned out, we received the Presidential Unit Citation for that action and I, personally, was awarded the Distinguished Flying Cross for leading it. Soon after the target, though, the Jerries came after us with a vengeance. As I mentioned, the early bombing and turn by the 389th left a split in our formation which the Germans took full advantage of. They shot our plane's nose out and got one of the right hand engines so that we couldn't keep up with the rest of the ships. I was wounded in the leg and I believe the navigator, Howard Blumenkranz, was killed by the first burst.

There was a decision to be made in the heat of battle and it was a hard one to make but I made it. I haven't regretted it. It seemed to be the thing to do, since it was approved by command. The job was to get that airplane factory but the decision I made cost us. I lost some good friends there, including Blumenkranz.

I went for years being bitter at the stupidity of dropping bombs on Eisenach like they did. I found out later how it all happened. The wing lead's bombardier had just taken over and crouched down over his bombsight when his ship took some hits. He was killed and collapsed right on top of his bombsight, triggering the bomb release switch when he fell on it. That's why those bombs fell at Eisenach. I thought it was stupidity for a long, long time. It was just that the Germans were damn lucky and got the lead bombardier at the wrong time.

After our ship was crippled we couldn't keep up with the rest of our formation. The wingmen were overrunning us and we were heading toward a big mess. We either had to cut back, get out of the way, or everybody had to cut back and go slower and become even bigger sitting ducks for the Jerries. We were losing altitude and I couldn't make them all stay with me so I pulled out of the formation. I told the pilot to "pull up, over and out" and I signaled my deputy lead on my right to take command and fly in the lead position, which he did.

As we pulled out, the German fighters worked us over again, this time getting my face mask and what they hadn't gotten earlier of the nose and the rest of the stuff in the cockpit and the engines on the right side. That's when I told the crew to prepare to bail out. I really don't know what happened after that. I know that the pilot or the radioman dragged me — I was out of oxygen and maybe in shock, I really don't know which — and dumped me out of the bomb bay. I woke up in the air, swinging from side to side and thought how quiet everything was.

That quickly ended when a German fighter came by and took a shot at me as I was floating down. I've got a slug in my back right now where the bullet hit me. I couldn't have been wounded there in the airplane because my seat had a steel plate behind it. I came to long enough to see that guy come by and shoot me. The next thing I remember is waking up, lying in a snow bank way up on a mountain somewhere. There were pine trees all around but I hadn't hit a single one of them. As I looked up, I was startled to find myself staring into the business end of one of the strangest looking guns I had ever seen.

Saved by a Nazi Officer

After being wounded and bailing out of my stricken ship, I landed in a snow bank deep in mountainous woods. Once I came to my senses and was able to realize I had actually survived, I found myself facing the barrel of what looked like one of Miles Standish's blunderbusses. Behind the gun was a kid who looked no older than 12 or 14, shaking like a leaf. I guess I was, too. I don't know. He wouldn't touch me but just stood there. All I could do was stay still. I was hardly in any shape to do anything else.

An old man showed up with a one-horse sled. He searched me — I was unarmed — and rolled me over to the sled. The boy and "grandpa," as I call him now, took me down the mountain to a doctor in a little mountain village. They dragged me down the main street while the whole village turned out to see the American *Luftgangster* as they called us captured airmen. There was an old, gray-headed woman standing there with a little boy and the little boy spat on me as I went by on the sled. The grandmother hauled off and just flattened him. She was embarrassed and, I suppose, just trying to be a decent human being.

The doctor's office was located in his house. His little boy, who spoke good English, came in a few minutes later and acted as an interpreter. That doctor probed around and pushed some paper towel wrappings on my wound and told me someone would soon take me to a prison hospital. True to his word, a *Wehrmact* open-bed truck came around that night, collected about six or seven of us, and deposited us on the floor of the police station at Eisenach. During the trip, I passed the word to the boys to tear their parachutes on some nails we found sticking up in the bed of the truck. The Germans prized the nylon our chutes were made of and I didn't want them to have the pleasure of reusing the material.

Those chutes were torn to pieces by the time we got to the police station. A German air force fellow walked in, saw us there, and then saw our parachutes. He said, "Ah, parachute nylon." But when he pulled one of them out he noticed it was torn. We all started laughing at him so he hauled off and kicked me. He was mad when he realized what we had done to him. But that's all he did. I couldn't blame him. He just lost his temper and kicked me. That was the only time I was hit like that.

They put us in a nearby schoolhouse where we stayed for about three days. During that time they didn't feed us but simply gave us water. We were told we would be moved to a prison hospital. A bunch of us had gathered at the schoolhouse by now. We were all suffering from various kinds of wounds or sickness. The only help we got was from an orderly who would empty the chamber pots and give us some water. By the second day, infection was setting in and I was beginning to worry. That's when someone very interesting walked into our lives.

He was a major in the *Luftwaffe* who happened to be home on leave and had heard that we were there at the schoolhouse. He came by to see what was going on and I started raising Cain with him about our conditions. He could speak English very well. He had flown in the Spanish Civil War back in 1937 and 1938, having been burned badly about the face in a crash. During that time, he had been captured but had been treated well by his captors.

This major saw the shape we were in and it incensed him. "I apologize and I'm going to do something about it," he declared indignantly. By golly, it wasn't 30 minutes, it seemed like, when he came back with the mayor and just blessed him out right in front of us. Apparently, it was the mayor's responsibility to look after prisoners of war until the army took them. The mayor quickly left and came back with half a crate of Spanish oranges and lemons and even bean soup. That was the best breakfast I ever put in my mouth. It helped us survive.

Some of those boys were in bad shape. They had holes all through their legs. One boy had an eye out and another boy had an arm practically off. Infections were setting in and fevers were running high and I knew it was beginning to look desperate. But, thanks to this major, ambulances and trucks arrived. We were put in the trucks and taken to a railroad station where we were loaded onto boxcars and transported about 15 or 20 miles to a prison hospital. The hospital was actually a converted three-story schoolhouse. A number of U.S. Army people were already there.

As our train pulled out, I saw the German *Luftwaffe* officer standing next to the track, waving at us, smiling, and shouting "Good luck!" He was the nicest man that he could have been.

Schneider the Snake

On D-Day, June 6, 1944, I, along with other wounded prisoners, was moved to yet another hospital, this one at Meiningen. I'll never forget while we were waiting, a train came around with little heads sticking out of the slats of the boxcars. I asked a nearby German guard who they were. "Juden" came his terse reply. Those Jewish kids were waving to anyone they saw as they were being transported to a concentration camp.

At Meiningen, I had the "pleasure" of doing business with a real wheeler-dealer of a German. His name was Helmut Schneider and, as it turned out, our mutually beneficial relationship helped to make our existence as prisoners a little less uncomfortable while saving some lives at the same time.

Packs of cigarettes included in our Red Cross parcels were often used as bribes. We would assess everyone a cigarette out of a pack for the common fund. One day Dr. Wooding, our senior British medical officer, came to me and said, "Major, we've got a boy here who has a high fever. He has to have sulfa." Sulfa was so new I really didn't know what it was. "We need sulfa," the doctor said, "or this boy is about to die." "Let me see if I can get some sulfa," I responded. There were seven German army hospitals in this town and one POW hospital and they all worked from a common supply pharmacy. The Germans didn't have trouble getting the supplies but it was like pulling teeth to get anything for the POWs.

I called in my favorite goon, Schneider. "Schneider," I said, "we've got to have some sulfa tablets." He said, "Give me a pack of cigarettes" so I gave him some out of the common fund. He left and about two hours later he came back. He handed me a brown paper bag and said, "Here are all the sulfa tablets in Meiningen." I said, "What do you mean?" "I went over to the supply sergeant," he explained. "I light up the Camel cigarette. He is smoking an old Turkish cigarette. I blew a little smoke in his face and I said, 'Wouldn't you like to have some of these?' He understood. I told him that I needed some sulfa and I gave him ten cigarettes. He reached around, pulled this bag off the wall, and handed me the bag real quick before anybody saw him. I keep ten cigarettes, I give him ten cigarettes, you got your sulfa, and you got all of it in town."

If I had been the German commandant of that town and had found out what Schneider had done I would have had him shot at sunrise. How many boys do you reckon in those German hospitals needed sulfa that night and didn't get it? And I was rolling in sulfa.

Helmut insisted he wasn't a Nazi. His father was a judge. I said, "Why is he a judge if he is not a Nazi?" All judges had to be Nazis. "Well, he had to join the Nazi party to get along, you know, and keep the judgeship. Just politics, that's all." Schneider had gone to law school for two years and at one time had been in the *Afrika Korps* when he suffered some sort of wound that enabled him to return home and get a job as an interpreter instead of going back to the front.

I remember that election time was coming around in the U.S. and before that big day Schneider walked in to where I was. "Major," he said, "I don't understand it. I have here a letter from the Davidson County Election Commission for you." He gave it to me and it turned out to be an absentee ballot. Word got around and all the Germans were really curious about the document. I talked it up, even talked about President Roosevelt, and said I knew several people on the ballot. I made a point of saying what a great country it was that allowed its citizens to choose its leaders.

Taking advantage of my captors' interest, I offered to come down to the office and mark my ballot in front of anyone who wanted to learn more. "Ja, Ja," they said. So I voted, marking my ballot right in front of them in the medical director's office. There were 15 or 20 Germans standing around, each with a wistful look on his face. I saw a captain standing there and said, "Captain, when was the last time you marked a ballot?" "1926," he responded in a rather downcast voice. I made sure they saw I voted for Roosevelt. Later that afternoon, we were out in the yard when several Germans passed. One stomped his feet and shouted, "Damn, I don't understand it!" We go out there and get shot up and they get to vote for their commander!"

We reached a point during our stay at Meiningen when we needed a radio tube. We had a Royal Canadian radioman who said he could put a radio together for me but we needed a tube. So he told Schneider what kind of tube he needed. Schneider said he couldn't do such a thing since it would be a major offense if he were caught. We finally figured out how to meet our need. Soon Schneider's birthday rolled around so we told him to come on down to the ward and we would have him a birthday party. We might even break out some American cigarettes. I laid it on thick. Heck, we would even serve some jam and butter.

He took the bait and soon appeared at his own party. I had our plan all cocked and primed. I knew that Schneider was a camera bug so I told him to bring his camera with him so that some pictures could be taken and then shown to our families after the war. I maneuvered him between two of us with my arm around his shoulder and someone took some snapshots. Schneider returned two or three days later with the pictures. Oh, he loved them. With no one else around, he handed the pictures to me to let me see them. They were good, clear pictures that would put him away for a long time for associating with the enemy. Before he could react, I took a picture and put it in my pocket, telling him he could have it back when he brought me that radio tube.

Sure enough, about a week later in walked Schneider with the tube and my Canadian buddy got his radio fixed. We listened to the BBC and kept up with what was going on in the world. In fact, that radio kept going long after I was gone.

I returned home after the war and settled into a life of work and family. We had just moved into our house in 1951 when a big cold snap hit and the power was off for several days. The night the power came back on, the telephone rang. "Major Evans, this is Schneider."

"Who?" "Schneider. Helmut Schneider." "Well, what's on your mind, Mr. Schneider?" I was kind of ill-tempered at that point, having been cooking on the fireplace and without heat for several days. He said, "Helmut Schneider from Germany." Then it dawned on me. "For gosh sakes, where are you?" "Over at Vanderbilt. I'm on a Fulbright Scholarship." "Well, Schneider, you stay right where you are. I'm going to come get you. You have to come out here and have supper with us and tell me what happened after I left Meiningen and went to Sagan." So I got him and brought him out to supper and he told me about what happened to him.

Over a helping of my wife's fried chicken he talked about almost being recruited for work behind the American lines during the Battle of the Bulge because he spoke pretty good English. He also talked about leading a rag-tag bunch of ill-armed young boys and old men toward the battle lines in the final days of the war only to surrender to the Americans without firing a shot. And about his work with American doctors treating wounded soldiers while he was a POW.

Schneider was a slick one. He came to me one day and said he wanted to stay in the United States. I told him, "No. You were sent over here for a purpose. You got that scholarship for a purpose." I blocked any chance he had of becoming a U.S. citizen. He was a real snake. But he was very useful. He got that sulfa for us and when two or three boys needed fresh eggs he got them and brought them to us. He stuck his neck out every time he did it. I think, basically, he was a decent fellow and wanted to be as humane as he could be and not get himself in trouble. But if he had been caught giving us that sulfa there's no telling what they would have done to him. As the years have gone by, Schneider and I lost touch but the last I heard of him he was a very successful commercial lawyer in Hamburg, Germany.

Please, Mr. Blood and Guts, Let Us Stay

Our forced march as POW's through terrible cold and snow followed by riding in boxcars finally ended at Moosburg, where we found ourselves in February 1945. We were "guests" of the Germans until liberation day a few months later. That's when I had an up-close and quite uncomfortable episode with General George Patton.

General Patton had gotten into all kinds of trouble during the war because of his temper. His reputation had become well known throughout the army. If anyone had read *Stars and Stripes,* the service newspaper, they would have been pretty familiar with his escapades.

When we were liberated by General Patton and his troops all these young bucks — 19 and 20 year old lieutenants — were chomping at the bit to get home. They just knew they would be flown out in 24 hours. "Boy, they'll fly us out of here," I remember hearing. "We'll be in London and Paris tomorrow night and we'll be home next week. Yes, they'll get us right on home and we'll be out of this damn place." Everybody was impatient to leave. But the general quickly sent word that we were to "keep those boys right there. Don't anybody leave." "I can feed you," he proclaimed, "but I can't do anything else until I take Munich. Then I'll start helping to get you out." He warned all of us not to try going west on our own because "the Germans will kill you in the back alleys."

All of us senior officers had our hands full quieting the boys down. They were ready to mutiny against General Patton at that point and head out west on their own. They would have, too, if we hadn't interceded. They would have run into all kinds of trouble while foraging for food and demanding all kinds of things from the German citizenry.

To back up what I just said, an American sergeant saw me that very day. He was just one of the many American troops now streaming through our camp. He said, "Major, you look hungry. Come on, let's find something to eat." That got my attention, so I said, "Where are we going?" His simple response: "Come on." So we got in a jeep and drove for about six or seven miles to the next little village. There, we stopped at a farmhouse where an old man and woman lived.

The sergeant walked in and tersely addressed them. "I want some bread and potatoes!" he commanded. "Nicht got. Nicht got. Nicht got. Alle ist kaput," they quickly told him, obviously concerned about what might happen next. "I want some potatoes!" he repeated. To back up his demand, he fired three rounds into the floor. Bam! Bam! Bam! That got their attention. The old man ran into the back of the house and soon emerged with a basketful of potatoes and a loaf of bread.

Imagine that kind of situation going on everywhere. There had already been some fighting, killing, and just about everything else. I almost felt bad about seeing the sergeant scare those people like that. It was obvious that poor old couple didn't have anything and were trying to hang on to their last potato.

Back to General Patton. Everybody was mad because he wouldn't let us go. On day two of liberation Patton strutted into camp accompanied by some other self-important muckety-mucks. I happened to be the adjutant of the camp and it fell to me to call the troops to attention at the presence of our visitors. We walked into one barrack — I remember a little vestibule and a pot-bellied stove there — and I bellowed "Attention!" General Patton stood there flanked by two congressmen. I also remember bunks positioned very close together filled with big, long-bellied men lying on beds stacked five high.

All those men crawled down out of their bunks and came to attention. It took a little while but they all got straightened out. Patton stood there staring at them when way back in the back we heard a boy say, "Oh, Mr. Blood and Guts, this is home, sweet home. We love it here, Mr. Blood and Guts. Please don't make us move. Go away and leave us alone."

I thought, "Boy, the roof will come off this place now." Surprisingly, Patton didn't do anything. He stood there with his hands on his hips. I could see he was very mad but he just stood there, bit his lip, and controlled his temper. He never said a word. He stood there for what seemed forever, about a minute I guess, turned on his heels and stomped out, saying, "Let's go to the next building."

That's the only time I ever ran into General Patton during the war. "Oh, Mr. Blood and Guts, this is home sweet home. We love it here." I knew exactly who it was but he couldn't have found that boy in a year.

21

SERGEANT JOHN KATZ

DOB: December 21, 1925
Where: Clarksville, Tennessee
Air Force: 20th
Bomb Group: 499th
Squadron: 877th
Station: Saipan
Decorations include: Distinguished Flying Cross, Air Medal with clusters. A B-29 gunner, John flew 23 combat missions over some of Japan's biggest cities and major military installations. The fire raids, as they were called, were designed for maximum damage to break the will of the Japanese people. To the amazement of his father, a wounded German war veteran from World War I, he survived the war unscathed. Postwar, John spent 32 years as a chemical engineer before retiring in 1981.

Tail Gunner by Accident

Some of my training as a tail gunner occurred in a B-17 so I was surprised when my final assignment landed me on a B-29. The Flying Fortress was cold, very cold, whereas in the pressurized B-29 I wore shorts and t-shirts underneath my flight suit. Oxygen masks were used only in an emergency. The ride on a B-29 was smooth and quiet, even more so than the commercial airliners of today.

How I got to be a tail gunner on a B-29 when I was trained to be a radar operator involves a story with a leading character almost too good to be true. His name was B.B. Brice, a nice, fun guy whom everyone liked. B.B. was born with a silver spoon in his mouth. He came from a wealthy family, so wealthy in fact that his dad would send him and the rest of us money, as much as 20 dollars at a time. In line with his reputation as a fun loving kind of guy, B.B. had a convertible on our base at Clovis, New Mexico. He would use it for various recreational activities including taking himself and his friends out for steak dinners.

At the time, B.B. was our tail gunner. One night it seems he needed even more excitement in his life so he decided to "borrow" the general's jeep. The exact details of how and why he decided to take such liberties with the property of a high-ranking officer remain a classified secret to this day. B.B. had a little too much fun with the jeep and turned it over. I don't know what happened to B.B. after that, but his actions that night changed my life because I was soon "volunteered" to take his place in the tail, thus becoming the tallest man in a position that calls for the shortest man. But I needed a job and so a tail gunner I became.

On our missions we flew over approximately 3,000 miles of open water with each mission averaging at least 10 hours. I flew 13 fire raids to Japan over places like Oita, Akashi, Tokyo, and Kumamoto. The rest were high explosive raids. We had our orders to destroy as much of those cities as possible and with our firepower we delivered terrible devastation. At night and alone, we bombed from altitudes as low as 2,000 feet when using incendiary bombs. When they hit, they spread flammable gel over the wooden structures of the Japanese and created a virtual wall of flame. The scene was too incredible to describe what with the brilliance of the fires, the bursting anti-aircraft fire, and the blinding brightness of the Japanese searchlights trying to catch us in their powerful beams. It was a scary time to be caught in the searchlights, waiting for the next burst of anti-aircraft fire which always seemed to grow closer and closer. We tried our best to move away by swinging right and left but during that time I couldn't see so I felt like I had been singled out for death.

Part of my job called for me to arm the bombs on each mission. I would crawl into the bomb bay and pull the cotter keys out of the nose of each bomb. We usually carried ten tons of bombs so it took awhile. The whole time I never thought about all the people dying as a result of our raids. We were focused on one main objective: end the war as soon as possible.

Thankfully, we never took any direct hits although we had engines knocked out sometimes and many holes in the plane after most missions. All of this led up to the day when we were on a routine mission and had dropped our bombs. The pilot switched over to general radio reception and we all heard that the war with Germany was over. At the time it didn't make much difference to us because the Japs were still firing at us.

Why Didn't I at Least Get a Scratch?

In one sense, my dad, Carl Otto Katz, was like all the other dads with sons or daughters serving in the war. He was proud of me for being a tail gunner on a B-29 based so far from home on Saipan. I had survived 23 combat missions over Japan, enduring intense anti-aircraft fire, enemy fighters that often swarmed over us like so many angry bees, and probing searchlights that singled us out at night during fire raids over Japanese cities. In the process, I won the Distinguished Flying Cross and the Air Medal with cluster. Best of all, I came home physically and mentally intact.

John Katz (courtesy John Katz)

In another sense, though, my dad was very different from all the others. Carl Otto Katz was a true Prussian officer in the German army during World War I and, as might be expected, was very Prussian in his beliefs and behavior. His war experiences included being shot five separate times, being buried alive, and receiving the Iron Cross for his bravery. I've often said if he had been paid for his bravery he would have been a millionaire. After World War I, dad left Bremen, Germany, and came to America, settling in Clarksville, Tennessee, to work in tobacco sales. He wanted to be an American, part of what he considered the greatest country on earth. But the Depression ruined him and even though he remained a brilliant, honorable man, a series of low paying jobs meant he never had much money. Yet he was very proud to be an American and to have his son fighting for his adopted country.

So when I came back from the service without a scratch, dad, bless his heart, had a hard time understanding how I helped America win the war. Remembering his own sacrifices as well as all the pain and suffering he endured, he expected me to be a changed man. Physically, that is. "It would have been better," he said, "if you had lost an arm or suffered in some physical way."

Most of us would have a very difficult time trying to understand that type of thinking. But the love for my dad and the respect I had for his courage surpassed any sort of negative reaction I had to his words. I knew he loved me and that's what mattered the most to me.

22

LIEUTENANT BILL RICKMAN

DOB: April 15, 1923
Where: Nashville, Tennessee
Air Force: 8th
Bomb Group: 446th
Squadron: 706th
Station: Bungay, England
Decorations include: Air Medal with clusters

The villagers of Beselare, Belgium, were surprised to see parts of a B-24 along with parachutes falling out of the sky two days after Christmas 1944. One of the chutes belonged to Bill Rickman who, along with some of his crewmates, was rescued by Canadian forces. Bill flew 28 combat missions as a B-24 copilot. After the war, he remained in the air force, retiring as a lieutenant colonel after 20 years of active duty around the world including Korea and Indochina.

Chutes Over Flanders

I enlisted in the army air force in December 1942, ready to serve my country and start a new life. We were all hyped up about the dirty Japs and the terrible Nazis. Everybody wanted to go get them but there was another compelling reason for me—the attraction of the wild blue yonder.

I had always been interested in flying. In my younger years if I heard an airplane flying over I would listen and run outside to watch it pass by. That was the time of the bi-wing planes. The movies of World War I fascinated me as well with the daring pilots and their thrilling dogfights.

Dogfights would not be a part of my life as a B-24 copilot but I was excited to be up in the air nonetheless. I ended up flying 28 missions with the 8th Air Force, 446th Bomb Group with most of those occurring after one hair-raising trip we took over Germany. The date was December 27, 1944, when we were flying in support of our ground forces fighting the Battle of the Bulge.

The B-24J, number 42–51312, was carrying our crew of ten to Kaiserslautern, Germany, where we were to bomb the center of town in order to disrupt the traffic flow of materials to the German front. The weather was clear but cold. Bad weather had socked us in for about two weeks. Once the weather improved we were good to go. The mission wasn't supposed to be all that bad. Flak was expected, but not a lot of it. It turned out that this was one of those days when the amount of flak wasn't a factor. Instead, it was the accuracy of what they were throwing up at us. In our case, I mean deadly accuracy.

We took off from Bungay, England, 20 miles south of Norwich, on a trip that was designed to take no more than eight hours. Climbing up to about 10,000 feet, we began our racetrack pattern to form up as a group. This took the better part of an hour from the time the lead plane took off until the last plane got off the ground and joined us. Then it was off across the North Sea, crossing over the coast of Holland at about 20,000 feet, still climbing to our usual bombing altitude of 25,000 feet. The German anti-aircraft fire along the coast signaled the beginning of the shooting gallery. We were the targets.

Bill Rickman (courtesy Bill Rickman)

This was my sixth mission and it seemed things were normal, if the word "normal" can be used to describe a bombing mission. We proceeded to the target and dropped our bombs but several direct hits from flak left us on fire in the bomb bay and on the left wing between number 1 and 2 engines. I knew we were in serious trouble. Pilot Lieutenant Jesse Whaley and I began switching off, using all our strength to manhandle the plane so as to keep it in formation. We lost altitude and were forced to drop out of formation. In addition to the other problems, the tail was damaged and the autopilot, electrical, and hydraulic systems were shot out.

With fire eating through the left wing, Whaley wasted little time in sounding the jump bell. Meanwhile the fire in the bomb bay had been snuffed out by the radio operator. Thank goodness there were no German fighters around because we were little more than a sitting duck.

The ship struggled for a while as we moved away from Germany and toward Brussels, Belgium. We were falling fast as the first few members of the crew crawled onto the narrow catwalk over the bomb bay and jumped. The navigator, bombardier, and most of the gunners all made it down safely but were soon captured and imprisoned. Then the unexpected occurred which, in retrospect, probably allowed the rest of us to jump into friendly hands. Our tail gunner, Sergeant Richard Petrus, was afraid to jump. He was frozen with fear. That's when our radio operator, who had earlier put out the bomb bay fire, stepped up once again. Sergeant North Phipps was an exceptional person. In fact, of all the enlisted men I knew in my long military career he was top notch. Phipps had the presence of mind during all the pandemonium to create a homemade static line. He hooked the line to the d-ring on Petrus' chute so that it would automatically open once he jumped. Even with that, we had to push Petrus out through the bomb bay.

Then, another unexpected occurrence: Petrus was still so scared of falling that he desperately grabbed hold of the catwalk with his hands as he was going out. So Phipps had to stomp on them before Petrus finally released his grip and fell, the chute opening on schedule. During all this I was still in my copilot's seat trying to trim the plane, turning occasionally to see what was happening. I wanted badly to get out. Phipps followed Petrus out and I quickly followed. When Whaley finally let go of the controls, the plane rose up violently. He was lucky to get out because of the g-forces.

As I bailed, I counted to one, not ten, and pulled the ripcord. Now is the time, I thought, to hear that glorious sound of the chute opening. I didn't want any part of counting all the way to ten. For some reason, I had chosen to wear a harness with a clip-on chute that had only a 22-foot canopy. That meant I had more freedom to maneuver in the air but less time to do it before hitting the ground.

My parachute harness wasn't cinched up tight enough and when I bailed out one of my testicles got hung up. It was a long ride down with that discomfort. I remember several other things about going down. One of the tails of our B-24 had broken loose and was floating like a leaf, swaying back and forth in the air. I also had some concern about landing on the spire of a nearby Catholic church. Then I saw a huge haystack and thought how wonderful it would be to land there. Neither happened. The four of us who jumped roughly at the same time came down within sight of each other, listening to the plane crash within a few hundred yards of where I landed. It barely missed a school. I hit the frozen ground of a farmer's field pretty hard and banged up my left ankle, leaving it severely sprained.

My next vision was of a farmer hovering over me and threatening me with a pitchfork. Quickly I took all the survival stuff I had and emptied it on the ground, trying to explain that I was an American. He and his neighbors were suspicious because the Germans had dropped troops behind the lines dressed up in American aircrew uniforms. I showed him a piece of silk with an American flag on it. I also flashed an explanation that I was an American aircrew member and that his help would be appreciated, written in different languages.

Other people soon gathered and they took all four of us to a local official's house where we were treated, to our great relief, like royalty. Someone there had a camera and took a picture of us. Months later that picture was mailed to me. Another person spoke enough English to get by. That's when we found out we had landed near Beselare, Belgium. The Canadians were in the area. They got us to Brussels, then to an RAF facility near London where I was hospitalized for 10 days. I was the only one of the crew hurt.

If the tail gunner, Sergeant Petrus, had not hesitated about bailing out we probably would have landed in enemy-held territory, as six other members of our crew did. All of them survived their POW experiences. We had actually flown over a hundred miles farther after they jumped. We didn't have any hard feelings toward Petrus. Unfortunately, he was killed later in the war on April 11, 1945, while flying with another crew. His plane collided in mid-air over England with another B-24 while coming in on approach to their base.

Upon release from the hospital, I spent five weeks on "DNIF," duty not including flying, at two rest camps in Scotland and England. The next mission when I returned to the air was to Berlin. I was probably more frightened about that than anything else.

After the war, I put all my experiences behind me and really didn't think about them for 40 or 50 years. My family didn't hear me talk about how it was back then until recently. I didn't think what I did during World War II was special, just part of my life. But one thing is for certain. Even at my age, over 80 now, I still get goose bumps about flying the skies.

23

Lieutenant John McGonagle

DOB: January 22, 1922
Where: Boston, Massachusetts
Air Force: 12th
Bomb Group: 319th
Squadron: 440th
Station: Sardinia, Corsica
Decorations include: Purple Heart, Air Medal with clusters, POW Medal. John flew the Martin B-26 until he was shot down on his fifteenth mission by Me 109s over Mantua, Italy. Wounded and suffering from burns, he managed to bail out only to be taken captive once on the ground. From October 19, 1944, until the end of the war he was a POW at *Stalag Luft 1*. A graduate of Boston College, John worked in sales for building materials and cement companies after the war, retiring as vice president of sales and marketing for Marquette Cement.

Big Tail Birds

After advanced training and three weeks before getting my wings, I picked the P-38 as the plane I wanted to fly in combat. "We're sorry," I was told, "we're only taking B-17 and B-24 pilots." "I don't want to fly bombers," was my quick response. That's when, surprisingly, the government showed some flexibility and willingness to work with me. "Tell you what we'll do," an officer said, "we have B-26s available. The B-26 is a hot plane." And so it was. Thus began my relationship with one of the fastest, most thrilling planes that flew in the war.

No one was used to flying something as fast as the B-26, most especially me, who had never set foot in a plane before training. The Marauder, as it was called, had no glide pattern because of, among other reasons, its short wingspan. It killed a lot of people in training and soon earned some very descriptive nicknames such as "The Flying Prostitute" because it had no visible means of support. But I was young and fearless in those days and was excited to have an exciting plane. I was hooked on it from the beginning.

Flying the B-26 meant being very careful during takeoffs and landings. There was little, if any, room for mistakes since it was known to stall. You'll understand even better when I tell you about how we began and finished missions at our base. As part of 319th Bomb Group, known as the "Big Tail Birds," we were assigned to a field at Decimomannu, Sardinia. When I say field, I mean field. Our CO, Colonel Joseph Holzapple, took a big open field, put in six oiled runways side by side, and began what became known as "Colonel Randy's Flying Circus." Six B-26s would line up and, at a signal from a flagman, take off together. As we got up, we formed a box, three planes under the other three planes. This saved a half hour or so of planes forming in the sky and also saved fuel which allowed us to stay in the air longer, if needed. It was a real trick to get the same six planes back on the ground safely. The worst part was being the inside guy. That was a real tight turn coming down. The pilot had to be especially on guard against stalling because of the slower speed.

Normally we flew at about 10,000 feet. The B-26 was a precision bomber with a great reputation for having the most hits on ground targets. We would primarily hit bridges and sometimes the freight yards at Rome. Basically, though, we flew missions designed to disrupt supply lines which meant anything that moved: troops or equipment.

We also participated in supporting our troops invading southern France. We bombed beaches, fortifications, and troops while taking lots of flak.

On October 19, 1944, our mission took us from Corsica over Lake Como for our turn onto the target: bridges over the Po River near Mantua, Italy. I remember it being a beautiful day. The bomb bay doors opened when suddenly we were attacked by ten Me 109s. We never expected to see them so we had taken out the waist guns to lighten our load, enabling us to fly farther into Italy. The first pass of 109s knocked out our left engine. We dropped out of formation immediately, salvoed our 5,000 pounds of bombs, and dropped the nose wheel. I was flying copilot this day so I was doing all I could to help the pilot keep us flying. The second pass knocked out our other engine and started a fire. We knew then we weren't going back to base anytime soon.

The German fighters quickly figured out we had no waist guns because most of their passes started below us. By now, the fire had consumed the wing tanks and was making its way into the cockpit. Shrapnel was flying everywhere when the bailout bell sounded. Throughout all this I was trying to decide where to jump, either through the top or the nose wheel well. The top didn't sound good because I would probably hit the tail once out of the plane so I raised my right arm to cover my eyes, ran through the fire, and jumped through the nose wheel. Not long after that, the plane exploded. I

John McGonagle (courtesy John McGonagle)

didn't know at the time that I had been hit by shrapnel. In fact, it wasn't until 60 years later when I was having back problems and had an MRI that my doctor discovered the metal in my back and wanted to know if I had been shot.

The last three planes in our formation were shot down that day. The fighters had done their job well. "What do I do now?" I asked myself as I drifted to the ground. I remember a feeling of aloneness in the air and also the eerie silence after being in the pandemonium of a dying airplane. I remembered my medical kit and thought I would get it and run for the woods nearby. I also saw the Po River and knew I didn't want to land in it so I maneuvered my chute to land in an adjacent field. I hit the ground, undid my chute, pulled the medical kit off, and started to run when bullets were fired at my feet. I stopped and found myself completely surrounded by German soldiers who kept their guns trained on me. They kept motioning for me to throw what I had in my hand, my medical kit. I think they believed it to be a grenade. Anyway, I threw it. I had an ID bracelet my parents had given me with my name and serial number on it. It had been burned into my wrist. I tried to unbuckle it and a German ripped it off.

I've often wondered why the soldiers didn't shoot me. Maybe they thought I would provide them with information during interrogation. I was taken into a nearby town where the other fliers gathered. They put us all in a truck and paraded us around basically saying, "Look who we captured." I can still see the people staring at us but I don't remember any name-calling or things thrown at us. We were driven to a prison where we were all put in one cell. That's where we stayed for the night. I didn't know it at the time but it was the beginning of an incredible part of my life.

Stalag Luft 1

I spent a month in a German hospital recovering from the burns I received bailing out of my B-26 during a low level bombing raid over Italy's Po River. Then I was transferred to a recuperation camp at Spittal/Drau in the mountains of Austria where most of my barracks mates were primarily Australian POW's. They were a great group of guys. I remember Tom Hawks from Melbourne and Gordon Bode from Queensland both of whom had been captured at Tobruk two years earlier. They really took care of me, especially since they had been there long enough to get packages from home. When it was time for me to leave, all I had was a shirt and pants so Tom gave me a sweater. I don't know how he acquired the sweater but he said he had plenty others. I kept in touch with him and his wife after the war until he died.

The Germans decided to move me in January 1945. Two older soldiers were assigned to accompany me. They took me to Innsbruck for a trip to the interrogation center in Frankfurt. Along the way, we were stopped many times because of blown tracks. Each time we had to get off and pick up another train and then I would spend the night in a German jail. On one occasion we were high up in the Alps amidst very deep snow. I was being pushed around in the crowd trying to get on the train when I was separated from my handlers. So I got off the train and just stood there, freezing, trying to decide whether to make a break for it. "Where the hell would I go?" I said to myself so I turned around and got back on the train, hollering for Hans and Fritz. They found me and we managed to squeeze into a small compartment with lots of people. I was the odd-looking person in the group as a POW so I had the "honor" of sitting on the floor and giving my seat to a German.

I was turned over to some vicious people in Frankfurt, members of the *Gestapo*. They tried a few tricks on me like varying the comfort of my prison cell from hot to cold to hot again, little food, and the perfect English of one interrogator who said he was from Brooklyn. That shocked me. "Welcome," he said, "you are the last prisoner to come here since you got shot down at Mantua, Italy. You probably don't know this but your group has gone back to the states." And they had! They had flown till the end of the year and then returned to America. "I know everything," my interrogator continued, "I don't need anything from you." So I was assigned to *Stalag Luft 1*, put on a freight car with a bunch of other guys, spent the night in the Berlin freight yards, and ended up at Barth, Germany, on the Baltic Sea, the bitterly cold and snowy location of my new prison home.

When we arrived at the train station, we had to walk two miles to the camp. I remember the fellow who ended up in my room. He was a fighter pilot who had both his legs broken in a crash. He was having one hell of a time trying to walk so I put him on my shoulders and carried him as far as I could. Then two other guys carried him followed by two other guys until we arrived at the POW camp. Anybody who fell or who couldn't make it on our march was shot.

Stalag Luft 1 was a big prison camp with thousands of prisoners, all officers, I believe, living in four compounds. It was my home until the end of the war. We lived in long barracks-type buildings each with a hallway and rooms on each side. There were 24 men in each room. There was a pot-bellied stove in a corner with a table and some benches as our "furniture." It was a vicious winter. Many of us got frostbite even though we tried our best to huddle up by sleeping together and sharing what blankets we had.

Our food consisted of some German bread made of sawdust. We had a guy who could cut the bread into thin slices so that each man got two slices with his morning coffee. At noon, we got a pot of watery soup filled with maggots. Then at night we dined on two thin slices of bread and a cup of coffee. Since I was one of the older guys, at 23, I had to ration the food. Dick Dunbar was the bread slicer and he and I would count the bread. There were six slices for every guy, 144 slices to count out every day. We were the last two to eat. Then one day we discovered some bread missing. After carefully counting out the slices for the others, there was no bread for us. We thought we had made a mistake counting. The next day, damn if we weren't short again so we quickly decided that someone was stealing the bread. Dick and I didn't go to sleep that night, waiting for the thief. Sure enough, this kid came down out of his bunk, went over to the bread, took four slices, and went down the hall to the toilet. We caught him and warned him that no one would hear about it unless one more piece turned up missing. Then, the barracks would find out and God knows that the rest of the guys would do. We corrected the problem.

We had two West Point graduates in the room with us. You would think those bastards would have taken control of the room but all they cared about was taking care of themselves. They weren't helpful and didn't mix with the rest of us, choosing to talk with themselves and no one else. My respect for West Point dropped dramatically after encountering those clowns.

Here are some other brief observations of life at *Stalag Luft 1*:

The worst problem we had was the lice. We got a bath once a month, a cold shower. Then it was back to the bunk and the lice would cover me again. We had two young fighter pilots who thought it was great sport to pick the lice off each other and put them in a jar. "We don't want to kill them," they said. "You're two fighter pilots trained to kill people," I responded, "but you won't kill lice?"

Everyday we had to report to formation, morning and evening, sometimes three times a day, in all kinds of weather. Many of us suffered from frostbite as we stood in the snow waiting for the Germans to call our names. They just made it miserable for all of us.

I never knew anyone to escape from our prison. We endured the same routine day after day: playing cards, reading, and just trying to stay warm. The Germans had their Dobermans roaming around in the yard. We had our own way of dealing with them. We would open our windows and then put old razor blades into the sills. We just sunk them into the wood. Then we would take old, rotten potatoes and throw them at the dogs and they would jump up to the window to try to get inside and by doing so cut up their paws. Then we had to remove the razor blades quickly before inspection.

Max Schmeling, the German heavyweight boxing champ who knocked out Joe Louis and later lost to Joe, came by the camp one day with a group of Germans in tow. He wished us all well in his broken English and then went on his way. What purpose he served beats me.

Some guys would save their bread after getting a Red Cross parcel. They would use raisins and powdered milk and make what we called "*kriege* cake." They made a mush of the bread, milk, raisins, and some cocoa and then put it in a homemade oven and cooked it.

I never encountered jets in combat but two of them flew over the compound one day. They were going like hell. I remember thinking, "Oh, my God, what are we going to do about that?"

We found out that President Roosevelt had died by listening to the BBC through a handmade crystal set radio that was clearly contraband. We had to be careful not to get caught with one of those.

I weighed 170 pounds when I entered *Stalag Luft I* but when I got out I weighed just 125 pounds. My mother saw me and broke down crying.

On May 15, 1945, the Germans disappeared and some Russians liberated our camp. They were the most ungodly army I had ever seen. They wore different uniforms and some were riding old mares. We were told to stay where we were so we just sat there until four days later when a jeep showed up as the advance of American troops. We raided the Red Cross parcels that hadn't been delivered to us and I dug into the candy bars and Spam. We were a mess. I remember one guy couldn't take the change. He just sat on his bunk silently and appeared out of it. Another simply ran away once the barbed wire had been breached. He said he was going to America. We never saw or heard from him again. I overheard one GI tell another, "My God, look how thin they are." "We're going to start flying you guys out of here," another one told me. Soon we were on our way to Camp Lucky Strike in France where we were deloused with DDT, cautioned about eating too much too quickly, and given new uniforms.

On June 15, 1945 I finally made it home to Boston. My father, a World War I vet, wanted me to come with him to the American Legion dinner commemorating the battle of Bunker Hill. I went to the parade earlier in the day then accompanied my mother and father to the local armory where I became the air force representative at a table with a group of guys representing each branch of the service. The guy next to me was in the navy. He seemed like a nice, likable fellow so I turned to him and he introduced himself. "Hi, I'm Jack Kennedy," he stated as we shook hands. He told me about his PT boat experience and was generally very sociable but he looked thin as a rail. Of course, I knew the Kennedy name in Boston so I asked him why in the world he was at this armory in Charlestown, a tough place. He told me he would be running for office soon and needed all the votes he could get. We talked about our war experiences. He was a delightful guy.

24

LIEUTENANT ART DRISCOLL

DOB: December 11, 1922
Where: Stillwater, Oklahoma
Air Force: 8th
Bomb Group: 385th
Squadron: 549th
Station: Great Ashfield, England
Decorations include: Air Medal with clusters. Flying a B-17 was a "dream come true" for Art. He was credited with 22 combat missions before war's end. Yet he was a very religious young man who struggled at times with the nature of war and its effects on all involved. Once home, Art graduated from seminary and served as a minister to college students for 16 years. For the next 20 years he was a consultant in the National Student Ministries Department for the Southern Baptists.

Danger Over Dunkirk

Newly arrived B-17 pilots were required to fly as copilots on their first two combat missions. I flew my first one with Lieutenant Taylor to Dessau, Germany, just north of Leipzig. Flying as "tail end Charlie" in the formation, we ran out of fuel and had to land in France near the coast, returning to our base the next day. The second mission I flew was with Lieutenant Cooper to Kaiserslautern. We also ran out of fuel and landed in France.

My first mission with my own crew was to Mannheim to hit a tank factory. The weather was terrible so we flew on instruments and I looked hard for the square G marking that signified the 385th. Ultimately, we were unable to find our bomb group at altitude after takeoff so we tagged on to another group for the bomb run. Upon returning to our base, during debriefing, we learned that we were lucky to be alive because we had attached ourselves to the "Bloody 100th" Bomb Group, identified by our description of the markings on the tail. Many stories were floating around about why the 100th got hit so hard every time it went out on a mission. One story claimed that some of their planes surrendered to the Germans early in the war by putting their wheels down and while being led to a German base suddenly pulled them up and made their escape. Another story claimed that their commanding officer was incompetent and was sent back to the U.S. Whatever the reason, the 100th certainly had a bloody reputation.

My copilot was from Stone Mountain, Georgia, a slow-talking southerner we called "Slow Joe" Bachus. He was a real southern guy in talk and in manners but Joe was a good pilot and we had a solid working relationship. Often, after we got close to the target, we would trade off flying the plane every 15 minutes. I would also let him do landings and takeoffs and eventually got him checked out as a first pilot. As it turned out, he never got his own crew so he stayed with me. Some pilots wouldn't let their copilots fly so I believe we had a special understanding. The only thing about Joe was when he would call out the location of flak. Whenever the flak started exploding around us, he would always say, "Flak over yonder." To which I would respond, "Where's the flak, where? 10 o'clock high? 1 o'clock low?" "Flak over yonder" would always come the reply, "My gosh, Joe, where?" I would say while I looked for it myself.

My thirteenth mission turned out to be a "lucky" one for me. I remember that our target that day was an ordnance warehouse north

Art Driscoll (courtesy Mary Driscoll)

of Berlin. The trip didn't start out well since very few planes from our bomb group found the proper assembly point due to terrible weather. Many planes simply joined whatever formation was in the vicinity heading toward Germany. We learned later that our group diverted to a secondary target. We, on the other hand, hooked up with the 293rd Bomb Group and proceeded to hit the primary target. Even though it was tough flying in bad weather, we made it through the bomb run and headed back for our base at Great Ashfield, England, alone.

We were still flying on instruments through heavy overcast so the navigator kept telling me to drop down in order to find a landmark. We had lost the Gee Box, a device critical to our navigating, along the way and he needed to do some visual recognition to locate us, such as a town or a railroad. Meanwhile he gave me a heading and I brought the plane down to about 1,400 feet. Suddenly, all hell broke loose as our plane was riddled by flak and ground fire. We immediately realized that we were over Dunkirk, the only German stronghold remaining in that area of France. We had been briefed that the German installation there would be tough and it was.

We had lost much of the control of our Flying Fortress so I made a quick decision not to attempt a crossing of the English Channel but to make a slow, gradual left turn back over France. The navigator gave me a quick heading to an RAF emergency airstrip at Merville, France. "Suds" Sumney, our tail gunner, had been wounded when flak hit that section of our plane. Jack Sweeney, the bombardier, and one of the waist gunners pulled "Suds" out of the tail and administered first aid. I got back there to take a look and poured some sulfa on his wounds and that's when I realized I didn't have my chute.

The damage to our plane was extensive and we discussed our options at the time: we could bail, try to make it back to England, or land in France. Sweeney, the bombardier, asked the waist gunner for his chute. "Fuck you, lieutenant," came the quick, succinct reply. "Well," the bombardier said, "go get my chute and bring it back here." That's what he did and the bombardier continued providing medical attention to the tail gunner. At this point, though, I figured that "Suds" couldn't handle bailing out so I decided to land the ship in France. I had to bring her in "hot" at 150 miles per hour rather than the usual 110 for landing because we had very little control of flight with damaged wing flaps, ailerons, and tail assembly. We rolled to the end of the runway and got out as fast as we could, figuring she would catch fire. The plane must have had a hundred holes in it, some big enough to crawl through. There was extensive wing damage as well. That plane never flew again. As for "Suds," he planned on being a professional baseball player after the war but he lost the use of his arms due to his wounds. For him, the war was over. The RAF returned the rest of us to our base that same day. During our debriefing that evening, we used photos from our camera to convince intelligence officers that even though we didn't bring our plane or our tail gunner back, we hit the target for a successful bombing mission.

I went on to fly 22 combat missions before the war ended. After Germany surrendered, I flew displaced French citizens back to their home from Linz, Austria. These were people who had been imprisoned in concentration camps and they were pretty emaciated. As we landed at Linz, they were lined up along the runway already sprayed with DDT and waiting to board. We had benches built along the sides of the fuselage to accommodate as many as we could but even with that they would cram into the fuselage, tail, and nose of the plane. We circled Paris to let them see the city from the air before landing on their home soil.

I feel good about what I did during the war but not good about the fact that we lost 413 men from our bomb group during its service at Great Ashfield. When the war was over, I walked away from it. I never told my family any of my stories until 1995. I didn't even try to be in touch with my crew. "Suds," the tail gunner, hitchhiked from Michigan down to Ruston, Louisiana, to visit me just four years after the war and then I had no contact with him until 1995. My copilot happened to be in the control tower in Oklahoma City when I was at the University of Oklahoma in the 1970s so I visited with him for about 30 minutes but after that had no contact with him. After all the hair-raising experiences we shared, we went back to school, had families, started careers, and said little about the war.

Religion and War

An interesting thing happened during the assignment of what planes we would fly after receiving our wings and commissions. Our names were put in a big jar and 75 new 2nd lieutenants were told that the first two names drawn could fly the P-38, the "hot and fast" plane at the time, or have their choice of other types of aircraft on the list. As luck would have it, my name was the first one drawn. I surprised just about everyone with what I said next. "I don't want a P-38, I want to fly a B-17." So I got my choice and have never regretted it.

I shocked my instructors by choosing a heavy bomber but it was a dream come true for me to pilot a B-17. Maybe that's because during training I did some off the cuff, crazy kind of stuff that only a kid of 19 would do. Things like buzzing barges in the river, practically putting my wheels on them I was so low. I enjoyed watching the workers jump in the river. That was a daredevil kind of flying but I wanted to make it interesting instead of just floating around in the air. I also did some hedge hopping in three-ship formations as well. I could tell some stories about buzzing barges on the Mississippi River and flying under the bridge at Cairo, Illinois, or maybe swooping low over the women's college at Conway, Arkansas. All those stunts could have easily ended my flight training or worse, ended my life.

I was always very active in religious concerns. In fact, I was probably close to being a conscientious objector but with all my cousins going into the military my mother pushed me to be active in the war effort. Personally, I was satisfied with just going to college but all my mother's sisters had gold stars in their windows and her son was in college. She had several sisters living within 30 miles of each other out in western Oklahoma and my father was totally disabled from his service in World War I. During my youth, we moved around to cities with veterans' hospitals — Tucson, Denver, Muscogee. I had to be the little man of the house but when the war broke out I just wasn't serious about joining up.

I finally volunteered for the army air corps reserve on August 3, 1942, while a freshman at Oklahoma Baptist University in Shawnee. At that time, I was told I wouldn't be needed until after graduation. That was okay with me because I could finish my education. Six months later I was called into active duty.

After training I was stationed as part of the 8th Air Force, 385th Bomb Group, at Great Ashfield, England. Religion continued to play a major role in my life during that time. We had services once a week at a chapel on base and the chaplain himself happened to be a Baptist from Arkansas. He was an outgoing sort of fellow, nice, and funny. I remember him telling me after Sunday service to take him to the theater so he wouldn't go to the bar and get drunk.

As for myself, I had a funny feeling about praying. I had a hard time praying that God would protect me against another young man who happened to be a German and who had just as much a right to live as I did. I never did pray for my own protection but I certainly believe my mother and father did. I don't believe I ever hated the Germans. I had a job to do as a B-17 pilot and I just did it, obeying my orders in the process.

25

LIEUTENANT MYRON KING

DOB: October 22, 1921
Where: Southampton, Long Island
Air Force: 8th
Bomb Group: 401st
Squadron: 614th
Station: Benefield, England
Decorations include: Air Medal with clusters. A B-17 pilot, Myron was credited with 20 combat missions. On a mission to Berlin, flak damage forced him to land his ship, *Maiden U.S.A.*, in Poland. He and his crew were detained, moved around, and eventually released by the Russians. In an unusual twist to a fascinating story, Myron was then put on trial by U.S. authorities. Postwar, Myron owned a picture framing business and art gallery.

The Incredible Journey of the Maiden U.S.A. *and Her Crew*

There was nothing during our takeoff from Deenethorpe, England, on February 3, 1945, to warn us of the life-changing events we would soon encounter. In fact, everything was normal during the early hours of our trip to Berlin, if you could say anything was normal about flying a bombing mission right to the heart of our enemy's capital. Our ship on this day was the battle-hardened *Maiden U.S.A.*, a tested and respected B-17. As the pilot, I had full faith in my crew, especially my copilot, William Sweeney, who had finished his pre-med studies before being drafted. During the briefing prior to our flight, Sweeney and I noted the coordinates of a Russian airfield where we could land, refuel, and take care of any minor repairs following our bomb run. What an important part that information would play just hours later.

We were at 30,000 feet flying in the center of a 12 ship squadron which was in the center of 1,003 planes from the 8th Air Force. We had dropped our load and were heading off the target when the excitement began. In quick succession, I saw a 155mm flak shell burst just behind the ship in front of us, then another exactly halfway between our ships. Knowing what was coming next, I sat there in the cockpit just waiting for the end. "This is it," I told myself, fully expecting us to take a direct hit from the third shell. Instead, it burst between number two engine and the nose, pushing in part of the nose and hurling a piece of flak inside where it severed my navigator's throat mike but only left a scratch on his neck.

Whirling, red-hot metal punctured a hole about the size of a broom handle in the engine as well as the nearby oil cooler. Very quickly about 40 gallons of oil streamed out and coated the side of the plane. Later, it was described as looking like "a black rubber mattress was wrapped around the wing and appeared to be six to eight inches thick." Additional damage included three of the nose windows and a cut oil line to number four engine. By the time we could feather number two engine, number four ran away and would have burned up in a few minutes if we had not feathered it.

At that time, the first thing that came to me was the Russian field mentioned in our briefing. The field was approximately 15 minutes away so we called the flight leader and told them we were headed for Russia. We could clearly see the Russian artillery firing at the Germans below us, marking the front line of their steady advancement toward Berlin. I asked Sweeney what he thought we should do and he agreed with me that we should not try to get back to England primarily because strong headwinds would force us down before reaching the coast. Any attempt to try for Sweden was dismissed as well because I knew it have would taken much longer to get home due to issues surrounding that country's neutrality.

Myron King (courtesy Myron King)

We circled where the field should have been but if there was a field it was little more than one of those plowed fields used for reconnaissance missions. We were sure it was the field given to us for use in an emergency but my feeling was that we would have had to land wheels up and I wasn't about to do that. We had enough gas to possibly get to Warsaw or some field near the city so I picked up the Vistula River and followed it. We flew low while looking for a place to land, hoping to find the city's airport.

We flew across the city one way then across the city the other way and couldn't believe what we saw. Not one building was standing. The once proud city, the center of so much history and culture, had been obliterated. We could see a thousand chimneys standing but nothing else. We also saw many refugees, most on foot, streaming back into the city where almost all of them would find nothing.

We finally found the airport but the Germans had put charges all down the runway so no one could use it. There were piles of concrete also obstructing any attempt at landing. Hundreds of Polish peasants using one-horse sleds were piling dirt beside the runway, trying to create a new strip. We quickly decided we couldn't land there so we headed farther west where we knew there would be some big, flat, open fields. About that time, though, we were placed squarely in the gun sights of a Russian La-5FN fighter the pilot of which, I found later, was a hair away from blowing us out of the sky.

The Russian pilot, seeing our crippled, lumbering B-17 making its way over Warsaw, thought we were Germans flying a captured plane. As he related to us later, he flew a long pursuit curve, keeping us dead in his sights throughout, with his hand on the trigger of his 20mm cannon and the slack taken up ready to fire. All this time we couldn't see him because he flew with the sun behind him, a classic attack maneuver. He finally decided to ease off the trigger pressure and make a pass by us. Somebody in our plane saw him and I immediately fired a red flare to signal we were friendly. That, plus lowering our landing gear, kept us from being blown out of the sky. He flew around in front of us and we just followed him.

He took us to a very small fighter strip, nothing more than a 2,000-foot plowed field, where light planes were landing. This was in the middle of a very cold winter and this strip, about the size of a football field, had irrigation terraces cut across it. However, they were flooded with water which had frozen so light planes were landing on this frozen surface without a problem. I knew I didn't have a choice by now so I decided to set the ship down the best way I could. I never concentrated on anything in my life like I did when I landed that plane. The rest of the crew was in the back in crash positions as I took the *Maiden U.S.A.* down, dropping below 100 miles per hour and thinking we would crash once we reached 80 miles per hour. We stalled out over a fence and hit the ground hard. I thought I had come down too straight and the wheels had broken off then I realized that they were still turning. We traveled down the field at about 90 miles per hour with full flaps, breaking up the ice in big chunks as I prayed we would stop somehow.

We reached the end of the field, made a big, sweeping curve, and the plane came to a stop. We had landed at Kuflevo, Poland, southeast of Warsaw and about 600 miles from Berlin. The fighter pilot came over to greet us and I went with a Russian major to explain our presence. Our engineer stayed with the ship to start the work of repairing the oil cooler. When I got it over to the Russian officer that we had been shot up over Berlin, they couldn't do enough for us; they treated us like kings and even threw a party for us that night at a local one-room schoolhouse complete with food cooked by the local peasants. They sang Russian songs and we returned the favor with the air corps song as the vodka flowed freely. Later, we were parceled out to local villagers' homes the owners of which were told to provide us a place to sleep.

For the next three days the Russians tried to get us clearance to leave for Lublin, where we could obtain enough of the fuel we needed to reach Italy. During that time, we made repairs to our engines, including the important oil cooler. It ran hot, but it ran. Near the end of the third day we were running the engines — testing our repairs — when a Russian C-47 transport plane landed and taxied right up to our ship. We cut the engines and while I stayed inside to finish cutting all the switches, Sweeney, the copilot, got out and began talking to a Russian general with the aid of an interpreter. The interpreter, a young man who appeared to be in his late teens, was standing between the two.

The interpreter didn't know English very well so we had a hard time understanding each other, especially when trying to transfer the terms he would give us in meters and kilometers. We finally got over to the general our situation and that we weren't cleared to fly to Lublin. He told us we could fly with him to Lida, where a regular runway was located along with enough fuel to get us to the American base at Poltava. We had to leave quickly, he said, because the field at Lida was 30 minutes away and it was almost dark. After doing some quick but difficult calculations, we decided we had enough gas to go with the general to Lida. Just to be sure, we had the crew take all the guns, flak suits and ammunition — anything that didn't make it fly — and put them in the C-47. In addition, all the crewmembers who weren't essential to flying our ship were to ride with the general.

I knew our takeoff was going to be tricky not only because of the field's condition and its very short length but it was also about 15 degrees higher at one end. So we got to the end of the runway where I locked the brakes and broke the wire at the end of the throttle to give us war emergency power. I never had an airplane shake like that when we let go of those brakes. I yelled at Sweeney to take care of everything in the cockpit, all the instruments, "and if this big ass bird can fly, I'll get it out of here." At the end of the field was a road. We hit the road and bounced about as high as a telephone pole and then started settling down. All four props touched the snow that covered the ground. My wheels were up as we crossed a second field, making a flat turn to avoid trees looming in the distance. Then, over a third field with the props still whirling through the snow, *Maiden U.S.A.* started up like a rocket.

I was excited to be flying again but as I pulled the throttle back my elbow hit the kid who had been our interpreter. Obviously, it was too late to transfer him back to the C-47 so I made a decision that would haunt me for years to come: he would ride with us on the short hop to our next field. But immediately I knew we had trouble. "I want to go to London with you. I have an uncle in London," he told me. I was completely taken aback by his presence in our plane and had a strong suspicion that he really wasn't an interpreter after all. For lack of a better name, I decided to call him "Jack Smith," after a bombardier we once had. The situation was compounded by the fact that our new friend "Jack" was wearing flying clothes with no insignia that he had found in an emergency bag and had put on over his regular clothes.

The Russian general decided not to land at Lida but at Szczuczyn, Poland, a little over one hundred miles from Kuflevo. The runway was longer and made of lend-lease steel mat so there was no problem landing. While the rest of my small crew left the plane, I walked to the rear and found "Jack Smith" sitting in the radio room. He didn't want to leave the plane but I insisted. It was very cold so I allowed him to wear the clothes he had put on.

The next day the Russians motioned that they wanted to see me so I went into a room where they had gathered. This time there was no vodka to be shared. They wanted to know who was on our airplane. I understood them, through a Russian mechanic who could speak a little English, to want the name of each man on the plane so I complied. Starting at the top, they went down the list with one saying, "Amerikanski?" and I would reply "*Da.*" They pointed at the name of each man, saying "Amerikanski?" When they got to "Jack Smith," I said "Nyet." He said, "Polish?" I said I didn't know. Then they wanted to know if he got on the airplane at the last stop. Eventually they brought him into the room. I tried to explain to them that he did not hide on the plane and how we thought he was the general's interpreter. They didn't seem interested in that. They wanted to know if he was "Jack Smith." I said "Yes." As they took him out, "Jack" whispered, "Pray for me." That was the last time I saw him.

The next night two Russian navigators came to our room, one of whom spoke English fluently. They mixed with our crew, spending three or four hours at night and several hours during the day with us. I figured that this was the Russians' way of deciding whether we had told them the truth about "Jack Smith." In all, we spent about five weeks at Szczuczyn. For one reason or another — bad weather, no clearance or whatever the Russians wanted to tell us — we were not able to leave.

Finally, with the Russian line advancing, we moved with our friend the general to a base at Lida, about 150 miles farther east. We were treated well and I, for one, thought the "Jack Smith" incident had been dropped. After five days at Lida we were cleared to fly to Kiev, 300 miles to the southeast. Along the way we encountered good weather so I made the mid-flight decision to continue on to the American base at Poltava, another 150 miles farther southeast. We were back among Americans after having spent 43 days missing in action and held by the Russians. We caught our fellow Americans by surprise. They had no idea who we were, why we were there, or how we got there so cables were quickly transmitted among American authorities. It seemed to me that our long ordeal was coming to an end. How wrong I was.

A Kangaroo Court

When we got to Poltava, our folks there put in a clearance for us and *Maiden U.S.A.* to fly to Italy and it was granted. We felt that, after so many days, our mysterious odyssey was over and we could finally return to our home base. But we had a lot of major battle damage to repair on the ship and it had to be test hopped. I believe it was a week later, just as the ship was ready to go, when word came from Moscow wanting to know why we spent five weeks in Poland. It couldn't have happened at a more dramatic moment. We were literally in the plane with the engines running, set to return to Italy, when someone ran up the ship and delivered the message.

During our time on the ground at Poltava, diplomatic and military cables flew back in forth between the Americans and the Russians centering on our mysterious rider, "Jack Smith": who he was, how he received a ride on our plane, and what he was doing there in the first place. In short, the Russians were claiming the young man was a spy and that I was flying spies into their territory. We were told to cancel our flight home and later ordered flown to Moscow. Besides me, the crewmembers involved were William Sweeney, copilot, Richard Lowe, navigator, and Ernest Pavlas, the engineer.

I learned that I would face a general court-martial based on the following charge:

> *Violation of the 96th Article of War. In that 1st Lt. Myron L. King, 401st Bomb Group, 614 Bomb Squadron, did, in Poland, on or about 5 February 1945, while, as Senior Pilot, operating an American aircraft under the auspices of the Soviet Army, transport, without proper authority, an alien from near Warsaw to Szczuczyn, and did, thereafter, until such alien was removed by Soviet authorities on or about 6 February 1945, permit this alien to wear U.S. Army flying clothes, and to associate himself with the American aircraft's crew under the name "Jack Smith" known to be an alias, thereby bringing discredit on the military service of the United States.*

I went through a lot of grilling by the American military during the days after landing at Poltava, leading up to my trial. My feeling was this was the most stupid thing that ever happened. I really wasn't scared. I just figured the Americans were doing this as a show to please the Russians.

My court-martial was held on April 25 and 26 inside the very beautiful and ornate Spaso House, the American ambassador's residence located about one mile from the Kremlin. I faced a panel of American officers ranging in rank from colonel to major, each of whom seemed vitally interested in my actions during the time I first laid my eyes on "Jack Smith" until he was taken away by the Russians. Including my testimony and that of the other crewmembers, there was never any direct proof brought forth that we, in any way, deliberately smuggled "Jack Smith" aboard our ship nor that we had any intent to accommodate, much less hide, a spy while we were on Russian-held territory. But the verdict appeared to be set before the court-martial began.

It is known now that my predicament reached the highest levels of the Soviet government and became quite a point of contention between Mr. Stalin and our ambassador, Averell

Harriman. At least three meetings were held between the two to discuss my situation with Stalin claiming that I would fly in a spy and then a few days later fly back, shoot up my engines with my own pistol, and then be forced to land for repairs. During the time on the ground, he claimed, I would pick up a spy and return him home. Stalin and his crowd were determined I would pay for what he viewed as act of espionage. And it seemed my own government, at least publicly, was willing to allow me to twist in the wind to accommodate the dictator.

Shortly after the conclusion of all testimony, I was found guilty with the court issuing this finding:

Of the Specification of the Charge: Guilty except the words "without proper authority." Of the excepted words, not guilty. Of the Specification after deletion of the three words "without proper authority," guilty. Of the charge: Guilty.

I was issued what I thought was a particularly harsh reprimand and fined $600, payable at $100 a month. That was a lot of money back then but I viewed it as a lenient sentence in light of other examples of unauthorized flights by American officers who had found themselves in trouble. I regretted the reprimand becoming a part of my official record although I heard through my defense counsel that once the decision reached Washington it would be set aside.

The next day I departed for the airport in a sort of clandestine way accompanied by General William L. Ritchie who told me, as we approached a waiting C-47, to leave the car as soon as it stopped and board the plane quickly. I did and we were soon on our way back to Poltava, joining up with the rest of my crew. I also paid a sentimental visit to our ship, *Maiden U.S.A.*, during which I painted the name *Mission to Moscow* on her nose. Not long after that we returned to England and the 401st Bomb Group at Deenethorpe.

By the way, I eventually got all of my $600 fine back from the government. And on January 11, 1952, I was cleared of all charges for which I had been court-martialed. Below is the original reprimand in full.

To 1st Lt. Myron L. King, 401 Bomb Group, 614 Bomb Squadron
Subject: Reprimand

1. On 3 February 1945, having sought sanctuary for your aircraft and crew in a foreign country, you came under the jurisdiction of the military forces of an ally. Subsequently you transported an unauthorized foreigner to another airfield within the jurisdiction of this ally. Upon arrival, you failed to check the identity of this unauthorized person and did not report him to the proper authorities. You further aggravated this situation by allowing this person to be associated with your crew and to wear U.S. flying clothing, and by otherwise indicating that he was a member of your crew, thus attempting to deceive the military authorities of our ally, until he was sought out and apprehended by them.

2. This foreigner, transported and covered by you, was alleged by our ally to be an agent dangerous to their interests. As a result of your misguided and reprehensible actions, our ally assumed that representatives of the U.S. Army were engaged in activities with an ulterior purpose. So seriously were these events received that they were brought to the attention of our Ambassador by the Chief of State of our ally.

3. Your abuse of the hospitality and sanctuary offered you by our ally is totally inexcusable.

4. Your actions in this case have demonstrated a deplorable lack of judgement [sic] and common sense on your part, and have brought discredit upon your organization and upon the Military Service of the United States.

A copy of this reprimand will be filed with your record.
John R. Deene, Major General
U.S. Army Commanding General
U.S. Military Mission

26

LIEUTENANT DON PETERSON

DOB: March 9, 1925
Where: Renville, Minnesota
Air Force: 5th
Bomb Group: 22nd
Squadron: 2nd
Station: Philippines
Decorations include: Air Medal with clusters. Don flew 19 combat missions as a B-24 navigator in the southwest Pacific. Like others, he still has nightmares about one decision he made. After the war Don worked in sales before getting involved in the Democratic Party. In 1962, while in South Dakota, Don managed George McGovern's successful race for the U.S. Senate. He played an active role at the 1968 Democratic convention in Chicago and was a Democratic candidate for governor of Wisconsin in 1970.

From the Midwest to the Pacific

From December 1944, through the end of the war, I was a navigator on a B-24 with the 5th Air Force in the Pacific. I was a kid from Minneapolis, Minnesota, who had to have his parents' permission to enlist because he was one month shy of his 18th birthday. I knew I didn't want to go into the infantry. Life as a "ground pounder" just didn't appeal to me.

Instead, my sights were set on becoming a hotshot pilot. While at Kelley Air Base during training, my name appeared on a bulletin board to report to a designated office. I remember cadets walking down the hall and opening the door, never to be seen again. When it was my turn, I walked in, saluted, and was greeted by an officer's life-changing words. "You want to be a pilot but your test scores indicate you would be a better navigator. You want to be a navigator, don't you, mister?" I didn't know anything about navigating but I had an aptitude for mathematics.

I didn't know anything about a B-24, either, until reaching March Field, California. I didn't know how to get in one and had never seen one. (I quickly found out that you enter a B-24 through the bomb bay.) The sight of that big machine overwhelmed me. It was

26. Lieutenant Don Peterson

Don Peterson (courtesy Don Peterson)

not beautiful, certainly not glamorous, but it was functional, a real workhorse that got the job done.

One day I was walking among the barracks at March Field and I heard this peculiar noise above me; like a sputtering, crackling sound. I looked up just in time to watch a B-25 actually come apart. The tail section was falling off as the plane quickly descended on fire and eventually crashed just a few hundred feet from me. There was nothing I could do. Part of the prevailing thought at the time was that if we lived through our training, we would probably make it through the war.

My first combat mission was a bombing run on Clark Field in the Philippines, originating from the island of Palau and covering 500 miles over water to the IP, where the bomb run begins. Japanese fighters were hitting all around us but we, of course, couldn't deviate from our bomb run. I literally lost control of my bowels I was so scared. Once over the target, I crawled back to the bomb bay and tried to see where our bombs hit. I had been designated the "intelligence officer" on that flight. The good news was we weren't hit and we were only one mile and one minute off our IP. The other navigator overseeing me thought I was a genius.

We mainly bombed airfields on my 39 missions but we also hit some shipping. Several missions took us to Hong Kong where we bombed ships in the harbor. One time we went out looking for Japanese ships headed back to protect their homeland but the flight engineer forgot to have the extra fuel tank filled. We just dropped our bombs and jettisoned what we could to make our plane lighter. Upon landing on Mindanao, we ran out of fuel while taxiing.

Bombs weren't the only things we dropped. Sometimes during missions over the Philippines we dropped matchbooks that said, "I Shall Return." We threw them out the windows and watched them scatter below us. I felt a little foolish doing that. I always thought MacArthur was an asshole.

I remember a mission during which one of our planes had to ditch. We were always told that it would be bad for us if we went down. The water would present its own challenges and the land was rough; primarily it was jungle and mountains. In this instance, the crew survived the ditching but was captured by the Japanese. We were told those fellows were force marched and stoned through every village. The enemy showed no quarter.

We were also told never to drop our bombs in the water so on one mission I looked for something, any sort of target. We couldn't make the primary target due to bad weather so I just picked a town on the way back and dropped the bombs on it. I still have nightmares about my decision. I didn't even look through the bomb bay on that one.

I flew with different crews on my missions, a total of 104 men according to my flight logs. All our work was considered low level bombing, usually around 10,000 feet, so the flak was especially rough and dangerous. That type of combat would affect people in different ways. We had a young copilot who lost it. They found him sitting by himself in the jungle laughing and doing some unmentionable things. He was shipped home.

We returned from a mission over Shanghai, China, one day and found out the atomic bomb had been dropped and the war was over. Like the rest of us, I had no comprehension of what the atomic bomb was. Later, a few of our planes were assigned to a recon mission over Japan. We were to fly over Tokyo and Hiroshima and then back to Okinawa to see if we would be fired upon. No shots were fired at us but I remember Hiroshima being little more than a destroyed blob. There were a few structures sticking up but mainly there was total destruction. I didn't see a soul; there was no movement.

During the Vietnam War, I turned into a peace activist. That war was wrong and I believe Iraq represents Vietnam with sand — just a stupid thing to do on our part. Seeing war firsthand turned me against armed conflict. As a kid overseas, I was scared being away from home and getting shot at. I thought I would go to church but even there I got little comfort. One day, while we were sitting on the ground around him, the chaplain told us that the Japanese were terrible people and that God was on our side. I didn't believe him and slowly grew more distant from the church to the point that today I am an atheist. All the killing we do to each other during war is unnecessary. I still have visions of looking through our bomb bay at the explosions and destruction caused by our bombs. The images are vivid.

27

Captain Al Suedekum

DOB: January 30, 1918
Where: Cape Girardeau, Missouri
Air Force: 5th
Bomb Group: 38th
Squadron: 405th
Station: southwest Pacific
Decorations include: Air Medal with clusters. A veteran of 62 combat missions as a pilot and flight leader in the B-25, Al flew mainly low level bombing and strafing missions against Japanese bases and ships. On June 17, 1944, he flew his fifty-third mission: an extremely low level attack against enemy shipping and naval vessels in the Dutch New Guinea area. It resulted in heavy damage to two freighters and the sinking of a smaller vessel. Al then flew his damaged plane safely back to base and landed without any injuries to the crew. His actions earned him a recommendation for the Distinguished Flying Cross. Following the war Al was commissioned in the air force reserve, retiring as a lieutenant colonel. As a civilian, Al worked in the printing industry for 48 years.

Targets Aplenty

For me, the very nature of our low level strafing and bombing runs with all their challenges and unpredictability overrode any chances of being scared. I rarely flew our B-25 in a straight line, believing that a lot of evasive action was better than presenting us as a fat, juicy target. That doesn't mean we didn't have our share of close calls.

Mission number 53 took us over the islands of Samate and Jefman off the coast of New Guinea. The targets were a Jap airstrip and a ship sitting nearby. As we made our low level run on the ship, anti-aircraft fire started up all around us. I don't know where it came from. Anyway, we sunk the freighter but lost our right engine in the process. Almost immediately, my copilot shouted for me to keep the engine running if I could. It was spitting and sputtering and he had to hold the throttle down on it while I watched the temperature gauges. Somehow we made it back to base on what I would call an engine and a half.

Shortly before that exciting trip, we were returning from a mission over the same islands when one of the crew spotted what they thought was one of our C-47 cargo planes flying above us. "What's that C-47 doing up there?" he said to the rest of us who were, by now, stretching our necks and straining our eyes to see what he was talking about. "That's not a C-47. That's a Betty bomber!" somebody yelled back. The Betty was a twin engine Japanese navy attack bomber prevalent throughout the Pacific. Its pilot was flying straight and level, about 1,000 feet up top. We were running low on fuel at the time so I had all but ruled out a fuel-guzzling climb to get him. That's when he made the move we needed. Instead of climbing, which probably would have saved his life, the Betty's pilot decided to dive and make a run for it. I peeled off and started after him with guns blazing. I could see the tracers hitting his wings but the durable plane just kept flying. For a short while, at least, we got to use our B-25 as a fighter aircraft. Our "real" fighter pilots flying nearby in their P-47s and P-38s heard all the action as it took place and wanted a go at the Betty but we wouldn't give them our location. I was determined to make the kill myself so I made two passes, the last one with flaps down. I know I seriously damaged him but by then others had found us and joined in the fun. The last plane in the attack got credit for the kill.

We lost an engine and just about ended it all during a flight over Sorong, New Guinea, on June 17, 1944. Our mission involved an extremely low level attack against Jap merchant and naval ships in the area. Intense and accurate anti aircraft fire knocked out one engine early in our run but we were able to drop our bombs between two Jap freighters anchored side by side, scoring very damaging blows. One ship was left sinking and both were burning fiercely. Our plane was badly damaged and I knew enemy fighters would soon be on the scene but I couldn't pass up the tantalizing target of an enemy lugger plodding through the water down below. A lugger was a small craft that carried cargo from the bigger ships to shore. We attacked and sank it before we turned and limped for home, satisfied with the day's work but a little concerned that our one remaining engine left us vulnerable to enemy fighters and might stop at any moment.

I don't consider myself a hero for what I did in combat and I don't regret anything. I'm satisfied with how I handled what I was assigned to do. I just did my part to help my country win a war.

Windshield Wiper at 350 mph

My introduction to the army air corps was like something out of a dream. I had always loved airplanes as a youngster; their thrilling escapades in the movies helped lead

Al Suedekum (courtesy Al Suedekum)

me to build my own model planes out of wood but I never actually flew in an airplane until the service. I still have those little wooden planes today and they bring me as much joy as they did over 70 years ago.

The day I got my wings I was very excited and proud. It was then I found out I was assigned to a B-25 unit. So began another love story involving man and machine. The B-25 Mitchell was something special, easy to fly and exciting beyond anyone's imagination, especially the way we flew it in the southwest Pacific.

I flew 62 combat missions in that amazing plane, some out of Port Moresby and most of the rest from Nadzab, New Guinea. They were exciting missions, many of them low level bombing and strafing runs against Japanese installations. Many times we dove off the mountains of those islands, then turned and swooped in just as fast as we could. Often that meant going wide open at 275 miles per hour. We came screaming in at tree top level so the Japs wouldn't see us approaching; our twelve, .50 caliber guns blazing away, hitting anything that moved. All the while I flew the ship up and down, side-to-side so the enemy would have a harder time drawing a bead on us.

We dropped our bombs on targets we saw as we went along: sometimes runways, or, if we were flying to the side, perhaps revetments, planes, machine gun positions, or supply dumps. Mostly we made just one pass so we didn't have a lot of time to act and react.

We were coming in low one day and I had a copilot on his very first mission. I think he learned one of his most important lessons that day when a ship flying higher in front of us got hit and dropped out of the sky. "You see," I said, "that's why we're so low."

I had sort of a bad experience shortly after I arrived overseas. At that time, the older crews tried to get their copilots assigned as first pilots. So they stuck me with a guy who was a copilot, someone who didn't have much experience in a B-25. They basically forced this fellow into the pilot's seat and I had to fly alongside him. Trouble was, he was afraid of the airplane. There's just no other way to describe his problem. Someone with experience could tell he was afraid by the way he acted and how nervous he seemed. We flew a mission to Wewak one day which involved us lining up either six or three abreast, as we normally did for a low level run over a target. Machine guns were firing at us from both sides and tracers were peeling off all around us. When I saw what was coming in at us I instinctively ducked down but when I looked over at the pilot he had ducked down, too. We looked at each other and sat up real fast.

The worst thing he ever did, though, involved a mission on a Jap supply base situated between the sea and some mountains. Once again we dove down out of the mountains and on this day held the outside position of the turn. This was one of those times when we red-lined our engines, reaching a maximum speed of 350 miles per hour as we dove in to do our damage. During the run, we encountered a lot of dust kicked up by the planes in front of us, something that wasn't unusual. All of a sudden this pilot designate stretches his arm outside to try to clean off the plane's windshield, much like someone would do with their automobile windshield, except we're going as fast we can while firing and being fired upon and trying to drop our bombs at the same time. It's a wonder the wind stream didn't rip off his arm. After that, I decided I had better fly the plane back to base. I was fortunate not to lose my life on that mission.

28

LIEUTENANT JOHN LECHLEITER

DOB: January 8, 1923
Where: Nashville, Tennessee
Air Force: 8th
Bomb Group: 100th
Squadron: 350th
Station: Thorpe Abbots, England
Decorations include: Purple Heart, Air Medal with clusters. John's eleventh mission was his last. An engine explosion and fire forced down the B-17 he was piloting over France. He and a surviving crewmember still can't figure out if the engine blew up because of flak or mechanical malfunction. After the war John remained in the air force reserve and retired after 28 years of commissioned service as a lieutenant colonel. He was recalled for active duty during the Berlin airlift and the Korean War, flying C-47s and modified B-25s on supply missions. After earning an engineering degree, John spent 28 years in cement, ready mix, and concrete products sales.

Two Point Landing in France

Contrary to a lot of the guys whose stories appear in this book, I flew when I was young, having soloed when I was 16. My daddy used to take me to the airfield and even though he wasn't interested in flying, he was all for entertaining his son. My love of flying, coupled with the fact that I was mechanically inclined, made it natural that I would volunteer for the army air corps.

After the usual lengthy training period, I was assigned out of the replacement pool to the 8th Air Force, 100th Bomb Group, as a B-17 pilot. The "Bloody Hundredth" it was called and for good reason. We weren't the group with the highest losses in the 8th, but it seemed that many of them came in significant bunches so that we got the reputation of being a hard luck outfit. Out of 306 missions, we suffered 177 aircraft missing in action. Our "square D" marking on the tail became a sign of fascination to some, but to others it was something to avoid. As for me, the 100th's reputation wasn't a bother. I was so busy trying to do my job that I didn't think about it.

28. Lieutenant John Lechleiter

John Lechleiter (courtesy John Lechleiter)

I certainly had my moments, however. On my second mission, a trip to Merseburg to bomb a synthetic oil refinery, I knew I would get killed. The anti aircraft was hot and heavy and the plane on our wing simply blew up. Clouds of black flak greeted us but we had nowhere to divert or hide: it was straight ahead or nothing. The Germans were running out of oil at the time and they needed to protect their refineries. They did a good job that day. We made it back but the tail gunner in the plane next to our hardstand took a hit. Part of his head was blown off and I could see the scalp on the window. Being so young at the time, though, I tried to think that the enemy was not going to get me but my buddy instead. I guess that's how most of us thought.

Coming back from missions was even scary. A weather change often presented problems for us. We let down over the North Sea and picked up a beacon signal to get a heading back to Thorpe Abbotts, our base, just south of Norwich. At the same time, thousands of other planes were also returning to their bases. We couldn't really relax until we got on the ground and drank the post-flight medicinal whiskey. I drank other crewmembers' whiskey when I had the chance.

February 20, 1945, was a day I'll always remember. Flying my eleventh mission, we were at 17,000 feet and experiencing fine weather. I didn't see any tracers but the top turret gunner said he did. The number 3 engine started smoking and soon burst into flames. There was no big jolt or jarring explosion. We quickly moved the plane out of formation and dove to try to put out the flames. By this time, the fire was trailing 10 or 15 feet past the wing and I knew there was nothing to do but get out.

The bell rang, alerting the crew to jump. Then I set the autopilot and got everyone out the best way that I could. There are several things I remember after leaving from the bomb bay. First, the noise from inside the plane was replaced by the quiet of the air while falling. I also remember seeing chutes around me and thinking that I would land in a lake that was looming larger and larger below me. So I pulled on the chute in the hopes of steering it away from the water and toward dry land. This scared me to death as the chute partially collapsed. A tree broke my fall and I was soon able to pull my chute down but after that I fell hard to the ground. The resulting pain left little doubt that I had broken my ankle. So here I was alone in strange territory, some part of France, not knowing if it was enemy-occupied, with no way of getting around.

Soon I heard voices in the distance and as they got closer I noticed two or three men who spoke French. I couldn't remember any of my high school French but I knew enough that I should try to make some new friends. I gave them my chute, which they were delighted to have, and shared my cigarettes with them. I was in obvious pain so they grabbed each other's wrists and held hands as I sat in the middle. They carried me several hundred yards to a vehicle and then drove me to Trelon, France. There, at the police station, I feasted on cognac and fresh eggs until some Americans showed up. As it turned out, the rest of my crew was spread out over miles and I never saw them again.

Eventually, I was put on a hospital train headed for Paris. The cars were full of wounded from the front. Cots were stacked six or eight high and the sights were gruesome — bloody bandages, stumps, and casts galore. I made friends with a tank commander and we agreed to meet up after the war but we never did. He was a young fellow just like me.

I'm curious now to know a lot of things that happened during my time overseas but there's no longer anyone to ask. I never really talked about my experiences; now I wish I had. I still wonder what caused my ship to go down. I knew the engines were frail and that engine failures were a common occurrence but we believed in that airplane. It was tough, durable, and forgiving.

Every year when February 20 rolls around, I think about my exciting day long ago. I'm thankful I survived and made it home. I wouldn't want to do it again.

29

SERGEANT BERNARD SANDERSON

DOB: November 19, 1921
Where: Nashville, Tennessee
Air Force: 15th
Bomb Group: 454th
Squadron: 736th
Station: Cerignola, Italy
Decorations include: Air Medal with clusters. An experiment in night bombing left Bernard with a crippled ship and concerns that bailing out would mean a quick death. As the ball turret gunner on a B-24, he survived 29 combat missions between 1944 and 1945 but that one, dark night is an experience he will never forget. Bernard returned home, earned a college degree in agriculture, and worked in residential real estate for 35 years.

A Long, Dark Night Over Germany

Day missions out of our base at Cerignola, Italy, were bad enough. Now we were assigned a rare night mission, an experiment we were told. The Brits flew a lot of night missions but not us. I wasn't very happy about it because we didn't know much about handling matters in the dark. The nights in that part of the world during the war were very, very dark. Any of us could back out if we chose but we were young back then. We didn't think of the possibility that we might not come back. I thought the other guy would get it, not me.

Our B-24s flew independent of each other so there was no formation flying on this night. The target was a German factory situated next to a concentration camp. That was a common thing for the Germans to do. The factory could make use of the slave labor and if we bombed it there would be a chance of hitting the camp, something we tried our best to avoid.

I was the ball turret gunner on our B-24. The turret was similar to the more widely known turret found on the B-17 except ours was fully retractable. Once lowered, it could be raised back into the ship. The way it was made, with its high wing, the B-24 sat too low to have a permanent ball turret. I didn't spend a lot of time in the turret anyway. That's because the guys before us had done a good job of destroying most of the German air force. Once the turret was lowered I usually sat on the edge with my legs and feet dangling so I could drop quickly into it. I placed two or three flak vests under my butt in case we took flak from below, which was often. During our long trips I would talk with the other guys, listen, think, and do some praying.

On this night, roughly half way to the target, we lost an engine to a mechanical problem. We listened over the intercom as the pilot and engineer talked back and forth about what to do and then we talked among ourselves. The decision was made to push ahead. We were no strangers to flying on three engines.

Over the target we lost another engine, this time to flak. The bomb run was always nerve wracking. It scared the hell out of us. That's why "bombs away" was always such a wonderful sound. The B-24s reputation was one of taking a lot of abuse but we were losing power aboard this one and we had a long way to go to get back home. Then, on the return, a third engine started acting up. It was only giving us half power at best. Our navigator, a good one, figured we would fly into one of the high peaks of the Alps if we couldn't find a way around it. So our pilot, Jack Nichols, told us to throw everything out of the plane that wasn't attached in order to make it lighter. Out went our guns and other heavy gear. Then he told us to be prepared to jump. Those of us in the back of the plane couldn't see what was going on up front but I went ahead and put my chute on. Then I started thinking. I'm Jewish and the last thing I wanted to do was jump out over Germany in the middle of the night. I didn't want to think about what would happen to me. So I propped myself against the bulkhead separating us from the bomb bay and put flak vests all around me for whatever good they would do. I sat there and prayed and prayed. And I kept waiting for us to hit.

Bernard Sanderson (courtesy Bernard Sanderson)

It's hard to believe that we lasted so long in the air with only one full engine. One of the crew from upfront came back to check on things. "What are you doing back here? We thought all you guys had bailed out," he said. Two of them had, as it turned out. I watched them go out the escape hatch nearest us. I was too scared to follow. Thank goodness the navigator had miscalculated. We made it around the peak but not before the pilot stopped others from jumping. Those of us in the back didn't hear any of that because our intercom was disconnected.

We managed to limp back and make an emergency landing on a fighter strip, barely stopping before the end of the runway. There were no dramatics. We were just grateful for being safely on the ground. Six weeks later the two crewmates who had bailed out walked back into our tent. We had given them up for dead but the Yugoslav partisans had picked them up. Those boys had quite a story to tell. The partisans led them through the German lines. At times they had to lie on the ground while the Germans walked right past them. It's an amazing feeling when two friends you think are dead suddenly reappear. There were lots of hugs, backslapping, and crying.

The nighttime flying experiment was discontinued, much to our relief. There was a hell of a lot of second-guessing about our night mission. The bombardier always insisted the pilot didn't handle things the way he should have. I don't remember whether he divorced us or we divorced him but the bombardier soon left our crew. We knew we were all dependent on each other and we were good friends. We didn't need somebody in the crew complaining all the time.

All our crew returned home from the war. One guy got nicked on the head with a piece of shrapnel. In the hospital some bigwig came by and gave him a Purple Heart. "Look what I got! Look what I got!" he kept telling us. He was awfully proud of that medal. As for me, even with all the flak, the dead engines, and the long hours in the air, flying sure beat the hell out of serving in the infantry.

30

SERGEANT CHARLES WHITEHEAD

DOB: August 8, 1921
Where: Greenwood, Mississippi
Air Force: 20th
Bomb Group: 330th
Squadron: 458th
Station: Guam
Decorations include: Purple Heart. Charles flew 9 combat missions as flight engineer on a B-29 during raids over the Japanese homeland. He received the Purple Heart for injuries sustained during the final mission aboard aircraft K-37, *City of Osceola*. As a civilian, Charles was a life insurance agent, retiring in 1982 after 21 years.

The Last Flight of K-37

Here is the story of our old bird, K-37, finally written by someone who was on board that awful day. I have read other accounts and it is quite natural that some errors crept in. But as anyone who ever got into this type of thing will tell you, you just don't forget most of the details until you meet your Maker. I can still close my eyes and see what my fine young aircraft commander looked like slumped in his seat and I can still hear the air roaring through that God-awful hole in the airplane.

In the records of the XXI Bomber Command, it was Mission Number 187, an attack on the urban areas of Osaka, Japan, by B-29s of the 58th, 73rd, 313th, and 314th Wings. Flown on June 1, 1945, the mission saw 509 planes airborne, with 458 bombing the primary target, an arsenal, with 2,788 tons of bombs. Altitude was from 18,000 to 28,000 feet and the time over the target was to be from 10:28 to 12:00. After the raid, 81 of the big bombers limped into Iwo Jima in various stages of distress. Ten aircraft were lost.

This is the story of one of the ten lost aircraft, a Renton-built B-29 of the 458th Squadron of the 330th Bomb Group, based on North Field, Guam. She was named by her crew *Behrens' Brood* but was later seen to have *City of Osceola* inscribed on her nose. K-37s serial number was 4293995.

Several articles have been written about K-37 and this mission and all of them I have read contain errors. This is the way it happened. I was flight engineer of her crew and I was aboard that day. How I got there is a story in itself. I enlisted in the army air corps in 1939 and was assigned to airplane mechanics. I instructed mechanics who were to work on B-24s. One day I was plucked out of mechanics and the next thing I knew I was on a troop train bound for B-29 ground school at Amarillo, Texas. After that, I met up with my assigned B-29 crew in New Mexico for further training, then assignment to the Pacific.

On that fateful June day Paul Schade, the 330th Group chaplain, visited the crew of K-37 at her hardstand in the small hours of June 1. The airplane commander, Captain Arthur I. Behrens, summoned the chaplain to one side and told him, "Paul, I'm not going to make it back from this one." How prophetic those words were.

The crew climbed aboard and in a short time the *City of Osceola* was airborne en route to Japan. Bad weather in the form of a front was encountered off the Japanese coast making rendezvous with the other B-29s a harrowing experience. I recall frantic exchanges between our pilots and radar man because many other planes were milling about in the heavy "soup." Danger of a mid–air collision was very real. Later, I learned that 27 Iwo Jima-based P-51s with 24 of their pilots were lost.

Charles Whitehead (courtesy Charles Whitehead)

In spite of the weather, rendezvous was accomplished, formations were assembled, and the run to the target began. At our altitude of 18,000 feet, and at 10:54 hours (the time my panel clock stopped), K-37 found herself apparently in the middle of a barrage of exploding flak. There was a sudden explosion inside the nose from a projectile burst inside the aircraft. It pulverized the thick armor glass in front of Captain Behrens, blew off the upper third of his control column, and continued by striking him full in his face, killing him instantly. The blast continued rearward and upward, blowing a huge hole in the "greenhouse" with such force that the barrels of the four, 50 caliber machine guns in the upper forward turret were bent like so much spaghetti. The young copilot, 2nd Lieutenant Robert Woliver, suffered flak wounds on his nose and left forearm as well as impaired vision in his left eye.

I faced rearward at the time, my back to the copilot, separated from him by a sheet of armor plate. That's probably what saved my life. I knew the pilot was dead because part of his face was now on my instrument panel but I didn't know the extent of our damage. Temporarily losing control of the aircraft, Woliver was not able to control our descent until he got us leveled off at about 10,000 feet. The gunners said later several Japanese fighters chased us down but lost sight of us in some clouds. K-37 was finally brought under control but proved difficult to fly. Some undetermined damage made it necessary to keep pressure on the controls to keep her nose up. After a major course correction (the ship was first headed west toward China), Lieutenant Woliver headed in the general direction of Iwo Jima. After what seemed hours of staggering across the ocean, it appeared that all our luck had run out. No other aircraft were sighted but we droned on, not even aware of our power settings or fuel remaining since almost every instrument on my panel and the pilot's was blasted into uselessness. My log went out the roof with the blast when the plane was hit. I sat there wondering how I could help. I did a whole lot of praying.

Finally, when it seemed that we would probably have to soon ditch, the pendulum of luck swung back toward the good side. This luck came in the form of an Iwo Jima-based P-61 Night Fighter that was flying a "squint" hop — a flight in daylight hours to spot any flaws in its airborne radar so that it could be put in top-notch working condition for night missions.

It was piloted by Arthur Shepard. His radar man was Arvid Shulenberger. These two had flown through a squall and their radar was out, but Shulenberger notified the pilot that he had spotted a blip on his IFF (Identification, Friend or Foe) scope. The blip turned out to be the IFF on K-37. Shulenberger soon told his pilot that the B-29 would miss Iwo by a

Charles Whitehead's stricken B-29 *City of Osceola* escorted by Arvid Shulenberger's P-61 MiD-NiGHT MiSS over Iwo Jima on June 1, 1945. Shortly after, the P-61 shot down the B-29. (©Eric Shulenberger)

Another view of the B-29 *City of Osceola* passing over Iwo Jima. Note the dangling nose wheel, believed to have been hand-lowered by crewmembers in order to bail out over the island. (©Eric Shulenberger)

hundred miles if it continued on its present course. They intercepted us and soon guided us to Iwo. The brakes on K-37 were out. Lieutenant Woliver had been weakened by loss of blood and all but blinded by the explosion on the flight deck. It was evident that there was no one aboard who could land the plane so he made the decision that everyone should bail out. In two passes over the island, that is what we did. I went out the wheel well, hoping that the parachute rigger was a Christian who paid attention to what he was doing when he packed my chute. Woliver exited with the help of 2nd Lieutenant John Logerot, the bombardier. We landed on the island, no one got wet. I landed among a bunch of battle-weary marines and their tents. Instead of asking about my condition, they yelled for me to give them my chute, saying I could get it back tomorrow. I never saw it again. I figure they tore it up, made their own Japanese battle flags out of it, and sold them as the real thing to new replacements. Those marines had seen so much death they weren't in a mood for anything except making a profit.

Island authorities ordered Shepherd to destroy the K-37, now a derelict showing a tendency to turn. It could not be allowed to stay aloft because there was the possibility that it might crash on the island. So K-37 met her fate at the hands of one of our own. She went down near the Iwo Jima coast with the body of Captain Behrens still aboard.

The crew was hospitalized for observation and those of us who could travel were sent back to Guam. There, we were given the choice of flying again or staying on the ground. The loss of K-37 was the last flight for me. Surviving a badly damaged plane and a jump from 7,000 feet up was enough.

31

LIEUTENANT ARVID SHULENBERGER

DOB: September 1, 1918
Where: Wessington Springs, South Dakota
Air Force: 6th
Squadron: 548th Night Fighter Squadron
Station: Iwo Jima, Ie Shima, Saipan, and Okinawa
Decorations include: Air Medal with clusters. Arvid was not a member of a bomber crew but his connection with the B-29 number K-37, *City of Osceola*, will always be a unique part of World War II bomber history. Arvid was the radar officer aboard the P-61A Night Fighter *MiDNiTE MiSS* that intercepted the crippled K-37 over the Pacific near Iwo Jima. After the war he became a professor of English literature at the University of Kansas. Arvid published novels, plays, and poetry, some of which was based on his wartime P-61 experiences. He died in an auto accident in 1964 while returning home from teaching night classes in English literature to inmates at Leavenworth Federal Penitentiary.

Splash One Dreamboat

You know me, Al, they kicked the game away behind me. It was a letter from Shep. The first in thirteen years, since we had been two-thirds of a night-fighter team off Iwo Jima and Ie Shima in '45. Major Arthur C. Shepherd, now of Saigon, training the Vietnamese in fighter tactics. Thirteen years ago my own name was Al, and I was a lieutenant, a radar observer on a P-61 (Black Widow).

Shep got hold of my address somewhere, and wrote me. It was a good letter. The opening gag line was from the book that had been Shep's favorite on Iwo. Lardner's *YOU KNOW ME, AL*. There was only one line of disturbing news in it. "There was a printed story, Al, about shooting down the B-29, in *TRUE* magazine. All fouled up. They got the names wrong. Somebody wrote in a correction, and they got the names wrong again." It was the first I had heard of the matter — I had missed the stories in *TRUE*.

Shep and I shot down that Superfort. Nobody else. I found it, he shot it down. We got our names in the papers and on the air. There was a syndicated feature story about it. I could look it up. It didn't mean a thing, except that it was our only contact with public relations and fame during World War II. Besides, it was a funny thing. It's the only instance I personally know of in which a B-29 was shot down **from the air**.

I remember it as if it were yesterday. Yesterday was June 1, 1945. We had been a month on Iwo Jima, Sulphur Island, Volcano Island, a wind-bitten five-mile stretch of rock and ashes, seven hundred miles south-east of Tokyo. (The beaches were black sand on Iwo, and you couldn't stand long in one spot because the fire underneath would burn your feet.) Five thousand marines had died on Iwo, and something like 19,000 Japanese. There was still fighting going on, on the northern end of the island.

It was a beautiful day — blue sky, bright sun. The night before had been our night off duty; we hadn't flown night patrol. So we were awake that day to enjoy the weather.

At three o'clock the night before, we had heard the Superforts going over, going north for an Empire strike. Tokyo. Hour after hour, it seemed, the 29s droned over, hundreds of them coming from Saipan and Tinian. "Dreamboats" they were called in the fighter code. A terrific thing — a sound like a long promise in the sky. We knew that they were winning the war for us, coming in endless echelons, not bunched and high but a steady stream of aircraft at 10,000 feet — Angels Ten — the way the new General — LeMay — was firing them at the Japanese. Every afternoon, we nightfighters checked our ships and radar by a short daylight flight, to see that we were ready for night operation. Squint hops, they were called. ("Squint" was any error in radar calibration; it could be corrected in daylight, by a visual check on our readings.)

Sometimes our squint hops turned into something bigger. We would be put on air/sea rescue patrol, at the same time. That's what happened on June 1. The Dreamboats were coming back now, by the hundreds, a steady stream overhead on their way back to Saipan. A few were crippled, a few going down, some of them would have to stop on Iwo Jima if they were lucky enough to get back that far. Some of them were shot-up enough so that they couldn't land; those would be abandoned close to Iwo and the crews would bail out. By mid–afternoon on a sunny spring day like that one, there might be as many as thirty parachutes coming down around the island at once. Against the blue sky they looked pretty, drifting like dandelion seeds floating down over a calm ocean.

Shep and I were up, on a squint-hop/air-sea rescue patrol. The airstrip was hot, the inside of the airplane hotter, whenever we took off in the afternoon under the Pacific sun. I was sweating in the radar cockpit. The intercom clicked, once we were airborne.

"Warm enough back there?" Shep asked.

"Hotter'n Dutch love," I said. The dialogue was standard operating procedure. "OK," I said. "Generators off."

Arvid Shulenberger (©Eric Shulenberger)

"Generators off," he said.

I switched on the radar. "Generators on," I said. The set warmed up, a dot appeared on the A scope. I switched the nose spinner on, and the dot became a streak across the scope, then a dance of "snow" to be tuned down and tuned out so that targets would register. A 720 scope, with ranges of two, ten, and a hundred miles on it.

"Weapon flashing?" Shep asked.

"Flashing," I said.

We were vectored out on a heading a little west of north — three-four-zero. A hundred fifty miles out, we would pick up a destroyer which was on rescue patrol — a "Bird Dog" — and be directed by her for the remainder of our own patrol. Meantime we could check our radar set for squint, on the Dreamboats flying past us overhead, going south. They were still at Angels Ten, while we patrolled at 6,000, Angels Six.

Half an hour and a hundred-odd miles out, we ran into a towering squall line, and flew straight on, straight through it. That was a mistake. The rain streaked across the plexiglass and we were nice and cool. It sprayed in the tiny air vent, reminding me to close it. At fifteen miles range a bright blip marking a Dreamboat moved cleanly across the darkened scope and registered cleanly a few degrees above us on the B or elevation scope. No squint, we guessed.

Then suddenly there was nothing but light on the scope. It was out. I knew why, though that didn't help. Up ahead in the nose the driving rain had got through or around the fiber composition nose-cone, and the spinner was shorted out.

"Hell, Shep," I said, "Weapon bent. She's out."

"Unh?" he said. "Bent? Hell. Wet."

"Yeah," I said.

No sound for a minute or two while we digested the bad news. Neither of us wanted to abort a squint hop, but there was nothing else to do.

"We're out of the squall," Shep said then. "Think it's worthwhile to wait a bit to see if she dries out?" "I doubt it, but we can see." I glanced down from the scope. "Wait a minute," I said.

"Yeah?" he said hopefully.

"The IFF," I said. "It's working like a charm." It was. The little green old-fashioned scope, nothing but the round end of a cathode ray tube with a green light dancing on it as a "Christmas tree," was registering the B-29 at ten miles distance now. A clean signal, code four, two small blips then a big one, dit-dit-dah, on the starboard side of the scope. "You know," I said, thinking fast for an excuse to avoid aborting the flight and having to do another, "we might hunt for Dreamboats with the IFF. I can get a range and azimuth reading, and if they're in trouble they ought to be flashing their emergency signal. We could report any ships in trouble."

"Unh," Shep said. "Would that work?" "Never heard of it being tried," I said.

Shep did not want to give up the flight, and do another. "I'll call Bird Dog," he said. "See what you can find."

Bird Dog was ahead and off to port some thirty miles, coming in loud and clear on the radio while I switched the IFF to the hundred mile range and checked it hopefully. The little scope was never intended for this purpose, but only for what its name indicated — Identification Friend or Foe.

Shep spoke to me again. "I didn't tell 'em the set was out," he said. "I'll keep an eye peeled. It's Cavu." Ceiling and visibility unlimited.

"What they don't know..." I began. "Hey, wait a minute."

31. Lieutenant Arvid Schulenberger

Shep clicked his button to show that he heard me and said nothing.

"I got one," I said. A big blip which opened out over the scope face. "It's emergency all right," I said.

"Where?" Shep said, a note of hope verging on belief in his voice.

"Sixty miles," I said. "I think." The calibration on an IFF scope was pretty uncertain.

"Where." "Where."

"Well," I said, "it ought to be either over on the starboard side ahead or over on the port side behind." It was a trick of such primitive scopes, that a target could give the same signal from either of opposite directions. I was about to explain this to Shep, in case he had forgotten, when he spoke again, this time with heavy irony.

"You want me to fly both directions at once?"

"Turn starboard," I said. "Climb gently."

Our two engines took on a deeper roar as the Widow dragged her great acreage of smoky black wing upward towards Angels Ten. A great, powerful airplane, with more wingspan than any comparably powered ship in the service. More guns and horsepower than any other fighter.

The guess turned out to be good. The emergency blip got wider, then stronger, then closer. It moved onto the center of the scope. "Level out of your turn," I said.

We were approaching the signal almost head-on, and the blip moved visibly down the scope. For some minutes, we flew toward it. We were making history, perhaps. I had never heard of intercepting a target on IFF. "Angels," I said.

"Eight."

"Climb. Range ten. Starboard again. Turn starboard."

"There's a Dreamboat over there," Shep said. "I see it."

We climbed again in a gentle turn, holding the target at scope center for a head-on interception which ought to bring us onto its tail.

Shep called. "You sure it reads emergency? That ship ain't in trouble. Still above us, going like a bat out of hell."

"Yes, dammit," I said.

"I'll swing up on it," he said. On the scope, the target was moving starboard at three miles now though our turn had steepened.

"Climb," I said. "Steepen your turn. Firewall your throttle."

"You said it," he said. He didn't need me to tell him. The Widow roared and shook and climbed.

The target swung to port at a mile. "Look out there," said Shep. "That son of a gun doesn't need help. He's indicating 220 at ten thousand. Two-twenty was fast, something near 300 true air speed. I looked out as we swung closer and higher. It was a Dreamboat, big and shiny in the sunlight, flying high-tailed and steady, all its props going, not a mark on it.

"Hell," I said. I looked back at the scope. The emergency blip was so big it almost covered the scope when it flashed.

"Dreamboat, this is..." Shep tried calling the B-29. No answer. We moved in closer. "I can't get him," Shep said.

I was looking at my compass. "On this heading," I said, "he'll miss Iwo a hundred miles."

"I'll swing under him," Shep said.

The Dreamboat moved over us, over to our starboard side. We came up close, almost in formation off its wing.

"Holy...Cow!" Shep said.

"Look at that!" I said.

Half the big plane's nose was shot away. From the other side, we had not even seen the damage. Framed in the gaping wreckage, a man sat waving at us. The pilot. No. There was no pilot. The copilot. The pilot's half of the cockpit was gone. The pilot was gone. The co-pilot sat there with what looked like half the instrument panel before him, the air blasting past his left side whipping his sleeve. A direct hit had blown the whole port half of the nose away, not neatly but effectively, leaving a ragged, twisted-metal hole too big to be called a hole. Almost a decapitation of the airplane.

"We'll give him a steer," Shep said. "Wave and point." We waved, close enough to see the co-pilot's teeth as he opened his mouth. The Dreamboat kept beside us as we corrected our heading for Iwo. He had been heading out over the vacant ocean, flying beautifully blind.

He stayed beside us now — or we beside him, for the 29 flew fast and clean, at a true air speed a good deal faster than normal cruise. We learned later that there were no gauges left in the ship and the co-pilot couldn't know his speed, heading or altitude.

In half an hour we were over Iwo, calling in to say what needed to be told. The Dreamboat couldn't land, we could see, for the nose wheel was gone. We crossed the island, turned gently in formation, and came back.

The crew jumped. Just off our wing, we watched them flying out on each other's heels. The air blast caught them by turn, whipping and tumbling them like dolls thrown into a hurricane. The expressions on their faces are still in my memory. Their chutes popped open and then swung below, coming down over the island. The co-pilot jumped.

The crippled 29 was now headed northwest, still flying. Flying straight and level toward Japan. "Stay with it," was the word from Control. We flew formation on the derelict.

"Splash it," said Control. The order startled us, but it was natural enough. The Dreamboat appeared to be on its way to Japan if not Siberia.

We pulled up and Shep made a pass, taking his time but giving it the works in a long burst. Four fifties, four twenty-millimeters, firing at once, enough to set the Widow momentarily back on her heels. Our plane filled with powder-smoke and stink. We pulled out of the pass.

"Hell's bells," said Shep. Looking out, we saw the 29 flying as straight and level as ever, apparently untouched.

"You didn't miss," I said. "There were chunks as big as dishpans flying past."

Shep clicked his button and snorted.

Another pass, and a longer burst. Another look at the 29, still flying for Japan on its own. This time there was a lace of yellow fire down its starboard wing. Nothing else. It was a ghost ship, a flying Dutchman, it couldn't be shot down. It was on its own and going places.

Two more passes, taking the wings and engines. Spraying the bomb bay recklessly, not knowing whether it was still loaded or not. All that happened was that the 29 swung into a gentle turn, dragging its fire-laced wing a little, back towards Iwo. We began to feel desperate. Pieces flew off the ghost. A propeller windmilled. The ship flew on.

We had 450 rounds of ammunition and used them all. By the time the gleaming bomber had steepened its turn, and started spiraling towards the ocean, we were on the edge of feeling defeated, whipped, and disgraced. In full view of ten thousand men on Iwo we had been all but beaten by an empty ship. We had never heard of an aircraft absorbing such punishment.

We circled, empty-gunned, above the 29. She flew disdainfully and grand, steepening her spiral, her great wings gleaming in the sunlight, streaming flame. The spiral became a dive. The sea below was like a flexing mirror in the sunshine. She was not shot down, at last, but **flew** into the sea as into a mirror.

She touched. A roar of napalm bombs and gasoline, a great bloom of smoke, and an explosion that rocked the air about us, far above.

We turned steeply, looking down for a bit. Shep called in, with more relief than happiness in his voice, "Splash one Dreamboat."

32

SERGEANT BILL ROBERTS

DOB: February 28, 1919
Where: Brooklyn, New York
Air Force: 15th
Bomb Group: 376th
Squadron: 513th
Stationed: San Pancrazio, Italy
Decorations include: Air Medal with clusters. After graduating from Duke University in 1940, Bill returned home and enlisted in the army. Once the war began he went through several stages of pilot training before being sent to gunnery school. A radio operator/waist and top turret gunner on a B-24, Bill was credited with 50 combat missions. After the war this diehard Brooklyn/Los Angeles Dodgers fan worked as a sportswriter (witnessing Don Larsen's perfect game in 1956), and for over 30 years in newspaper layout and design.

Professional Air Cadet

After graduating from Duke University in June 1940, I found it difficult to get a job. Selective Service was pending and if my number came up for early call I wouldn't be able to continue work. Everyone at the newspapers I applied to said, "Get your year in and come back and see us." So I did get my year in. I volunteered with the first group to be inducted under Selective Service in New York City. I was inducted on November 29, 1940, at Church Street in Manhattan and sent to Camp Upton, 1222nd Reception Center, outside Patchogue on Long Island. I performed clerk-type duties including handling the classification officer's correspondence, marking up classification cards, and on extra busy days interviewing the new inductees.

When my year ended I received a U.S. Army Certificate of Service and was placed in the enlisted reserve corps as a corporal. A week or so later Pearl Harbor was bombed and war was declared. After one month and 7 days on reserve I was re-inducted on January 5, 1942, at Camp Upton and returned to the same job, the same barracks, the same bunk that I had left on November 28. "Uncle Sam" was nice. He gave me the Christmas holidays at home, without pay of course, before recalling me.

32. Sergeant Bill Roberts

Bill Roberts (courtesy Bill Roberts)

After returning to the classification section, I was given the military classification of specialist. As spring arrived, more and more limited service personnel started being used in the desk jobs to allow healthy men to serve in the field. Knowing someone would replace me, I volunteered to join the aviation cadets in July 1942. I passed the physical and my 118 pounds just made the lowest weight allowed by the cadets.

I was sent to the classification center at Nashville, Tennessee, that same month, never dreaming that after the war I would spend the rest of my life in Nashville. After taking a series of tests, I was sent to pilot preflight at Maxwell Field, Montgomery, Alabama. That lasted nine weeks. I was shipped to Dorr Field, Arcadia, Florida, for primary training in Stearman PT-17 biplanes. Never having flown, I got airsick many times. Also, I couldn't land the plane without bouncing in or diving into the ground. It didn't take long for the instructor to wash me out. I was back on my way to Nashville.

Remember, I was still a cadet. This time the army put me on a troop train with about 200 others and sent me across the country to Santa Ana Air Base, Santa Ana, California, for bombardier preflight training. About the only notable event of my time at Santa Ana was having baseball star Joe DiMaggio as an assistant PT instructor. He stayed to himself, though, which kept me, a big Brooklyn Dodger fan, from talking baseball with him.

I was sent to Kirtland Air Base, Albuquerque, New Mexico, for bombardier training. Finally, it looked like I was going to get my wings! In late July 1943, I went for a final check ride. I was given four bombs to hit a target and ended up missing on each one. By now, my instructor was so exasperated he demanded to try the fifth and final bomb. He missed the target, too. I think I made a mistake pre-flighting the Norden bombsight. After that, I had to go before the colonel. "Son," he said, "we made a mistake with you. By your excellent ground school marks, you should have been sent to navigation school but I'm not allowed to do that after you failed pilot and bombardier training." That ended my aviation cadet days, but I think I set a record. I wore the cadet wings more than a year.

The army gave me back my sergeant's stripes, the ones I had earned at the classification section, and sent me to Sheppard Field, Wichita Falls, Texas, for reassignment. That was the worst place during my time in service, including my time in Italy. It was midsummer; 115 degrees during the day, mid–90s at night. All we did was close order drill in the mornings and calisthenics in the afternoon. We ex-cadets were waiting to be assigned to radio, mechanics, or armorer school. I went up to the classification section and told the sergeant to please get me out on the first train. He noticed my classification card indicating that I had worked at Upton as a classification specialist and said he had a sergeant's job open, would I like it? I told him I wouldn't stay there for double the money. He laughed and said he would get me out.

True to his word, in a couple of days I boarded a troop train bound for Sioux Falls, South Dakota, trading the heat for the cold so that I could go to radio school. That lasted 20 weeks. Despite the cold and a few snowstorms in November and December, I passed. Then it was on to aerial gunnery school in Yuma, Arizona, and to crew assignment at Fresno, California. As a B-24 crew, we were sent to March Field, Riverside, California, for transitional training. We were about to finish when our pilot, Don Sawyer, got sick. We had to wait for the next class so we could be sent to Hamilton Field, outside San Francisco, the last stop before going overseas. At that time our navigator had surgery for appendicitis and we got another navigator who had gone AWOL when his original crew was sent out. He turned out to be a great guy who was a superb navigator.

This is now 1944 and I have yet to get overseas. Everyone expected to be sent to the Pacific theater when, one morning in late August, the CO called out 30 crews (300 men) and said there was an emergency in Europe. We would be sent over there instead. We were told to turn in all our equipment for the Pacific including machetes and were soon on a troop train to Camp Patrick Henry, Virginia. After that two-week, cross-country trip, we waited a week before boarding a Liberty ship and joining a 7-knot convoy headed for the Mediterranean. It took us 30 days to reach Bari, Italy. So much for an emergency.

A few days later our crew was trucked to San Pancrazio (San Pan to all of us), a small village deep down in the Italian boot where the 376th Bomb Group (512th, 513th, 514th and 515th Squadrons) was stationed. We were sent to the 513th and I went on my first mission on October 16, 1944, to Steyr, Austria, to bomb the St. Valentine Tank Works. After being inducted on November 29, 1940, it took almost four years to get into combat. That's a long time to wait just so I could risk my life high over Europe.

I'm Hit! Wait A Minute...

My combat career began as a waist gunner on a B-24 out of San Pancrazio, Italy, as part of the 376th Bomb Group, 513th Squadron. I flew five missions as a waist gunner before moving to top turret gunner. This made it handy for me since I was also the radio operator on our ship, sitting behind the copilot. I flew 37 sorties and got credit for 50 missions. Some missions qualified for double credit because of their length. Out of all my missions, the one that really sticks out for me — the one that was more terrifying than all the others — was the one we flew to the Bressanone railroad bridge in the Alps in northern Italy.

On the days when our target was beyond the Alps, those mountains were beautiful to fly over: snow-capped peaks, lush, green valleys, and even the hint of tiny villages dotting the landscape along the way. We knew that the chances were good heavy flak awaited us at our primary target but, for the moment at least, looking down on those mountains from high above gave me the briefest of serene moments. If your target for the day was in the Brenner Pass, chances were good you were in for some scary moments. The Brenner was Germany's conduit to Italy. Thousands of tons of supplies were shipped via the railroad every day to the Germans and their allies in Italy. Often our job was to disrupt those shipments as much as possible by attacking bridges and viaducts. This type of mission was particularly scary. The anti-aircraft fire thrown up by the Germans was formidable almost everywhere we went but in the Pass it represented a whole new dimension. The guns were effective there because they had been moved high up in the mountains, meaning the distance between us and them was much shorter. I've heard the term "sitting ducks" to describe our predicament when bombing in the Brenner Pass.

On December 29, 1944, we experienced some of that very accurate, heavy flak and I thought for sure we were going down. We all had on our flak helmets and flak jackets and throughout it all I'm ducked down thinking, "God, get us out of this mess." I was scrunched up trying to make as small of a target of myself as possible when I heard the flak hitting our plane, sounding like machine gun fire right in front of me. In fact, I thought my guns in the top turret were going off on their own. That's when I looked up and saw a cloud of smoke. I knew then we were either on fire or we were getting hit.

We dropped our bombs with all hell breaking loose around us and quickly turned for home. I guess it was good not to know for a while how badly damaged old number 47 was but we soon found out. The number one engine was lost, all navigation instruments shot out, the tail turret rendered inoperative, and we had a fuel leak in the bomb bay. That's a hell of a place to have a fuel leak. Suddenly, during a damage check requested by pilot Don Sawyer, tail gunner A.J. Norris (Bill, as we liked to call him) began screaming, "I'm hit! I'm hit! I'm hit!" Sawyer quickly tried to calm Norris by saying, "Take it easy, Bill. Take it easy." and he sent the ball turret gunner back to see about Norris. But before he could get back there, Norris yelled, "Never mind, it's just hydraulic fluid." Norris, in his panic, had mistaken the red-colored hydraulic fluid for his own blood. It's funny today and certainly understandable that Norris would make such a mistake but at the time the humor escaped me. (Norris was trying his hardest to finish his combat tour as quickly as possible since his wife was expecting a baby back home.)

Just about this time the ball turret gunner reported in, saying we had two wounded waist gunners. No one knew how badly they were hurt but each of them had holes in his flak jacket. On top of all this, we were flying back to base alone on three engines. We couldn't keep up with the rest of the planes in our group. Suddenly we had become a big, fat, slow-moving target for German fighters. About that leak in the bomb bay: flak had ripped the fuel lines in that area and the gas fumes were extra heavy. I was about to witness one of the most courageous acts of bravery I saw during my time overseas. Our engineer, John Sparks, took it upon himself to go out onto the narrow catwalk in the bomb bay and with his bare hands, in temperatures reaching minus 30 degrees, temporarily connect the ruptured lines, thus fixing that leak. To this day I'm not sure how he did it. I was so impressed and grateful that later I put him up for the Distinguished Flying Cross. He didn't get it but he should have.

So here we were flying a crippled ship back to San Pan, key instruments useless, our navigator using dead reckoning to get us back home, several wounded aboard, and then we hit a violent thunderstorm about 50 miles from the base. This is where Sawyer, our pilot, was at his best. He calmly shepherded our ship through that storm. As we approached the runway we fully expected to receive the priority landing that befitted our hazardous situation. Surprisingly, Sawyer found himself fighting with the guys in the tower who told us to keep circling so that planes arriving ahead of us could land. Sawyer was livid. "Goddammit, chase those guys away, we're coming in," he says. "We've got a leak in the bomb bay and two gunners are hurt." By the time he made a smooth landing on three engines the ambulances were waiting for us, all set to take our wounded to the hospital. The medics hurried aboard and quickly reached the two gunners who, once their flak jackets were removed, were found to be suffering from only slight, superficial scrapes on their backs. Their skin was barely broken.

There were some hot people on the ground that day but our guys' "wounds" were judged significant enough to get them each the Purple Heart.

Old number 47 needed more than just a few small patches, though. She was shot up through and through but she got us back.

When Christmas Was No Holiday

It was dark at 4 A.M. and cold even in southern Italy when a shivering corporal from operations awoke a sleeping B-24 radio operator with the words, "Merry Christmas, Rob. Let's go." Outside of actually sweating through a bombing run, getting out of a warm bed in the middle of the night to fly on a mission, not knowing whether or not you would return to that bed the same night, was the toughest part of flying combat in World War II.

"What's merry about it?" you grumbled to yourself as you struggled into your flight gear. "Today, of all days, we oughta get a day off. Wonder where we're going? Please not Vienna or Munich with all those guns. Please let it be a *baksheesh* (easy) mission." At the radio operators' briefing you found out. And it didn't sound too bad. We were going to hit the railroad yards at a little town named Hall, a few miles east of Innsbruck with only six or eight guns. But there was a warning. The bomb run would be east to west and a sharp left turn was necessary after "bombs away" to avoid the heavy flak at Innsbruck. The three other groups of the wing (the 97th, part of the 15th Air Force) would be hitting Innsbruck's rail yards — a rough target.

The briefing ended just as dawn was breaking and you joined your crew inside one of your favorite planes: No. 51, *Rugged Rosie*. Old Rosie was a veteran and plenty tough. She insisted on staying in the air no matter how many holes they shot into her and she nibbled daintily on gasoline so that she always made it home without a refueling stop. With eight 500-pounders in her belly and Lieutenant Don Sawyer of Houston, Texas, at the wheel, *Rosie* rose lugubriously into the air carrying you on mission number 20. For her, it was mission number 100 plus and for the group close to mission number 400. You were a part of the 513th Squadron in one of the most famous groups of the war — the 376th, known as the "Liberandos." The enemy knew it well, for the 376th carried its distinctive tail markings into the North African campaign, the invasions of Sicily, Italy, and Southern France, and on the celebrated strike against Ploesti.

As radio operator, you get a break this morning. While still in friendly territory you didn't have to remain on the intercom within the plane. On the way north, while in a slow climb to 22,500 feet, you tuned in on the BBC. On most days you listened to popular dance music but today, of course, familiar Christmas hymns came through the earphones. When the announcer said, "Peace on Earth, goodwill toward men," you could only give a humorless smirk. Too many men would face death; too many men would die that day.

You thought of the freezing infantrymen fighting in the Battle of the Bulge. No heated suits for them. You were thankful your war was relatively clean. THEY were fighting the dirty war.

All too soon you entered enemy territory and you climbed into *Rosie*'s upper gun turret. Just ahead was one of the most gorgeous sights ever seen: the magnificent Alps, shimmering in bright sunlight under the cloudless sky. It had snowed in the mountains on Christmas Eve and their virginal whiteness was broken only by occasional wisps of smoke rising out of the chimneys of snug homes nestled in the valleys. If only you were a Santa Claus carrying toys to those chimneys. But you weren't Santa Claus and you weren't carrying toys. "Dive for the cellar! Go to the shelter, everyone! We don't want to hurt you, just your railroad. Our *toys* are bombs! GET AWAY FROM THOSE TRACKS!"

You were on the bomb run now and the briefing officer was right. Scant flak, inaccurate. But up ahead a solid curtain of bursts aimed at the groups hitting Innsbruck. After "bombs away" your pilot needed no urging to make that sharp left turn. Sawyer stood old *Rosie* straight up on her left wing and she peeled off out of danger, seemingly as happy as you were to get that bomb load out of her belly.

It was a happy crew high-tailing it home. But there was a sobering note. The bombing pattern was poor which meant that too many bombs missed the target. You could imagine where they landed but you tried not to think about it. You could only thank God that you didn't take a swan dive down amidst the rubble and you couldn't help thinking: what a way to spend Christmas.

33

LIEUTENANT BOB SMARTT

DOB: April 24, 1921
Where: Smartt, Tennessee
Air Force: 8th
Bomb Group: 490th
Squadron: 850th
Station: Eye, England
Decorations include: Air Medal with clusters. Bob Smartt piloted a B-17 through 35 combat missions, mostly in *The Judge*, a plane named in honor of his father. Ending the war as a 1st lieutenant, Bob retired from the air force reserve as a lieutenant colonel. He received post war degrees from LSU (agriculture) and University of Tennessee (engineering) then spent 35 years as a civil engineer.

The "Old" Man

My first thoughts upon seeing a B-24 were full of doubts. "I don't know if anyone can fly that thing," I remember saying to myself. It just looked like it wouldn't fly, even with its four big engines. The hardest day's work I ever did was at Ozark, Alabama, in August 1944, the hottest time of the year. I did three-engine takeoffs and landings when my instructor pilot would cut one engine, then two engines sometimes. We did that for four or five hours while I was trying my best to muscle the plane. It was a good thing I was young and strong.

I was young but when I got overseas I was considered the "old man" of my crew at 23 years of age. While I had learned to fly the B-24, my bomb group, the 490th of the 8th Air Force, had switched to B-17s. I had done a lot of bad mouthing about the B-17 in the past but my move to the Fortress turned out to be a promotion. She was much easier to fly. I suppose the hardest part of changing planes was learning how to use a different type of landing gear. The B-24 had a tricycle gear while the B-17 was a tail dragger. That, plus upon landing, the B-24 tended to drop right down rather than engage in a glide like the Fort.

We flew most of our missions aboard *The Judge*, a plane named after my father, Robert Smartt, a circuit court judge in Warren County, Tennessee. He appreciated having a plane named after him. He would write letters that were intended not only for me but the entire crew. They were positive, encouraging letters filled with small but important phrases like, "want you home safely" and "we're all for you" while minimizing the danger we faced. The crew appreciated my father's letters.

April 18, 1945 found us over Pilsen, Checkosolovakia, hitting an oil refinery. As we approached targets on our bomb runs, the crew encountered the most frightening time of a mission. Flying straight and level, there was nowhere for me as a pilot to go. Furthermore, the bombardier was flying the plane anyway at this time. We saw the flak exploding in front of us, hitting planes here and there and we knew our time was fast approaching. I remember one time on a bomb run with flak popping all around I came on the interphone and just made the comment that I wished I had a camera. "What a picture out here," I said. To which my flight engineer, in the top turret, quickly responded, "Camera, hell, just fly this airplane and let's get out of here."

The April 18 mission proved dramatic for us because the Germans hit us with something we had never seen. On the bomb run, one of our gunners yelled out, "Jets coming!" And here they came, just

Bob Smartt (courtesy Bob Smartt)

some blurs straight toward us with cannon fire blazing. Since they had a longer range, the German pilots opened up on us sooner and out of the range of our guns but they couldn't hang around very long because of our P-51s. Those Me 262s made three passes straight through our formation on that day. I could see their tracers hitting targets all around us but we just kept flying. On one pass, the planes above me and to the right of me were knocked out of the sky. One was on fire when it peeled out of formation and soon it exploded with the loss of its crew. The pilot, copilot, and navigator shared my hut.

The plane above us was rammed by one of the German jets. I can only think that the jet was knocked out of action and the pilot might have been dead or simply lost control. The landing gear, engines, 500-pound bombs, and anything else from that plane should have showered down on us since we were just below but for some reason they dropped ahead of us and we cleared the area.

Officers from three crews shared my hut at our base at Eye, near Norwich. My crew was the only one to make it back that day. I remember it being a very sad time. I helped pack the personal belongings of those who were gone including the pictures of his wife and two children that a navigator had proudly displayed for everyone to see. We had an understanding that if anyone didn't make it back the survivors would get the booze and it would become community property so we grabbed what we could before the operations officer came through to collect everything else. Any money or valuables, of course, was returned to the families.

Even though we never really knew what our fate would be from day to day, I never took off on a mission when I thought I wouldn't come back. Nothing was ever said among us about not returning. At the same time, no one ever said to another crew, "We'll see you later." We would tell them goodbye and wish them good luck but never did we say, "see you tonight."

34

Captain J.O. Grizzell

DOB: December 19, 1923
Where: Paris, Tennessee
Air Force: 15th
Bomb Group: 99th
Squadron: 347th
Station: North Africa and Italy
Decorations include: Air Medal with clusters. Jim flew as a B-17 copilot and pilot on 50 combat missions over France, Italy, Greece, Germany, Austria, Yugoslavia, and Bulgaria. Post war, he was promoted to major in the air force reserve. In private life Jim worked at Wright-Patterson Air Force Base.

Regensburg, Monte Cassino, and Ploesti

On our way to Regensburg, the group got separated into two formations because of weather. The flight over the eastern edge of the Alps was uneventful. For three hours I said to myself, "This is it." That thought came from the earlier 60-plane, 8th Air Force loss which was headlined in most newspapers and on the radio. Regensburg was a tough target but I later realized the heavy losses came not from the target area but from fighter intercepts as the 8th passed over and near air bases going and returning. The first of the two separated formations went over the target taking the brunt of the losses and we followed shortly when the fighters were on the ground refueling. As I remember, our squadron did not take any losses. Some 25 years later, a classmate told me at a 99th Bomb Group reunion of his plane's being hit in the first formation, eventually losing three engines and the crew throwing everything out of the aircraft to get over the Alps only to crash land in the Adriatic off Trieste. He was a POW for 15 months.

For our mission to Monte Cassino, there was an early wake up for what would turn into a two-mission day (the first and only one I knew of for the 99th Bomb Group). I had checked out as first pilot in late February 1944, but was copilot for our squadron CO on this March 15, 1944, dual mission. On the first mission we encountered some flak but nothing out of the ordinary. We returned, ate, and were off again by around noon. By this time a front had

J.O. Grizzell (courtesy J.O. Grizzell)

moved in and as we got closer to the target we hit white clouds where formations broke and then reformed when visibility permitted.

This happened three or four times with the clouds getting darker each time. Fewer aircraft could return to formation and eventually we were on our own. The CO flew on, hoping that the clouds would break and we could drop. As we got near the target (still on instruments) we started getting flack and the CO immediately started evasive maneuvers. I called a ground radar station to ask for directions. I still remember the "Grubstake" call sign for the station. As I made the first call, the radio went "Gruuuubbbbbb" and that was it. Our radio had been hit. Their radar (or sonic equivalent) was up on mountaintops and since we were flying perfectly straight and level we undoubtedly presented an attractive target for their accurate aim and altitude timing information.

We evaded the ack-ack and flew west, breaking out over the Tyrrhenian Sea, identifying an island, and landing in Naples. Per SOP, the engineer opened the fuel tank petcocks to drain any water that had condensed from the clouds. When he opened the first one, gasoline ran from a crack at the edge of the plate to which the petcock was welded. We left the plane and were flown back to our base at Tortorella [formerly a no-building railroad stop] east of Foggia. With an engineer as copilot, I flew our Naples aircraft back to our base in late April or early May. It took that long to repair it.

The first high altitude mission to Ploesti, on April 5, 1944, was my last mission. Of course, everyone knew of the failed August 1943, low altitude mission to the oil fields there. No one knew what to expect this time around. It was a seven and a half hour mission. The flight to the target was uneventful. Of all the missions I was on, Ploesti had the most flak. It covered the entire oil field area. Other targets were normally small areas such as factories, marshalling yards, submarine pens, etc., and had concentrated flak. Miles of oil fields meant a great number of ack-ack batteries were necessary so as we flew toward and over the target, flak could be seen for miles. Explosions (not thick, concentrated flak) could be seen everywhere. It seemed to me to be more show than any sort of effective defense.

J.P.

After about three hours to our initial point at Sofia, Bulgaria, our planes found the target — marshalling yards — covered with low clouds. We knew the target since we had been there before. We flew past looking for secondary targets but to no avail. No bombs were dropped as far as we knew.

On our return, we passed Sofia and when out of fighter and flak range let down to about 12,000 feet for an easy return to base. Unfortunately, no one knew that a front with cloud buildups to around 30,000 feet had moved between us and Foggia. We had started the climb back to altitude when J.P. Wheeler, our pilot, pulled out of formation, flew perfectly level, and told me to level up the tanks. He didn't say what we were going to do but I knew it was serious. "Irish," Paul Raser, our engineer, and I leveled them with the fuel transfer pumps down to the second.

J.P. asked for the heading home and was told the reciprocal of the heading out. We never got a change of heading from there to the Adriatic coast, since we entered the front soon after leaving the formation. We gave ourselves 3,000 feet more altitude than the highest mountain in the area since we were heading into a low. Then we bored on through. We hit ice and almost lost the airspeed indicator but got the heat on in time.

Luckily, just as we hit the Adriatic coast, a few quick holes opened along the jagged, island-studded coastline. J.P. and I almost missed seeing any land since it happened so quickly. It was impossible to accurately identify where we were. The navigator, with us for the first time, said 15 degrees to the right, but our bombardier, C.K. Jankousky, who knew visual navigation, said five degrees left. J.P. called a conference in the cockpit and decided five degrees left.

Shortly out at sea, the clouds broke up and we dropped down to clear skies. To conserve fuel we had leaned out the engines till they coughed and then cracked them open a hair. We also dropped our bombs, not knowing what would happen after we hit landfall. Pretty soon we saw the mountain above Manfredonia and went straight in to Tortorella. Ours was the first airplane from the whole air force to land and since we were way overdue, Operations and S-2 followed alongside us in a jeep to the hardstand. I'm reasonably sure they were scared that possibly much of the 99th and other groups had been lost. J.P. debriefed the mission, providing information about the front. Then we waited for hours, getting reports on where planes from our group and other groups had landed.

As I remember it, there were seven or eight aircraft lost from the 15th Air Force. Three or four ran out of fuel and ditched, their flares being within sight of Bari air-sea rescue boats. Most landed south of Bari on any kind of runway they could find. One aircraft landed 100 miles south at a fighter strip near Brindisi. Aircraft were strewn all over south of Foggia so it took a while to get everyone together again.

The 20-degree spread between 5 degrees left, which was on the money to Tortorella, and 15 degrees right would have put us hitting landfall near Pescara, the eastern end of the front at that time. I'm sure we wouldn't have gotten that far, but trying to get to a field ASAP we could have been looking for a fighter strip like the one at Brindisi.

You might say we were lucky but I say it was smarts. J.P. Wheeler had a sixth sense about flying.

35

CAPTAIN ROBERT FESMIRE

DOB: May 6, 1923
Where: Lexington, Tennessee
Air Force: 8th
Bomb Groups: 801st/492nd
Squadron: 856th
Station: Harrington, England

Robert's accounts of his "carpetbagger" flights over enemy-held territory are compelling and reveal a chapter of the war rarely made public. The secret missions, flown in a black B-24, dropped agents and supplies behind enemy lines and were crucial to the success of the Allies. After the war, he briefly worked as an oil engineer before completely switching professions and becoming a dentist for the next 40 years. He also flew the C-46 in the air force reserve.

The Secret War

During World War II, folks back home knew about what was going on overseas from the newspapers and newsreels — the raids, the bombing missions. And to be sure, most of the Eighth Air Force (the Air Force to which I was assigned) was part of those activities. Three of our Carpetbaggers squadrons, the 857th, 858th and 859th of the 801st/492nd Bomb Group, did some night bombing with black B-24s. Sometimes their bombs were only propaganda leaflets, but other times perhaps 15 to 20 of our planes would fly as decoys for RAF bombers on joint missions. As the British planes neared their target, the decoy aircraft would veer off course and drop aluminum chaff. The metal particles confused German radar, and the planes served to direct the anti-aircraft fire away from those carrying the real bombs. These squadrons were like "Jack of all trades." They did everything.

The public didn't and couldn't know about the overwhelming amount of covert activity by underground forces in countries occupied by Germany. Their activity was very important in Hitler's defeat, but they had to have a constant and reliable source of weapons and supplies. That job was the primary responsibility of the 865th Squadron in our 801st/492nd Bomb Groups. Thousands of flights of B-24s dropped canisters over occupied countries. These canisters, floated down by parachutes, provided the materials the underground needed to continue the secret war. Many OSS agents were also dropped to become involved in the covert action.

I was especially proud to be a Carpetbagger. As a bomber pilot in formation combat flying, I would be like a robot. Moreover, I would have to rely on other, unfamiliar crews to do their jobs. I always preferred doing it myself. I was a maverick, and as chief of a Carpetbagger plane on a lone mission, I could make my own major decisions. All missions were flown at night, and drops were made from a few hundred feet above ground. The underground resistance fighters turned on the signal lights as soon as they heard the roar of our plane and saw the outline of our black B-24 when it approached the target.

We flew another successful mission over Denmark during the night of March 9. It was a good drop, and there was no enemy fire. But even though it was routine, it had more meaning to me than any other mission I flew. I was exhausted from a lack of sleep, and during most of the mission we had cloud cover above us that blocked the moonlight and gave the features on the ground a dull appearance. Suddenly we entered an area of perfectly clear sky with a beautiful moon shining brightly. I was flying at about 500 feet and could see several features of the ground distinctly.

We were over a small village when I looked down at the terrain. I saw a white painted church with a tall steeple. It looked exactly like the beautiful Methodist church in Nolensville, Tennessee, where my father was pastor. I suddenly felt a strange feeling inside me, and to this day I can only describe it as a spontaneous religious experience. This was the first time I had even thought about religion in several months. I thought about the church all the way back to our base, throughout the debriefing, breakfast, and as I was getting ready to sleep. Later that morning a messenger woke me up. "Lieutenant, the chaplain wants to see you." My eyes were open in an instant, and the memory of the church came flooding back. "I'll be right there," I said as I swung out over the edge of the bed. I felt as though I had received a message from above.

When I got to the chaplain's office, he invited me to sit down. "I received a letter from your parents," he began. "Are they all right?" I asked. "They're fine, lieutenant, but they tell me that they haven't received word from you in several weeks, and that they're worried about you. If you could spare a few minutes, I'm sure they'd love to hear from you." "Yes, sir. I'll write them as soon as I can." "Immediately would be better, lieutenant. I'm sure that every day for them that goes by without a letter makes them feel worse." "Yes, sir." I left the office feeling guilty, but believing that these events were so perfectly synchronized that they must have been sent by God. I was motivated to do better.

Mission to Sweden

Robert Fesmire (courtesy Robert C. Fesmire)

After returning to our Carpetbagger group on April 5, Robert Parks officially became our navigator.

Parks was easy to get along with, and I could see that he was team-oriented. In fact, I treated him just like a brother from the moment he joined us. Everyone welcomed the addition of Parks and Lancaster (the new copilot). This was a happy crew, and we were ready for action.

We received more information about the operation in which we were to participate. We were to be temporarily assigned to Metfield Air Transport base, a base in eastern England, and close to the southern part of the North Sea. Our mission was to transport military supplies in containers to Stockholm. We would wear civilian clothes, and each of us would have an official passport showing he was an airline official. This way, we wouldn't violate Sweden's neutrality — at least not officially. Once there, these secret containers of military supplies would be unloaded from our plane and trucked across the boarder to Norway to be used by Major Colby, his OSS men and other underground forces.

On April 9, Robert Parks, John Lancaster, John Carnevale, Jack Keeley and I made the one hour flight to Metfield ATC. When we arrived, a military van was ready to take us to our barracks. During this short ride we were amazed at the beauty of the airfield. The barracks and all of the buildings were modern stucco structures, and the grounds were beautifully manicured.

The next morning I reported to Colonel Bernt Balchen, the commanding officer at Metfield. I was astonished that he showed an unfriendly attitude toward me. He said as little as he could to me; then another officer took me across the room to take care of other business. It was there where I overheard a remark made by the colonel to the other ATC officers around him. "I don't know why they sent 8th Air Force crews for this operation," he growled in a heavy Norwegian accent. "Their pilots are no good. Our pilots are much more qualified. It's going to be a failure!"

That pissed me off, and I made sure I would remember his name. His attitude gave me the impression that he didn't give a damn whether we succeeded or not; in fact, it almost seemed that he wanted us to screw up so that he could justify his opinions. I decided to be cautious in following any order given by him.

Our crew was free for the next couple of days, so I decided to find out more about the colonel. I learned that he was one of the most famous pilots in the history of aviation, having flown over the South Pole with Admiral Byrd. He was Norwegian by birth, and he had become an American citizen. From what I could gather from the other ATC pilots, Balchen wanted to be the man responsible for freeing Norway from German occupation. It was a lofty goal, but one entirely fueled by ego.

But this love for his native land just inspired him to be more ambitious. He wanted to be promoted to general, and he made sure everyone knew about it. Balchen also resented that the OSS was in charge of all Carpetbagger covert operations, and he was convinced that he could do a better job. By the time I had talked to two or three pilots, my opinion of the colonel improved. His pilots had great respect for the old codger.

Our crew received a notice to fly our first covert mission to Stockholm on April 12. I expected no briefing, but was still disgusted when one wasn't given. Our only directions were to fly to Stockholm with a planeload of military supplies. We were to take off early that evening. Before takeoff we were given our passports, Swedish *kroners* and Swedish ration coupons. Our flight to Stockholm was routine (and) the weather was perfect. We landed at the Broma airport a little after midnight. We put on our sport coats and ties, then reported to the Swedish officials so they could stamp our passports. After this routine we were taken to an apartment complex where we would have a few hours of sleep.

Very early the next morning Parks, Lancaster and I were ready for sightseeing. We put on our coats and ties, and with our passports we became regular American civilians. Lancaster suggested going to mid-city Stockholm where we could find a restaurant. The ATC group had given us a liberal amount of Swedish money for eating and enough to pay for other limited activities. We also had ration coupons for food.

We ended up in the main area of downtown Stockholm. I thought it was a beautiful city. The bright sunshine felt good in the cold air. Thousands of bicycles crowded the streets, their riders busy pedaling to work. What few automobiles there were each had a small, 3-foot high stove attached on the side of the hood. It was obvious that there was a fire in the stove, but little or no smoke was coming from it. There was a metal tube from the stove to the engine of the auto, and I realized that the cars had been converted to run off the hydrocarbon gases produced by the burning fuel. The top speed of these vehicles couldn't have been more than 10 miles per hour. One car stalled, and the driver was refueling the stove on his car with what appeared to be coke or a wood product. These automobiles moved very slowly with this inefficient fuel. I reasoned that Sweden had no petroleum production, and gasoline was not available.

After walking around the city for a while, we found a very nice restaurant. We had our Swedish phrase books, but we didn't have to use them. The waitress could speak and understand English. Lancaster, Parks and I enjoyed a late breakfast of reindeer steak, fresh fried eggs and rolls, and we washed all of it down with lager beer. We learned that the beer was brewed in Nazi Germany, since the two countries enjoyed normal trade relations. "It's the only good thing to come out of that country," Lancaster said, raising his mug.

We were at the restaurant during midmorning. The workers hadn't had their lunch breaks and the restaurant was almost empty. There was only one other table with customers, and we couldn't keep from looking at the Oriental men seated at the table in the back of the restaurant. "Who are those men?" I asked our waitress as she passed. "I don't know," she replied, "but I think they're Japanese." The men indicated by the waitress watched our actions closely and suddenly began to speak rapidly among themselves. They threw some money on the table and rushed out through the back door. "Huh!" I snorted when they had gone. "Now what do you make of that?" "Looks like we scared 'em," Lancaster replied. "They probably thought we were gonna capture and torture 'em." Parks drank his beer. "Maybe they'll drop dead."

After a busy day we learned that we would fly back to England that night. An electric streetcar took us back to the vicinity where we had slept after our landing at the Broma airport. During our ride on the streetcar, Lancaster, Parks and I did a lot of talking. Some of the women on the car began listening to us, and one woman with a British accent exclaimed, "These Americans don't know how to speak English!" Several people laughed loudly, and it was obvious that they were making fun of our accents. We were amused and irritated. I began to think that some Swedes were pro–German.

Our April 13 flight to Metfield was routine. The ground crew welcomed us home, and we expressed our appreciation to them. After returning from our first covert flight to Stockholm, we gave our passports to a sergeant in the operations office. Later that afternoon our crew made a quick flight to our Carpetbagger base to check on our mail.

The next morning as Lancaster and I were walking to the mess hall for breakfast, we looked up to see approximately 20 B-17 bombers maneuvering into formations. The planes were approximately two miles away, and it was a beautiful sight. We watched as two B-17s approached each other to get in wing-to-wing positions. Bombers always fly close together when in formation, but these two maneuvered too close to each other. Suddenly, their wings locked together, and before we knew what was happening, both planes were in slow spins, diving straight down to the ground. They crashed with tremendous force, and there was a loud explosion as the fuel tanks burst into flames. No one had the chance to bail out, and it was obvious that crewmembers in both planes were killed.

It was an emotional sight for Lancaster, and it showed long after the event. He had enough trouble talking about his first crew without getting upset, and I'm sure this crash made him relive the night his crew perished in northern Scotland during a mission to drop OSS men and supplies to support Major Colby's operation. Lancaster was alive because he was sick that night and did not fly with his crew.

William Colby and the Norway Mission

It seemed that I had only been asleep for a short time when a messenger awoke me. "Wake up, sir. You have a briefing at 10:00." I opened my eyes and looked at my watch. Only two hours of sleep out of the past 26. Why did we have to brief now if we had to wait until night to fly? We had become adjusted to flying two night missions in a row; however, we had been able to sleep until mid-afternoon before receiving a message to fly that night. I felt hung over from the loss of sleep.

The early briefing wasn't the only thing unusual. Eugene Calhoun, the navigator, and Pete George, our bombardier, were not ordered to attend; only (copilot) Elliott and I were summoned. Whatever happened, I had the feeling Calhoun would resent missing out on the action. The fact that so many high-ranking officers were gathered indicated the importance of the operation, and I quickly became alert.

When we entered the large briefing room, we saw almost 100 people sitting around. Each crew sat together. We were joined by Captain Charles McGuire, navigator in the 856th Squadron, and Captain Robert France, 856th Squadron bombardier. I knew their records were excellent, and that they were the best at what they did. About 30 men I had never seen before were grouped into a corner. They, along with military supplies, were to be dropped over northern Norway from our B-24s that night. As I watched the Joes, I could tell they would be successful in any type of military action. Every man had a quiet demeanor about him, but you could see the intelligence and determination in their eyes. They were athletic and looked ready for the mission.

Major William Colby was their leader, and I soon learned that he and some of the men were to fly with our crew. We would be the lead crew, and I was pleased to be their pilot. I considered it an acknowledgement of my flawless record. (None of the crews were briefed prior to takeoff on the significance of an operation. Only later did I learn the importance of the operation which Colby and his OSS men undertook. Their task was to blow up the railroad and bridges that went from northern Norway to the main portion of the country. A few hundred thousand troops that had escaped from the Russian front had taken this route into Norway. Hitler wanted those forces back in Germany to boost the strength of his armies fighting the Allies. The successful destruction of railroad and bridges prevented German armies from getting back). I figured that after this mission was completed I would have two hours sleep out of 50. Nevertheless, the adrenaline pumped through me, and I was excited.

The distance from our base to the drop site created the main difficulty of the mission. A B-24 could fly for only 10–11 hours, and it was at least a 14-hour flight between our base and the target. In the early afternoon of March 24, our planes left for a Royal Air Force airfield in Inverness on the northern coast of Scotland. We would refuel there, then take off for a long journey to Norway. Even with the reduced distance, we still had to fly a 10-hour round trip to the Norwegian target and back. Between the extra weight and the unusually long flight, we knew that we barely had enough fuel to get to the target, make the drop, and return.

The Inverness control tower gave us clearance. Darkness was approaching, but it didn't bother me. I had learned to enjoy night flying. The runway lights had not yet been turned on, but I still could see the whole length of the runway. I opened up the throttles and roared down the runway. Suddenly the lights came on along a cross runway, making the one I was on look like the wrong one. I had gotten used to the darkness, and the sudden bright lights in front of me blinded me. I didn't know what to do — was I even on the runway? Confused and scared, I pulled back on the controls and risked stalling out by getting airborne so quickly. We wobbled, but stabilized as our speed increased.

Just as I let out a sigh of relief, the tower called. "Sorry about that, mates," the British control officer on the other end said. "We turned on the wrong lights. Hope we didn't confuse you." The smooth British accent only angered me even more. "Hell, yes, you confused us!" I shouted back. "We're damn lucky we didn't crash!" "Whose side are they on, anyway?" Elliott muttered. I snorted. This maverick was ready to be on his own while flying. I didn't want anybody telling me what to do or how to do it. But by the time we got across the North Sea, we were on our own, and I began to relax.

The five-hour flight to the frozen lake in Norway was uneventful. During the time over the North Sea, Major Colby and I discussed how to make the drop. "Listen, Fesmire," he said. "I need a low altitude drop, two, three hundred feet. Think you can do it?" I didn't want to say no, but I wasn't an idiot, either. "Major, I'm concerned about those mountains we'll be flying toward. How about a thousand feet above the lake? Colby shook his head. "Too high. I want to make sure my men and supplies are on target. If we get scattered, we'll have to take the time to regroup, and I'd rather not do that." Once again I thought of the mountain range we'd have to clear after we made the drop. "I can drop you at five hundred feet if I think the conditions are right." Colby grinned. "Deal," he said. He seemed to have confidence in me.

I admired Major Colby and his OSS team, and I was determined to drop him at five hundred feet. But if Colby had known what I knew about our crew's training and experience, he probably would have left us stranded back at Inverness. We had completed only three months of high-altitude bombing training before becoming Carpetbaggers. Our night flight training was limited, and we had received no training in dropping men. To further complicate our inexperience, some of us had slept for only two hours out of the past forty. We had never flown a mission over Norway; and we didn't fully understand the dangers of the mountains. We just knew that they would be ahead of us and not to hit them. Despite all of this, I tried my best to give Colby the impression that I knew what to do, that I was a pro. On the first count I think he gave me the benefit of the doubt. On the second, I knew he knew I wasn't.

Colby and I fell silent, and I began to think of how far I had come in two years. I had grown up in small towns, and had never been out of Tennessee until I was on active duty. In fact, I had spent less than twenty hours in driving an automobile. By now I had logged more than 1,000 hours as a pilot, most of them in a B-24, and here I was — the lead pilot for an OSS mission in Norway. It had become a different world for me.

Talking with Colby and reminiscing made the long flight seem shorter. As we approached the drop zone, I was amazed at how well we could see the snow-capped mountains. It was a beautiful sight under a shining moon. Captain McGuire had us on a perfect course, and soon saw the large signal bonfire. I turned and headed for it. When we were a few miles away, I lowered the flaps, changed the pitch of the propellers, and reduced the airspeed. I quickly lowered our altitude as much as I dared. Philbrick (the dispatcher — the man responsible for seeing that men and supplies were successfully dropped from our plane to the underground) opened the Joe hole for the drop of the OSS men. He told them to wait for his signal so that their jumps would come at proper intervals.

We were about 500 feet over the frozen lake when we made our drops. Philbrick did a perfect job of coordinating the jumps, and Captain France dropped the supplies without incident. The whole thing was over in seconds, and we were delighted. But there was no time to celebrate. A high, snow-covered peak was directly in front of us and we were closing fast. How I did what I did next, I'll never know. I banked hard, flipping the plane almost upside down into a vertical and parallel path with the mountain, and turned 180 degrees in seconds. When it was over I looked at Elliott. "How close did we come?" I asked him. Elliott was silent for a long moment before he whispered, "At least a hundred feet." I thought how lucky we were to be rid of the excess weight from the supplies and men; otherwise, we would not have made it. "Somebody was watching us tonight, men," I said.

After we escaped the peak, I climbed to a safer altitude, and we began to feel better. Since there were no enemy planes or gunfire, we could take the time to take a closer look at Norway's terrain. The shining moon on the snow-covered mountain peaks was a beautiful sight.

36

SERGEANT BILL JONES

DOB: October 14, 1925
Where: Nashville, Tennessee
Air Force: 8th
Bomb Group: 95th
Squadron: 336th
Station: Horham, England
Decorations include: Air Medal with clusters. Bill climbed down into the ball turret of a B-17 and flew 33 combat missions as a gunner. Part of *Milspaugh's Milk Runners* crew, he ended the war as staff sergeant. Postwar, Bill spent 33 years with Sears as salesman, department manager, and store manager. Then he pursued his love of golf by working 13 years at a golf course, playing whenever he had the chance.

Life in the Ball

During training at Kingman, Arizona, they didn't ask me what kind of gunner I wanted to be. They simply conducted a line test. Here is how it worked. A line was placed across the door. Everyone who went under the line became a ball turret gunner. If you touched the line, you were destined to become a top turret, waist, or tail gunner. I didn't have a choice about being a ball turret gunner even if I didn't like it. At the time, I thought it would be a good position and I still feel that way today. I have to admit, though, that it was a little more dangerous than being up inside our B-17.

I had a standing agreement with the pilot. If the ball turret was ever hung up and the landing gear wouldn't come down, he would pick a long ditch to land in so that the turret would come in right over the ditch. The truth is that in the ball turret I was apart from everyone else, suspended in space. To this day, I wear my watch on the inside because as I reached up for my guns, I could tell the time better.

On a typical mission, if there ever was one, I would wait until after takeoff before stepping down into the turret and into my small seat. My legs folded up around me into a position I would maintain through the journey to the target, the bomb run itself, and most of the way home. I would reach behind and with the help of another gunner close the hatch over me, knowing that if all the systems worked correctly I could unlatch it from the inside in case of emergency. Because I was short I felt relatively comfortable. My hands fit the two, .50 caliber machine guns at head level. There was a round windshield in the middle of my protective Plexiglas bubble that had a sight on it for aiming and leading enemy planes.

My own technique of dealing with the flak coming up to meet us was to twirl the turret in a circle so that it had a better chance of bouncing off the thick Plexiglas. Throughout all this I was usually perspiring heavily under my fur-lined flight suit. Then, once our bombs had dropped, I would freeze until we reached lower altitudes.

One of my jobs was to watch where the bombs hit. I could turn the turret and tell the pilot that the bombs

Bill Jones (courtesy Bill Jones)

were ejected and then I would watch them go down by pointing the turret straight down. I had a perfect view of the explosions and their aftermath such as flying railroad tracks and freight cars. I didn't really worry about any casualties on the ground. We just had a job to do and we all wanted to do it to the best of our abilities. But I have to say this: the images of the explosions don't just go away. I can still see the bomb bursts in my mind.

On our very first mission there was a friend from East High School in the same formation. His name was Grabel Hill. We were in the lower left slot and Grabel was in the same position ahead of us. As I was looking toward his ship, I saw it take a direct hit and disappear in a big, black puff of smoke. I knew what had happened but all I could do was cringe as we flew right through their smoke, thinking we might meet the same fate. Grabel was a fun guy and a good student. Like me, he was a ball turret gunner.

After flying two or three missions, we named our plane *Milspaugh's Milk Runners*, after Lieutenant Milspaugh, our pilot. In 33 missions, none of our crew was wounded. I never did dwell on why I was spared and others weren't and I never talked with a single member of my crew after the war ended. Now, though, I'd very much like to know if my pilot is still alive. He's not listed in the roster of the 95th Bomb Group, neither are most of my crew. Lt. Millspaugh was a good pilot, a smart young man with character and strong leadership abilities. He controlled his crew and we all worked well together.

37

LIEUTENANT BEN ERNST

DOB: June 2, 1918
Where: Bedford, Ohio
Air Force: 9th
Bomb Group: 12th
Squadron: 81st
Station: Tunisia, North Africa
Decorations include: Purple Heart, Air Medal, POW Medal.

On July 14, 1943, Ben bobbed about in the Mediterranean for 17 hours before finally making it ashore into the waiting hands of Italian soldiers. He had bailed out on his fifth combat mission, a trip to Palermo, Sicily, as the copilot of a B-25 bomber that appeared to be too uncontrolled to fly. But it did fly and Ben became the only member of his crew from that mission to bail and be captured. He spent the remainder of the war as a POW. After his release at war's end, Ben returned home and became a mortgage banker as well as a state official.

The Only One to Bail

Upon reporting with my crew to the 81st squadron in Tunisia, I was taken from my crew and assigned to ride as copilot with an experienced crew for a while to receive combat mission training. It was July 14, 1943, four nights after the invasion of Sicily when we took off in our B-25. We had a drop-dead bomb time of 10 P.M. over Palermo. But when we got there at about 13,000 feet the searchlights and anti-aircraft guns so overwhelmed the "experienced" pilot that he threw the plane into all kinds of gyrations trying to escape. His moves caused him to lose control of the plane, throwing it into a flat spin. He soon ordered all of us to bail out. I decided that if we didn't do something the pilot wouldn't get out so I got up from my copilot's seat, put on my chute, kicked the hatch open, and went out of the plane. It was approximately 10 P.M. I didn't find out until months later, while a POW, that the plane suddenly leveled out at 1,000 feet and the rest of the crew made it back home safely. I was the only one to jump.

37. Lieutenant Ben Ernst

Ben Ernst (courtesy Ben Ernst)

Opening my chute at high speed caused physical problems which haunted me the rest of my life. I tried to guide the gyrations of the chute with the shroud lines but that just dumped it so I let myself swing. With all the anti-aircraft guns firing, I inevitably was hit in the wrist with a piece of flak. My crash bracelet prevented too deep a penetration so I was able to stop the bleeding with a handkerchief.

Knowing I was soon to hit the water, I had unbuckled the chute strips so that I could get out of it quickly and not be drawn under. As soon as I got loose in the water, I cut a hole in the silk bubble for it to sink. Next, I pulled one cylinder of the Mae West and blew the other by mouth to save one. At the moment, I didn't realize how far I was from shore in Palermo harbor. I could see where the mountain came down to the water so I started swimming to get around it by daylight. I had tied my boots under the Mae West. When I noticed one was missing, I let the other go. Also, when the chute opened it tore the Mae West leg strap loose so I had to keep pulling the vest down. When dawn started breaking I saw a white spot on the mountain and I realized it was a house. Seeing how far I was out to sea, I just turned and headed for the harbor.

Throughout the day, the sun got hotter and hotter and I got a real burn. There being no boats in the harbor, I had to keep going till I got to the docks. The sun was setting when I pulled myself out of the water and was met by some Italian soldiers. They took my jacket and shorts. A kind soul brought me a bowl of what I think was warm, cooked cherries. It was a lifesaver for my parched throat. As I was walked along a line of bystanders, I noticed they were giving me the "V" for victory signal.

Along came an elderly Italian colonel in a little car who took me, now called "Benyameen" by my "new friends," to his headquarters building. There he gave me some sandals and an overcoat. With much ceremony some soldiers ripped the stars from the lapels. A German officer soon came in and interrogated me but all I could give him was name, rank, and serial number. That night was spent in a cave near the Palermo Aerodrome, modest quarters that I shared with a couple of RAF fellows and one other American. The next day we were joined by members of another B-25 crew and six Canadians.

After a couple of days, we left for Messina at 2000 hours by bus. The moon was out so the small villages shone white just like they did in the movies of that time. Once the sun rose, we saw German artillery digging in on the slopes of Mt. Etna. We arrived in Messina at noon and for the first time I saw German troops. Right in front of the bus was an open-topped 6 × 6 with young, blond German soldiers filling it, most of whom were half asleep. These were the first actual combat troops that I saw. We didn't know where our troops were but later learned that Patton's army was just two days from Palermo.

We never knew where, when, or why we went places but during our odyssey we managed to travel by barge, truck, train, and railroad car. Across the Straits of Messina, arriving in Regio Calabria, then toward Naples by way of Agropli and Battipaglia, along the high cliffs above the port of Salerno, and then to Mount Vesuvius. We circled around the mountain and Naples to arrive at PG 66, Prisoneri d'Guerry, located in Capua. There we watched our bombers going over at noon each day on their way to their targets. The Italian fliers would rise to simulate attack and as soon as the U.S. fighters turned on them they would dive straight down below the mountaintops and then come up and roll around like victory had been won. One day a German fighter circled around our camp heading to an airbase about five miles west. He was in trouble as he had smoke trailing from an engine. Suddenly, we saw a form come over the side of the plane and it went down like a stone, his chute failing to open.

The daily routine as a prisoner included being counted once and fed three times a day. This lasted until August 20 when a B-26 with a hung bomb eased out of formation to wedge it loose on an opportunity target, the rail station at Capua. We could see it coming down. We did know there was an ammo dump next to it about 500 yards from our camp. All hell broke loose with burning shells flying through the air in every direction. All the buildings in camp were cracked and soon it was determined to abandon the place.

So, on August 27, we headed up the Appian Way, the roadway from Roman history still with cobblestones and chariot wheel ruts in them. We climbed aboard some rail cars and moved north, through high mountains and low valleys, finally descending steeply into a very large valley in the middle of which was a cone-shaped hill with a monastery on top. This was the location of PG 78 and the town of Sulmona.

The next day we hit the road again, not knowing where we were headed. We traveled in trucks along a river in a narrow canyon for about 30 miles to PG 21 at Chieti. Still not having much in the way of clothing and still with no shoes, I was outfitted with British battle dress and shoes along with a greatcoat. It was here that I became acquainted with Frank Fisher, the son of the Bishop of London, later the Archbishop of Canterbury. He gave me some unworn white woolen socks which, a year later, I used to darn wings and emblems on an inner flight jacket.

On September 8, 1943, Italy capitulated and the Italian guards left the walls. For a few days we even stood guard on ourselves as it was expected that British invasion boats were to arrive at anytime to pick us up. Unfortunately they were too slow. When we awoke a few days later German paratroopers were on the walls.

In less than a month we were evacuated and sent to Germany, where I was to remain in prison camps for the duration of the war. I was a POW of the Italians and the Germans for almost two years, all because I was the only one of my crew to bail out of our B-25 while it seemingly spun out of control toward the water below.

38

Captain J. Ivan Potts, Jr.

DOB: September 10, 1919
Where: Shelbyville, Tennessee
Air Force: 20th
Bomb Group: 40th
Squadron: 25th
Station: India, China, Tinian among others
Decorations include: Distinguished Flying Cross (2), Air Medal with clusters, Personal Commendation from General H.H. Arnold. B-29 number 42–63420, *Rankless Wreck*, heavily battle damaged, limped back to Iwo Jima on June 5, 1945, with Ivan Potts, Jr. at the helm. Ivan was awarded a DFC for that as well as one for piloting a B-29 on a record-breaking trip from Japan to Washington, D.C., as General Curtis LeMay's personal pilot. Postwar, Ivan achieved the rank of colonel in the Tennessee Air Guard, served as a foreign service officer in Lima, Peru, and became a successful Ford dealer in his hometown.

Near Tragedy Over Kobe

On June 5, 1945, the 25th Squadron, 40th Bombardment Group (VH) flew its tenth mission from Tinian and its 48th of World War II against the empire of Japan; a daylight mission using incendiaries. The day prior to the mission, Myrel Massey and I walked over from our tent to the briefing room a little before 10:30 P.M., joining the rest of the crew who were already gathered outside. This was our seventeenth mission together. Myrel was careful and conservative: extremely calm and concentrated over a target. I had developed a great deal of affection for him and admired his skill.

On this mission we had a new bombardier and a new central fire control gunner, Dick Moore, who had requested to join our crew. An unreconstructed rebel from Texas, he carried his Confederate flag into battle in his glass blister atop the mid section of the aircraft. We welcomed our new members, entered the briefing room, and quickly took our seats.

In the briefing room, each crew sat together in a row in front of a stage and a large covered wall map. We whispered to each other as we nervously speculated on the target, soon to be revealed. When the group commander entered the room, the order of "atten-shun!" snapped us to our feet and into absolute silence. At his, "as you were," we settled back into our seats.

The briefing officer ascended the platform and uncovered the mission map. "Kobe is the target...takeoff is at 0200 tomorrow. Your assembly point is Murato on Shekoku Island. The base altitude is 15,000 feet." A loud "Oooh!" spread through the gathered crewmembers when the altitude was announced. They knew that every gun in the area could zero in at that height. The worst thing about Kobe was that there was only one approach — straight up the bay.

"Be at your aircraft at 0100, take your stations at 0130. Your altitude going out to Japan will be 4800 feet. Assemble at your bombing altitude off Murata and join your formation leaders over Shikoku Bay to the south. First formation will assemble and bomb at 15,000 feet, second at 15,500 and the third at 16,000." The briefing officer went on, "The dock area is the primary aiming point. The mission code name is 'Dragon Leader.' Guard D radio channel. Radio silence is required. Estimated time to leave the assembly point is 0856, time to drop is 0916. Maintain your current bombing precision and you won't have to go back. Maintain base indicated airspeed of 200 miles per hour on the bomb run and over the target. Good luck to you!" We were going to need it! Our 25th Squadron was the third formation, last in line and last over the target — 56 minutes after the first group had gone in. We'd catch it from all sides! We knew it would be rough because we had been there before.

The trip to Japan was routine. At 0820, Joe Biersteker, our navigator, came up front and indicated it was time to start our climb to our assembly altitude. After a long thirty minutes, we reached assembly altitude and, leveling off, began to look for our formation leader. He was in his wide circle, nose wheel down, with six or seven planes already in position. We had seen the red flares from his location about ten minutes away. Soon we were all in place. We pulled in behind the other squadron formations and headed for Kobe. The 44th Squadron was lead squadron at base altitude with Captain Carter McGregor in command. The 45th was second under Major Neil Wemple, and our squadron, the 25th, was last in the group formation with Major George Wescler as our leader. Our bomb run would take us straight up Osaka Bay. Osaka lies at the head of the bay and Kobe stretches along to the south. We'd be just like a flock of geese on opening day of hunting season.

The day was beautiful below the scattered clouds. The morning rains had cleared the air over Japan, leaving only a light haze. As we flew the 20 minutes from Murato Point and started up the bay, all hell broke loose. Since the first group had gone over the target at 0800 at 16,000 feet, we were coming in almost an hour later and at about the same altitude. This gave the Jap fighters time to refuel and climb back up to get at us. The anti-aircraft batteries had our flight path in their sights and were warmed up as we moved into the target area.

J. Ivan Potts, Jr. (courtesy J. Ivan Potts, Jr.)

As we neared the target area, the flak became intense. The very accurate concentrations of bursts were spectacular. Japanese navy ships were in the harbor and their guns were mercilessly accurate. My mouth was dry as I looked around at Myrel. There he was, a picture of coolness and composure. Now it was requiring all our physical strength and concentration to keep our B-29 tucked into formation. I winced as each shell exploded ahead and to our right. Great black balls with their orange-red flashes could be heard as they exploded. Every time we would catch a flak burst above or below the wing the plane would shudder. You could hear pieces of flak puncturing the outside of our Superfortress. Two minutes before bomb release the fighters began to come at us in droves. They were flying through their own flak.

As we began the bomb run, I could see a "George" Jap fighter circling far out in front and slightly above in a great arc from the right. "Fighter at one o'clock," I called out on the intercom. All at once he decided to make his move. As he completed his arc, I had a sickening feeling in my stomach that he had picked us — a premonition. As he came in almost level we could see the large round circle of cylinders behind the propeller and the stubby, low wing that carried his armament. Several hundred yards away, he zeroed in on us, closing at a tremendous rate of speed. The moment he headed for us the four, 50 caliber machine guns in the front turret above us and the two in the turret below us cut loose with a deafening roar, adding to the intensity of the battle. At about 100 yards we could see the flashes from the center of each wing as he began to fire at us with two, 40 mm cannon. He came straight on, firing again, and flipping quickly on his back as he slid barely under our belly.

Dick Moore reports on the fighter attack: "We were firing away as he attacked. As he approached, I was firing six caliber 50s at it in short bursts of ten. Soon it appeared he not only was inflicting a great deal of damage to our plane, but was going to ram us. Under those circumstances I really didn't worry too much about burned out barrels and gave him continuous fire. He continued to approach and as he slid under the bomber, his plane exploded and bits and pieces went sailing by."

Back up front, Myrel and I had our hands full. One of the 40 mm shells hit our left outboard engine. Suddenly the engine went out in a bath of oil, smoke and orange flame. The plane felt as if someone had put on the brakes; the windmilling propeller was retarding movement rather than aiding it. The fuel pressure fell to zero. I hit the feathering button hard and fortunately the propeller responded. Zane Bloom, the flight engineer, pulled the fire extinguisher and the engine flames went out.

Another shell struck the fuselage just behind the front bulkhead where radio operator George Kelly sat and exploded inside the front bomb bay, knocking a large hole in the tunnel and severing the main electrical cable. Shrapnel flew all over the bomb bay, severing the hydraulic lines to the landing gear. All the electrical systems to the cockpit were out, including the turbo-superchargers on the three remaining engines. One-third less power was now being delivered. I wondered if we'd make it. There was no assurance the plane would stay together and we were four hours from the nearest refuge, Iwo Jima.

Fortunately for us the bomb bay doors had just closed when the shell struck the electrical cable, otherwise we would have been unable to close them. The increased drag would have consumed a great deal more precious fuel. In our stricken condition, we slowed and since we could not keep up, the formation moved away from us. We knew we were in trouble. We did not know whether we would suddenly be hit again and go down, or even whether we could keep *Rankless Wreck* flying. The coast was fifty miles away. In what was only a second but seemed like hours, we looked around and there was a buddy B-29 snuggled in close on our right wing, slowing down to stay with us. He had seen the hit we took and would help us get out to sea. With no operating guns we would have been at the mercy of any fighter that happened to spot us. We were under attack a couple of times, but our buddy fended the fighters off without further damage. Without our turbo-superchargers and with only three engines at two-thirds power, all we could do was start a power glide from Japan and hope we could get *Rankless Wreck* as far as Iwo Jima four hours away. Tinian was out of the question.

A quick word about our buddy system. The missions of the B-29s were the longest in history. Over Japan we were 15 hours from home and our fighters on Iwo Jima seldom made contact with us. Being alone, we were prey to Japanese fighters which searched for damaged 29s. To combat such danger, we devised our buddy system. If a 29 was in trouble, the nearest plane would move in formation with it and would shepherd it out to sea or until it ditched, standing by until an attempt was made to rescue the crew by our submarines or PBY rescue planes flying from Iwo Jima. The plan saved many planes and we thanked God for our buddies.

Now back to our struggle with our crippled plane. After the immediate confusion, Zane started to the back of the plane to determine the damage. Dick Moore started from the rear crew compartment and they met at the huge hole in the tunnel caused by the shell blast. Working together, they tried frantically to patch some of the wires from the severed cable. After a while Dick burned his hands badly and the project was abandoned with no success.

Now we were over the water flying on only three engines. I reduced the propeller rpm's

The crippled B-29 *Rankless Wreck* limps toward Iwo Jima with J. Ivan Potts, Jr., and crew aboard. Two 40mm cannon shells fired by a Japanese fighter struck the plane in the left outboard engine and the front bomb bay. With one engine gone, no turbochargers, all electrical and hydraulic systems gone, and 148 holes in the bomb bay, the plane landed on the gravel fighter strip at Iwo. She never flew again (courtesy J. Ivan Potts, Jr.).

to 1400 and the airspeed fell to 160 mph. Our props were turning so slowly you could almost see each blade as it cut through the air. This slowness set up a terrible vibration and everything not tied down was dancing about the flight deck. The flight home was a strenuous ordeal for both Myrel and myself. Most of the instruments were out, we were having to do everything by brute force, and we had eleven men whose lives were in our hands.

After an eternity, we approached Iwo Jima. We could barely see the island to our left. We were now just 300 feet above the water and running out of fuel. Zane had tried to transfer fuel from the dead engine tank, but all that did was spray gasoline all over everything. To complicate our situation, weather was poor over the island and deteriorating and the air was filled with other aircraft attempting to land. We could hear no signals from the control tower. Suddenly we saw a B-29 crash into the water just off the island.

Zane crawled back through the tunnel and told Don Jones, the tail gunner, to start the gasoline engine that powered the small electrical generator. Zane then resumed his position at his console. The emergency landing gear mechanism miraculously worked and the gear came down. With no indicator light, we would have to hope that the gear would stay down under the impact of landing. We turned on to our final approach. We were now committed.

The center runway was dimly visible. We could see almost a hundred B-29s scattered in every kind of condition, on and off the runway. There was no room for us to land! We glanced to the right. There was the short, gravel-covered fighter strip along the cliffs overlooking the beach, barely 2,000 feet long. Massey banked sharply right and we headed for it. As we lined

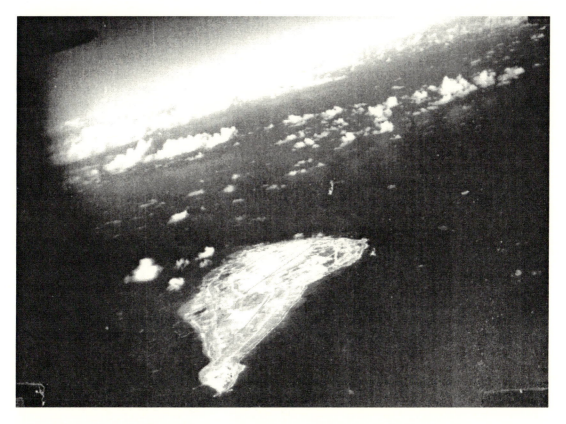

Iwo Jima in August 1945. Motoyama airstrip No. 2, center, had been lengthened for B-29s. The fighter strip, lower right, had been lengthened and paved (courtesy J. Ivan Potts, Jr.).

up with the gravel strip, flames began again in the dead engine but there was no extinguisher this time. I moved the propeller pitch fully forward. Massey reduced the power. With no flaps, we hit the gravel. We both applied the brakes hard! Nothing happened — the lines had been ruptured by the shell blast. The end of the runway was coming up fast; we cut the master switches and hung on. With no brakes, we quickly ran out of gravel. When we crossed the end of the runway we were still indicating 95 miles per hour.

Dick Moore remembers: "In the rear gunner's compartment, we were jammed against the front bulkhead in a crash landing position as we came in with no flaps and on fire. The airplane reeked of gasoline fumes. As we touched down and realized we were on the runway, we all jumped up and cheered. Then we realized the brakes were not operating. We again assumed the crash landing position as the plane sailed off the end of the runway, dropping several feet into a rough, muddy area, pock-marked with hundreds of shell holes. We were riding a 150-ton 'bucking bronco,' out of control and lurching and bouncing crazily at just under a hundred miles an hour. Finally the lurching and bouncing stopped, barely missing the cliff by a few feet. The plane had turned half way around at a right angle to the runway."

Everybody scrambled to get out of the plane, fearing explosion. I ran about a hundred feet, then I stopped and my knees buckled under me from the fright of it all. I couldn't rise! Our tail gunner, Don Jones, reacted differently. He ran and ran until they finally caught him with an ambulance. The fire was out. Shortly, a damage assessment officer informed us we had three minutes to get our gear out. All of us were taken to the Iwo hospital and released after the medics determined we were all right.

Ground personnel gathered around *Rankless Wreck* to count the shrapnel holes. There were holes everywhere and a count from the shell in the bomb bay alone accounted for over 140. She would never fly again. Incredibly, not a member of our crew had a scratch. A few days later, each crewmember received the Distinguished Flying Cross.

It was the end of the line for *Rankless Wreck*. She had served us well after we had gotten the bugs out. She would be scrapped at Iwo Jima. We wouldn't have to go back to Kobe, since eight square miles of it were destroyed. Another Japanese city had been stricken from General LeMay's list. The price: 11 B-29s lost and 176 damaged.

The Japan to Washington Flight

I had been flying with Lieutenant Colonel Bill Kingsbury, Squadron Commander of the 25th Bombardment Squadron. Late in the war he and I had become good friends. One morning Lieutenant Colonel Kingsbury came over to me and said, "They are picking a crew from the 58th Wing to compete in a selection down on Guam for a flight back to the United States and I think we have a pretty good chance of being picked as part of the crew to go back."

After a couple of days, he informed me that we were in fact going to Guam to represent the 58th Wing. I didn't know at the time that we were going to attempt a non-stop flight to the United States. Kingsbury, Tisdal Jones, Jerome School, and I were the members of the crew from the 25th. The rest of the crew was hand picked from among the combat veterans of the 40th Bombardment Group. I was in elite company.

On Guam, our plane was modified for our non-stop attempt. Five, six hundred-gallon tanks were installed in the bomb bays. Everything was stripped that was not absolutely necessary for the flight. All the guns and gun turrets were removed and the skin of the airplane re-covered. The blisters atop and on the sides of the plane were replaced with square flash

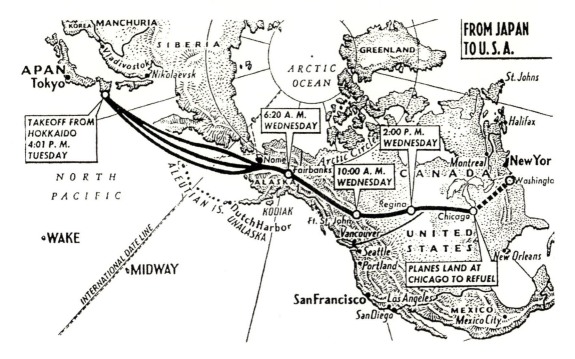

Route of the three B-29s across the top of the world on the record-breaking Japan to Washington flight. (Courtesy J. Ivan Potts, Jr.)

windows. The 40th Group markings were removed, leaving a solid silver bird which was waxed and polished to an almost new finish. The only marking remaining was our air force star. Then our new tail insignia was installed, the emblem of the Twentieth Air Force. Nothing was spared to assist our Superfortress prepare for its challenging mission.

Colonel William Blanchard joined us at Guam. He was now chief of staff of the Twentieth Air Force. We were crew Number Two. Plane Number One would fly Lieutenant General Barney Giles, Deputy Commander of the United States Strategic Air Forces in the Pacific and Commander of the flight. Major General Curtis E. LeMay, Chief of Staff of the Strategic Air Forces, would command our plane. The Number Three plane would carry Brigadier General Emmett O'Donnell, Commanding General of the Seventy Third Wing.

Our course to the United States would take us from the northern Japanese island of Hokkaido over Nome and Fairbanks in Alaska, White Horse in the Yukon and Edmonton in Alberta, Canada. The only field large enough to accommodate us was Mizutani on Hokkaido, the northern-most island of Japan. An alternate southern route was planned in case of bad weather. It would have covered Kiska, Adak, Dutch Harbor, and Juneau, Alaska, a total of 6,762 miles.

Our airdrome was chosen for our take off because it was one of the fields in Japan with long, concrete runways. It was built by the Japanese to send four-engine bombers on one-way suicide missions against our west coast cities. The runways were 8,200 feet long and were virtually at sea level which would give greater lift to our heavy planes.

On the morning of Tuesday, the 18th of September, we were awakened long before dawn to make final preparations for our take off. A weather ship was taking off about an hour ahead of the flight to explore winds aloft and report any unexpected storms. Far in the north, Super Dumbos and Dumbos, B-29s and B-17s, equipped for air-sea rescue, were standing by on alert. They would take off instantly on word that any of our three planes were in any kind of trouble.

Mizutani airfield was very dark and very chilly in the heavy mist of the early morning on Hokkaido. The field was unlighted and flashlights and truck headlamps lit our way to our sky giants. General LeMay decided he would let Lieutenant Colonel Kingsbury and me perform the task of getting airplane Number Two airborne. We had 10,000 gallons of gasoline on board, as much as a railroad car. We weighed 144,000 pounds, the heaviest overload ever attempted in a B-29. As the light began to appear in the eastern sky, we taxied out. As General Giles' plane, Number One, began its roll down the runway, we moved out and into position. Brakes were set, engines checked, lift flaps were lowered, propeller pitch run forward and the checklist completed.

It was now our turn. Lieutenant Colonel Kingsbury ran the throttles forward while I was at the controls. As our engines developed their full power, the brakes were released and we began to move down the runway. Little by little our speed increased. We used up all of the 8,200 feet and were in the gravel past the end when we finally left the earth at 142 mph indicated air speed. The tension was heavy as we broke away from the ground. There was no room for error or malfunction. If anything had gone wrong, it would have been goodbye to crew and airplane. We were so heavily loaded that if one of our four engines had failed or partially lost power on takeoff we would have crashed off the end of the runway. For hours into the flight we struggled until enough fuel was used to make it safe for three-engine flight. Then, for several more hours, our airplane would not have flown on two engines. If we had been forced to ditch or bail out in the Arctic water, we would have faced almost certain death.

We were off at 6:15 A.M., Hokkaido time (4:15 P.M., Washington time). Our expected arrival in Washington was to be 5:00 P.M. Eastern War Time the following afternoon, after 26 hours elapsed flying time on the trip that would take us a quarter of the way around the globe.

General Giles had our only weather officer on board his plane. Only two or three hours out he reported that we were running into slight headwinds, but changed his report when the general threatened to throw him overboard unless he did something about it.

The purpose of our route over the top of the world was two-fold; first, it was the most direct route to Washington; second, we were hoping to take advantage of the 200 mph winds of the "jet stream." Our B-29s had discovered these tremendous winds over Japan and we expected to use them to extend our range over Alaska and Canada. But things weren't going to wash out that way. A typhoon had been off Okinawa for about a week prior to our flight. We didn't realize it at this time and would discover later, the typhoon had actually reversed the winds over Japan and over the path of our flight. General Giles' weather officer was right. We were beginning to encounter some headwinds.

Somewhere over the Aleutians and almost on top of the magnetic north pole, the gyro compass started tumbling and it became increasingly difficult to be exactly sure where we were at any given time. To compound the navigator's problems, the radio compass went out shortly thereafter. It would come back into operation later in the flight to be of some help.

About 12 hours out of Hokkaido, we were southwest of Nome, Alaska. It was quite dark. We had finished the shortest day of our lives. It was now 1:00 A.M., Washington time. In another hour we were just south of St. Lawrence Island and had crossed the Bering Sea. Cold was now beginning to penetrate the airplane. Even our fur-lined flying suits were unable to keep out the cold. Over Nome we were treated to our first display of the Northern Lights. The long ribbons of eerie lights were magnificent from our ringside seats, four miles up.

The Northern Lights continued in view from Nome to Fairbanks. At 6:20 A.M., Eastern War Time, the temperature was 25 degrees below zero. The *New York Times* reported, "the men inside the planes lolled in shirt sleeves, warmed by the planes' heating systems." The facts were that we were very cold. Although our pressurization was still operating, the cold Arctic air had overcome our heating systems which seemed to have completely broken down.

By 9:00 A.M., we were 370 miles southeast of White Horse in the Yukon. It was about 5:30 A.M. Yukon time and the sunlight was now visible in the east. It was dawn again but we had had practically no rest during the night. Sleep had been virtually impossible. Not only had the excitement of the trip kept us awake, but we were very, very cold. We were now 17 hours into the flight.

The headwinds continued to increase. The first decision that a fuel stop would be necessary was made as we neared Regina. General Giles' plane was to land at Minneapolis, General O'Donnell was to land at Detroit and since our plane had more fuel, we were to continue on. The three bombers separated. By now the air speed had slowed so General Giles amended his decision to land at Minneapolis and have General O'Donnell land at Detroit. He had concluded that both fields were too small for our big planes. He and O'Donnell then both changed course for Chicago. General LeMay asked our radio operator to send a message to the War Department that we would keep coming. As we flew on, New York papers were headlined, "Two B-29s will land to refuel as third roars on to Capitol."

As we approached Chicago, General LeMay radioed to check on the weather in Washington and was informed it was marginal. Bill Townes and Captain Theodore Finder, the flight engineer, estimated we had enough gasoline to make Washington. General LeMay talked to Washington again and then decided to return to Chicago and stay with the other planes. Our plane had been the last to give up the non-stop to Washington attempt. We still had close to a thousand gallons of fuel in reserve. Some of the members of our crew thought the fact that General LeMay had two stars and General Giles had three had more to do with our turning back than with our ability to complete the flight alone.

General O'Donnell landed in Chicago at 5:43 Eastern War Time. General Giles landed at 6:30. We landed 13 minutes later, a total of 27 hours and 30 minutes out of Japan. We crew members all crawled out in Chicago and drank some very welcome coffee while waiting to resume our flight. The only people who talked to the press in Chicago were Captain Kermit Beahan and General Giles. Beahan was the bombardier of the plane that dropped atom bomb number two on Nagasaki, Japan. After we refueled, we were ready to take off again. "The silvery sky giants, manned by their blue ribbon crews, which had streaked across Alaska and Canada on the homeward leg of their ambitious mission, roared over National Airport in formation at 9:30 P.M. Eastern War Time." This was the way one national correspondent reported our arrival.

We encountered a short delay before deplaning from our aircraft. LeMay wouldn't leave until he had firmly implanted a freshly lighted cigar in his mouth. We were literally agog at the large delegation meeting us in the half-light as we deplaned. Secretary of War Henry L. Stimson was first in the receiving line. General Arnold, our air force commanding general, was next. General Arnold was later to write a letter of commendation for our record-breaking flight. The army air force had flown all of our parents into Washington earlier in the day from all over the country. A tired, bearded and grimy group of fliers was greeted by wives and parents for the first time in over a year.

The morning of September 20, we all gathered with our generals in the grand showroom of the Statler where Hildegarde had welcomed some of us the previous evening. General

General Carl "Tooey" Spaatz, left, Major General Curtis LeMay, second from left, and Brig. General Emmett O'Donnell, Jr., right, stand by as General Hap Arnold and Lt. General Barney Giles speak on a nationwide broadcast at the conclusion of the record-setting flight of three B-29s from Japan to Washington, D.C. Standing to the rear and between LeMay and Arnold is Lieutenant J. Ivan Potts, Jr., copilot of LeMay's crew (courtesy J. Ivan Potts, Jr.).

LeMay gathered us all around him. The atmosphere was completely relaxed as a contrast to the previous days. Later that morning all the members of the three crews met with General Giles in the same room. We were presented with the Distinguished Flying Cross, my second. General Giles gave us all our equipment as a remembrance of the flight. I packed up everything I had brought home with me except my parachute. General Giles said we could even have that if we wanted it. He also said he'd send me home in an air force plane. I told him, "Thank you, general, I think I'll take the train!"

General Arnold said, "The purpose of the flight was to see what might be expected of existing long range aircraft. The B-29 had gone into production with no service test. This was a service test."

It was the longest non-stop flight in air force history.

It was the first Grand Circle flight in history.

It was the fastest non-stop flight of its distance in history.

It was the first non-stop flight from Japan to the United States.

But records are made to be broken.

39

SERGEANT BILL EASTLAND

DOB: August 14, 1923
Where: Sparta, Tennessee
Air Force: 8th
Bomb Groups: 492nd, 467th
Squadrons: 859th, 788th
Stationed: North Pickenham and Rackheath, England
Decorations include: Air Medal with clusters. Bill's first bomb group, the 492nd, was disbanded after suffering 52 lost planes in 66 missions. He transferred to the 467th Bomb Group where he completed his 35 combat missions as a B-24 flight engineer/gunner. Bill remained in the air force reserve and retired after 30 years with the rank of colonel. His professional career was spent with the U.S. Corps of Engineers as a civil engineer.

The Comforting Sound of Rain

I grew up in Sparta, Tennessee, and had hardly been to Nashville, much less anywhere overseas. I ended up knowing more about London than Nashville. I was a flight engineer/top turret gunner on a B-24, usually on a plane called *Feudin' Wagon*. I flew with the same crew for the duration of combat, 35 missions in all. I am happy to report that everyone made it back safely.

It was a pure accident that I became a flight engineer. I certainly didn't ask for it and, in fact, the day before we shipped out for air corps training everyone in that group was shipped out to quartermaster school instead. At gunnery school, which I didn't ask for either, I had the most fun I ever had. That's because I grew up on a farm and there were times when ammunition cost just a little too much for my family and so we couldn't buy what we wanted to shoot. Thanks to Uncle Sam, though, I shot as much as I wanted, especially skeet. They would put us on the back of a pickup truck with a platform and the truck would go around on an oval track while I tried to hit pop up targets with different kinds of shotguns. We were told to shoot a hundred rounds and I soon ended up with a bruised, sore shoulder. Scores were kept and there was a lot of competition, even some betting.

I had never been off the ground in my life, actually never higher in the air than the loft of a barn. We went up for some aerial target practice on my first flight and the pilot told me the intercom wasn't working so when he wanted me to shoot he would rock the wings of our plane. As the target approached closer and closer I had no idea whether it was time to start firing but it wasn't long before our plane hit a bit of rough air, causing the plane to dip and rise, and I decided for myself. I blasted that target all to pieces. That's because I could have thrown a rock and hit it. It was no surprise, then, that I was high scorer for the day. Everyone thought I was a great shot but I didn't reveal my little secret that the target was less than a hundred feet away. I think my pilot would have thrown me out if I hadn't been fastened to the plane. When we got back to the base he used words I had never heard before but he never reported what really happened.

Eventually, I joined my combat crew and underwent training with them. The pilot, as it turned out, could play classical piano and he knew how to fly our B-24 well. The copilot was a fun guy but he thought the mandatory checklist requirement before every flight was amateurish. He decided he didn't need to read the checklist. One day we took off from Topeka headed for England loaded with freight. The plane wouldn't get off the ground and since I stood between the pilot and copilot on takeoff I saw what was happening. We weren't getting airspeed because the superchargers weren't turned on. The switch controlling them hadn't been flipped. After we took off the tops of some pine trees getting airborne, the pilot made it clear that no matter how long we flew together we would never take off again without going over the checklist. I just told the guys in the back that our load was a little too heavy. I didn't want them to lose confidence in the pilot.

Bill Eastland (courtesy Bill Eastland)

My first combat mission was on July 12, 1944. We had a battle-proven copilot accompany us just to make sure everything went all right. He sat on a plank between the pilot and copilot so he could watch everything firsthand. My original bomb group, the 492nd, had suffered a high casualty rate — so high that it was eventually disbanded — so this guy was very nervous. Prior to the flight, he gave me the third degree, testing me on everything. He walked with me around the plane to make sure I knew what to do in an emergency such as how to transfer fuel from the wing tanks into the main fuel tanks. This was the only testing that I got since my own pilot didn't test me on anything.

This mission, to Munich, was a long one. Flak knocked out our oxygen system and so we had to drop down to around 10,000 feet where we didn't need oxygen. That meant we had to fly back to base by ourselves. This being

A typical pre-mission briefing for bomber crews (courtesy Bill Eastland).

our first mission, we didn't know enough to be concerned but the fellow who accompanied us was really upset. He was sure we were going to be found and shot down. In fact, he had the radioman shoot off every red flare we had to see if fighters would come to our assistance. We got back to base without seeing any planes, friendly or enemy, and the guy eventually settled down.

A couple of our very early missions were to St. Lo where we dropped bombs near our troops. What I remember is how strongly we felt about helping the GI's breakout of that area. I've tried to reconstruct this action by talking with our radioman since he was on the command radio and knew more about what was going on but he doesn't remember much about it. We were supposed to drop on the enemy side of some red flares that had been set up on the ground. We did that except the smoke from the flares drifted too close to our own troops who were located very near the drop site. I don't know if our bomb group dropped in the wrong place but I do know hundreds of our troops were killed. This bombing was one of the tragic episodes of the war.

Soon after that we headed to Kiel to bomb the heavily protected Nazi sub pens. We were flying slot that day and because of my position in the top turret I got a good view of the action whether I wanted to or not. About a hundred feet away from us the low left plane took a direct hit and disintegrated. We lost two planes of our four-plane element that day. There were times when I would think, "Well, we're next." I just had to accept that and not let it interfere with what I had to do.

I prayed the nights before our missions — just a simple prayer — usually the 23rd Psalm. I didn't have trouble sleeping since I was so tired but the tail gunner occupied a bunk underneath me and he smoked cigarettes all night long. If we were on the alert list I knew we would fly unless the weather washed us out. Our Quonset hut homes were metal and we slept near the metal so if I turned over in my sleep and heard the rain I would say, "Well, I've got one more day to live." The rain was a very comforting sound to all of us.

Bringing Home the FEUDIN' WAGON

My sixteenth combat mission as a B-24 engineer/top turret gunner was not the roughest I endured but was probably my most memorable. I remember that the early part of the flight was routine: takeoff, formation, and even the unpredictable English weather all cooperated. Our plane, *FEUDIN' WAGON*, was one of 396 B-24s from the 2nd Bomb Division headed for different targets on September 11, 1944.

Even as our 45 planes arrived over the target — a synthetic oil plant at Stendal, Germany — nothing appeared unusual. The Germans were putting up their usual blanket of anti-aircraft fire when a burst of flak near our plane hit our gas line. It wasn't a direct hit but, in terms of damage, a critical part of our ship was affected. We dropped out of formation and immediately there were concerns as to whether we would make it back home. Anytime nearby crews reported seeing a stream of gas running from your plane you knew there was a serious problem, including the possibility of a midair explosion.

The pilot sent me back to check the bomb bay where the transfer valves for the gas tanks were located. Quickly I saw gasoline vaporizing in the air. I couldn't see where it was coming from since the air was so thick and the smell was very strong. At the same time I was getting soaked with gas. What I thought at that very moment I wouldn't want to put into print.

Four selector valves in the bomb bay controlled the gas content into the four main gas

FEUDIN' WAGON, the B-24 saved from a fiery explosion through the quick work of Sgt. Bill Eastland (courtesy Bill Eastland).

tanks. They could feed all the tanks on a constant flow or the flow to each tank could be controlled individually. Under normal conditions, it was a simple matter of turning each tank's switch, using designated arrows for position changes. Each tank held the gas for each of our four engines.

I walked out on the bomb bay catwalk — little more than 12 inches wide — grabbed a bomb rack with one hand for support and leaned out, searching for the cutoff valve. I didn't know where the gas was coming from or what part of the heavy rubber gas lines had been hit. It was strictly a trial and error search. At the time we were probably about 20,000 feet up where the air temperature was minus 30 degrees centigrade. I had taken off my heated gloves but kept on the nylon inner gloves so my skin wouldn't stick to the metal. Normally I didn't wear my chest chute and this day was no different. It was standing in a corner of the flight deck.

I wasn't able to determine where the break in the line was so I went back to the flight deck and yelled to the pilot — Earl Borders of Richmond, Virginia — that I would experiment with the valves. By this time he had turned off the plane's electrical system that heated our flying suits, operated the gun turrets, and the radio. He knew, as I did, that one spark would cause a catastrophic explosion. Meanwhile he had a real battle on his hands dealing with engines two, three, and four which were receiving more air than fuel. When an engine received more air than fuel a runaway prop developed — a dangerous situation. For a while, it looked like all our engines would quit. In fact, we actually flew with one engine briefly.

I went back to the bomb bay at least three times before, somehow, I got the selector valves in the right combination. I couldn't tell you today what positions they were in but somehow the combination worked. The engines got enough gas to cause each to run and get us back to England safely.

All four engines were running when we got back to the base. We landed before the rest of the group and were taken straight into interrogation. I was soaking wet with gasoline and I sure didn't want anyone lighting a match or smoking around me. My questioning was cut short and I was taken to the base hospital where I was stripped down and greased up all over. I spent the night there but couldn't wait to get out, which I did the next day.

What happened to me wasn't that unusual. I didn't expect anything out of it like a medal or special recognition. I was just glad to be on the ground. Years later I saw the man who was our radio operator on that mission. He introduced me to members of his family as the man who saved the plane that September 11. I didn't save the plane. I was just saving my rear end. That same man saved my life on one mission when my oxygen supply was cut off. He noticed I had lost consciousness and quickly got me on the floor and gave me his oxygen mask. Then he passed out. The copilot came back and helped us both. After a few minutes the pilot yelled at me, "Are you all right?" I was probably too groggy to operate those twin .50 cals in the top turret but I told him yes. "Then get back up there." he said. "There are fighters in the area."

One more thing I remember about our missions was the vacant hardstands as we taxied by after landing. I can still see the ground crews looking, waiting, and hoping their planes would come back. There was no communication on individual losses so it was "wait and see." Hours after fuel time was exhausted they were still hoping for a telephone call that their plane may have landed at an alternate base. That happened to us.

Those planes belonged to the crew chiefs. They just let us borrow them and we were supposed to bring them back hopefully in good shape. You can't believe the pride of ownership exhibited by those crews. I have never seen fliers who didn't credit their ground crews with their success and even their lives. We trusted them so fully that most of us didn't even preflight the engines as that had already been done. We just got in, started engines, and pulled out.

40

LIEUTENANT BOB CHAMBERS

DOB: January 26, 1922
Where: Mifflinburg, Pennsylvania
Air Force: 10th
Bomb Group: 7th
Squadron: 9th
Station: Pandaveswar, India
Decorations include: Air Medal with clusters. From October 1943 through March 1944, Bob piloted his B-24 in the China-Burma-India (CBI) Theater. During that time he flew 20 combat missions including one during which he literally drove an enemy pilot into a nearby mountain. He retired from the air force reserve as a major after 20 years of service and spent his civilian life in sales.

Adventures in the CBI

We were assigned to the 9th Squadron, 7th Bomb Group at Pandaveswar, India, about 120 miles from the Burma border. Our bomb group was part of the 10th Air Force in the CBI (China-Burma-India) Theater, a part of Lord Louis Mountbatten's South East Asia Command.

We left the U.S. on September 9, 1943, and arrived at our combat base on October 1. This was just one year nearly to the day that I had started flight training in Orangeburg, South Carolina, and only four months from when my crew and I started our combat training together at Davis-Monthan Field, Tucson, Arizona. We were surprised when we arrived at our base to learn that the combat losses for our B-24 group were next to the highest thus far in the war, second only to the Ploesti oil refinery raid. Our mission in India included helping to prevent the Japanese from progressing far enough north in Burma to harass the construction of the Ledo Road, the ground supply route into China, and from attacking our airplanes supplying China over the Hump.

Our main mission was to destroy Japanese airports, supply depots, marshaling yards, bridges, and roadbeds as well as the seaport at Rangoon. We closed that seaport by sinking a ship in the channel with underwater mines. We then concentrated on the seaport, rail marshaling yards, a cement factory in Bangkok and the railway from Bangkok to Rangoon. The enemy's determination to prevent supplies from reaching China from India made combat against them costly.

There was only our group (four squadrons) of B-24s and two squadrons of B-25s to fight the American air war over Burma in the winter of 1943–44. Our missions were too long for fighter escort so we had to protect ourselves as best we could. Our bombardier was killed on one of our early missions. We were shot up badly on several other occasions. On those missions our navigator and radio operator were killed and ball turret gunner and nose turret gunner were taken prisoners and held for the rest of the war. The squadron commander took those members of my crew on one more mission after we had completed combat. They were shot down near Bangkok. That was a sad, sad day for those of us who were left.

Bob Chambers (courtesy Bob Chambers)

During this period, Japanese fighter strength was formidable because of their army's determination to stop Allied supplies from reaching China through and over north Burma. In daytime, they were often able to pit 10 or 20 fighters against our bombers whenever we were bombing targets within range of their major fighter bases near Rangoon, Mandalay, or Bangkok. Our major nighttime targets were these airbases. We would attack them during full moonlight and fly to the targets individually, usually bombing from 8,000 feet. We would have 15 or 20 airplanes taking off at two-minute intervals and scheduled to arrive at most targets around midnight. We were always very scared of being hit by anti-aircraft fire or that an enemy fighter might get under us by spotting our nearly white hot superchargers. Fortunately, during this period we lost very few airplanes on night missions but did have some planes damaged and crewmembers hurt. It was during the daylight, high altitude operations that we sustained many demoralizing losses and much damage.

We were on one night mission in mid–October when, soon after bombs away, the airplane shuddered and suddenly wanted to turn to hard right. It took the copilot and me pushing hard on the left rudder pedal to keep us flying straight in order get us back to home base. Various crewmembers using flashlights searched all around the tail surfaces, rudders, and rudder control mechanism to find what had been hit. They could find nothing damaged back there. With everything else seeming okay, we flew on until we got near home base and found that we would have to fly around the field and land in the opposite direction because of the wind. We swung way out so as to make only a gradual left turn, not daring to allow the right wing to drop because we might not be able to bring it back up. Powering up some on the right engines and back a little on the left, we were able to make a wide left hand circle to line up with the runway and land safely. When we got out and looked the airplane over, we found that some of the right aileron and wingtip were torn away apparently by ack-ack that didn't explode.

On another night mission at the beginning of November, a burst of tracers shot past the cockpit window near enough that we heard a loud *whoosh* as they went by. A few minutes later, with a loud rattle of bullets slamming through our airplane and the top turret operator shouting in pain, we knew an enemy pilot had us where he wanted us. The navigator shouted that he saw mountain ridges ahead in the moonlight and said he could guide me right down where we could just miss the hilltops. This would wipe out the fighter from under us. The enemy pilot couldn't take his eyes off our superchargers or he would lose sight of us and not be able to get back under us. We planned to lead him to his death. Also, for him to be able to shoot at us he had to be 300 to 400 feet below to give him room to turn up steep enough to fire at us. Then, to keep from flying into us, he would have to turn and dive back down to get ready for another try.

Guided by the navigator, I was able to just skim the top of a high ridge and see a large flash of fire as the fighter slammed into the mountain just below and behind us. A loud clatter came over the intercom from the crew as they celebrated the enemy's demise. Then, the bombardier finished dressing the turret gunner's superficial wound to his left leg. We were ten of the happiest men on the planet once we got out of enemy territory.

Terror Under Fire

The air war over Burma during 1943–44 was especially severe due to the strength of the Japanese fighter forces and their determination to keep their supply routes open into North Burma. On December 12, 1943, we were on a mission to bomb an important railroad junction and bridge complex south of Mandalay, a target we had bombed repeatedly, so we were prepared to meet heavy resistance. We weren't disappointed.

Upon approaching the target at 21,000 feet, we were met by a *swarm* of enemy fighters and a lone bomber with them. The Japanese didn't fly in an organized formation, they flew sort of mingling around each other, like a loose swarm of bees. The bomber containing some of their superiors would fly parallel with us, out of range, to watch and see how their fighter pilots performed. When we spotted that bomber out there we knew they were going to press their attacks viciously, which they did. They dove at us from high out in front, one after the other, and head-on while spraying our formation with bullets as they came. Then they rolled over inverted above us and dove straight down behind the last bomber.

The group didn't lose any bombers on this mission but we were shot up badly and our beloved bombardier, Bill Neuhause, was killed. Bill was about my age, 21. He was from Oakland, California. We had been together on all our missions so it just broke my heart when he was shot. He was hit in the chest through the ribs with the bullet coming out under his shoulder blades. He remained alive long enough for me to land the plane at a British field. I stayed with the plane while two of our crew accompanied Bill in an old rickety truck the Brits used to transport him to the nearest hospital. The going was rough over 12 miles of bumpy road. Unfortunately, Bill died along the way.

While under attack like this, the inside of each bomber was pure bedlam. The crew members were screaming over the intercom the location of each enemy fighter they saw while calling out damage to neighboring bombers, all under extreme stress. The very worst *spine chilling* scare was when someone screamed over the radio, "*You're on fire!*" without saying which one it was. Everyone ahead of the one that was actually on fire thought it was his plane. Fire on a B-24 was usually in the bomb bay where all the crewmembers in the front don't know it until someone screams it on the intercom or radio.

Everyone, when under attack, was scared to the point of being *petrified, numbed* to the point that all did their jobs methodically, almost like robots. Time seemed to stand still under attack; 20 minutes seemed like hours. Everything that happened, like an airplane beside you falling apart or burning or the enemy diving at you, seemed to occur in super slow motion. It was especially hard for the members of the flight crew not manning guns — the pilot, copilot, navigator, and bombardier. At least the gunners felt they were able to shoot back. When bullets slammed into the airplane, it sounded like someone hitting the side of a steel building with a hammer. The bullets actually rattled as they sped through. You did not know what damage they had done or system they knocked out. Enemy anti-aircraft fire from the ground wasn't very accurate but we were always afraid of a lucky hit.

When a plane lost an engine or was otherwise damaged to such an extent that it couldn't keep up with the formation there was nothing the pilot could do to keep up. One time I watched a plane go down and heard the pilot pleading with the rest of us to come down and help him. He said, "You sob's come on down, come on down! Save me, come help us! They won't get you!" but we had orders to move on. I found out later the plane was shot down. Some of the crew jumped but were shot up going down.

This is a generic description for the 20 plus combat missions I flew over Burma and Thailand in 1943 and early 1944. During this period, the enemy would usually down several of our bombers on a mission and only lose maybe two or three of their own. In total, we suffered almost unacceptable losses on our side, rivaling the losses over Europe at that time. By mid 1944, long range fighter escorts (P-38s and P-51s) began to appear which, along with our success at bombing Jap air facilities, fuel depots, and ammunition dumps, substantially reduced their combat ability, making bomber combat less stressful on into 1945.

Flying "Fun" in India

During my 20 months of duty in India I was involved in several airplane mishaps in addition to my combat experiences. While on combat duty, I was chosen to fly to headquarters, 10th Air Force, near Calcutta between missions for the bi-weekly "official mail" pickup in a Fairchild 24 (military designation C-61). I was chosen because I had flown small airplanes before joining the military. Two of these planes had been wrecked by pilots who were qualified only in larger types and headquarters didn't want to lose the last one.

This looked like a fun flying job to the higher-ranking officers in group headquarters. So, being outranked (still a 2nd lt.) by a major, I could hardly refuse when he asked me to check him out in this fabulous, fun airplane. Several trips around the airport revealed why those B-24 pilots wrecked the other C-61 Fairchilds. The rudder peddles on the Liberator are on tracks and move back and forth over 12 inches on rollers whereas the C-61 peddles only needed a little nudging to achieve lateral control. Over controlling the rudders required that I catch the major with the brakes to keep him from ground looping. He recognized his problem so he suggested that he get more practice in the plane by flying along on the next trip to

Calcutta, which he did. On the return trip he suggested we exchange sides since he was used to flying from the left. He thought that this would solve his problem. We changed sides in the air but it didn't help his over controlling on the landing. When he began to lose it, I attempted to catch the ground loop with brakes but found there were no brake peddles on the right side of this airplane. By that time it was too late. It sure did tear that plane up. Thankfully, no one was hurt.

When I arrived at my Air Service Command base, I found they kept several airplanes around for rated pilots to fly the four hours per month required to keep their pilot's rating active. One of these planes was a "war weary" L-5, a little Stinson Observation plane that I really enjoyed. One day as I was taxiing rather briskly along, a P-38 landed on the runway nearby. I had not seen one close up before, so I stopped looking where I was going to watch this prettiest of all World War II airplanes close up. Soon thereafter I crashed the left wing into a forklift that was coming in the opposite direction on the same taxiway. It was loaded so high that the driver could not see what was ahead of him, either. It was a case of neither of us watching where we were going.

After wrecking the little L-5, I took to flying a Douglas "Dauntless" [Navy SBD, Air Corps RA-24] that was used for administrative transportation by our HQ. It was really a delight to fly but I did get a couple of frights out of it. One of them occurred when I took a buddy to a neighboring air base and left him there. On the return flight home in rather rough air, the control stick was suddenly restricted in its rearward movement and the plane began losing altitude gradually. It was a spongy restriction but with all my strength I could not stop the loss of altitude. I soon realized that if I rolled in the proper trim, with a restricted elevator, the servo would become a little elevator and, sure enough, I was able to retain enough altitude to make it to the nearest airport.

Pilots would realize the ensuing wheel landing was tail high and hot. After the adrenaline slowed and I was able to check the plane over, I found the guy had not tied his parachute down with the seat belt in the back cockpit when he got out and the chute had fallen down between the seat and the rear control stick. In my desperation, I had pulled quite a groove into that parachute.

These incidents along with traumatic combat experiences, flying in the monsoon weather in India and witnessing a B-24 crash during training turned me into a "fair weather" pilot after the war. I flew only sporadically until the 1960s and 70s when my interest in flying was rekindled. I eventually acquired my commercial and instrument ratings, but remained just a "fair weather" pilot.

41

Lieutenant Jim Kirtland

DOB: May 18, 1917
Where: Pinckney, Michigan
Air Force: 15th
Bomb Group: 454th
Squadron: 738th
Station: Cerignola, Italy
Decorations include: Distinguished Flying Cross, Air Medal with clusters. Jim won the Distinguished Flying Cross for saving his ship and crew after his B-24 was severely damaged on one of his 50 combat missions as a pilot. He was a farmer before the war but returned home to graduate with a history degree from the University of Michigan. His postwar career included leasing a service station and investing in real estate.

Sleepy Time

I liked to fly our B-24 every day that I could in order to complete the required number of missions as soon as possible. Usually, I enjoyed the number four position, about fifty feet below the plane in the number one position of my squadron. Shell casings from the tail gunner ahead wouldn't fall on us and there was no prop wash from other planes. The position offered all kinds of protection since planes were on all sides of us. I have to believe our chances of survival were improved by flying there.

I had a copilot once who did some stupid things to endanger us from time to time. One day we took off from Natal, Brazil, in a tropical storm and soon encountered a powerful updraft. According to the altimeter, our rate of climb was 3,000 feet per minute. I pointed this out to the copilot who thought I wanted him to cage the artificial horizon. Now we were in total darkness in a tropical storm with no artificial horizon by which to fly. It was 3 A.M. I had to go back to basics that I learned in primary flight training. When you don't know, center the ball and needle and get the air speed normal. From Natal to Dakar over the South Atlantic everything was routine.

This guy should never have gone to pilots' school. He was one of those who resented authority. This copilot had a problem with falling asleep on missions. Returning from a bombing mission over southern France one day, his eyes closed and he was gone. I yelled at him, "Wake up and stay awake! An enemy fighter might make a sweep across us and take me out and here you are asleep!" He didn't say anything, but he heard me all right. The next thing I know he's asleep again. That's the last time he slept on my watch. I always thought copilots really didn't do much. Lots of times they just raised and lowered the landing gear, wheel jockeys of a sort. But if the pilot fell victim to enemy fire the copilot became the airplane commander so it was very important that he stay alert. After all, his life was at stake, too. So I went to Captain Stacy Brown, the squadron operations officer, and asked him, "What am I going to do with this guy?" His brilliant response was, "What do you want me to do?" I told him to put the guy's ass in the air the next day with someone other than me. I never saw Mr. Sleepy Time after that and never heard from him again.

I was soon assigned another copilot, a former first pilot who had a few early returns because of bends in his knees. With him, 1st Lieutenant James McGehan, everything worked out well. He was still flying with my crew after my fiftieth mission. In fact, he became the "Yank of the Week" sponsored by Camel cigarettes for the most outstanding performance by a serviceman during one week. It occurred over Vienna, Austria, when flak knocked out one of his engines. Since he couldn't keep up with the rest, he cut across to join the others after going over the target. As a loner in the skies he was jumped by a number of Me 109s. During the ensuing fight his gunners got three of the enemy aircraft.

On July 25, 1944, we were one of 33 B-24s on a mission to bomb the Herman Goering Tank Works at Linz, Austria. Before reaching the target our plane lost a turbo coupling, a rubber unit that fit on an engine's supercharger. As a result, I lost some extra power so that, when we were in a climb doing 155 miles per hour, I was trying my best to keep up with the group leader. I told Regan, the bombardier, to drop half our load of bombs. We then proceeded to lose a second supercharger which meant there was no question about dropping the rest of our bombs before the target. "What are we going to drop over the target?" Regan asked me. I said, "Don't worry about the target." That wasn't my biggest concern at that point but it became so later while on the bomb run.

Jim Kirtland (courtesy Jim Kirtland)

Why would I want to risk a plane and a crew flying over a heavily defended target when I had no bombs? So I peeled off and joined a bomber formation that had already been over the target and was returning to base. That's when Lieutenant Hilton came up and took my place in the formation. He was flying in the number seven position, otherwise known as the slot. So he moved ahead and up a little and began flying where we once were when all of a sudden his plane took a direct hit. His right wing fell off and before we knew it he was gone. No one ever found out if anyone survived. I still feel I made the right call about leaving formation but I can't help but think had our ship not had mechanical problems that would have been me.

ASAP

My philosophy of flying missions as a B-24 pilot with the 15th Air Force was simple: stay busy. I didn't like to sit around and think about missions. I told my crew that my goal was to fly every mission possible. Simply put, I tried to fly every day so I could get my required number of missions completed and then return home as soon as possible. That meant often flying deeper and deeper into enemy territory to bomb, but so be it. As a result, I began my combat flying on April 21, 1944 and ended on August 13. During that time, I flew copilot on 15 to 20 missions with a good friend, Gerald Bradbury. That way I ended up with calluses on both hands since, as copilot, I would hold the wheel with my right hand and control the ailerons with my left. I enjoyed flying everyday and the only thing that held me back was the weather.

The briefing room for those of us in the 454th Bomb Group, 738th Squadron, was the wine cellar of an Italian landowner's house. The runways, located in his vineyards, were part of our home base at San Giovanni, west of Cerignola, Italy. On flying days, the group duty officer would awaken us, then we would head for some early chow, and onto the mission briefing. I remember the always-present big map of southern Europe. A white bed sheet covered the map but we could see the bottom of it. The briefing officer would always raise the sheet, revealing that day's target. Then, we would get the lowdown on the number of guns and fighter opposition to expect as well as weather conditions. Our eyes followed very closely a red ribbon that extended from our base to the target.

This is about my experience on June 26, 1944, during a mission to an oil refinery at Moosbierbaum, north of Vienna. Refineries were usually pretty tough targets to hit due to extensive anti–aircraft guns ringing them. We had dropped our bombs and the air was smoothing out after leaving the drop zone. However, there was still some flak flying up at us and one shell seemed to have our name on it. I felt the concussion on my left side as it lifted the left wing up a little. There wasn't much time to think about the predicament we were in because all of a sudden the wheel controlling the ailerons went limp. A big fragment entered the cockpit from left to right, missing my feet by inches. It cut three of six crucial control cables, including two aileron cables and one to the rudder.

At that point, I still had control of the aircraft by controlling the rudder. Actually, we were fortunate because any other combination of cables cut would have meant bail out time for all of us. As it was, I could pick the right wing up using the left rudder. I left the formation and flew alongside it and then waited for everyone to land before I finally started to bring our ship in. The last thing I wanted was prop wash from a plane in front of us causing our ship to fly all over the place. I told the crew, "If you don't think I can land this aircraft, you have a choice. I can fly this thing over the base and let you bail out." No one bailed. That's sort of ironic because I really wasn't a praying man, all I was thinking about was controlling the plane. If I had been praying, I probably would have been saying, "God, take this plane, I'm leaving it."

Our radio operator always wanted to use the red flares stored on our plane for just such an occasion so I told him to use them all up. All the emergency equipment was out there for us but, as it turned out, we didn't need it. We all just sort of left the plane in a matter of fact way. Major Corwin Grimes put me in for the Distinguished Flying Cross for having saved an airplane and a crew and I'm happy to report that I received that honor. Today, the upper turret gunner says I was the best pilot over there. As for me, I treated it as just another flight toward my goal of getting back home as soon as possible.

42

SERGEANT JOHN CUNNINGHAM

DOB: January 29, 1925
Where: Nashville, Tennessee
Air Force: 20th
Bomb Group: 497th
Squadron: 871st
Station: Saipan
Decorations include: Distinguished Flying Cross, Air Medal with clusters. As central fire control gunner aboard a B-29, John was responsible for firing the .50 caliber guns in the plane's top turrets. He flew 35 combat missions and won the DFC for helping to bring a damaged plane back safely to Saipan during a typically long flight. In civilian life, John spent 50 years as a wholesale food broker.

Low Level Fire Raids

Thousands of us who wanted to be pilots were washed out in 1944 and diverted to other needs. I had the choice of armament school at Denver or radio school at Scott Field or even mechanics school in Texas. I chose Denver because it sounded better to me. At Lowry Field I was assigned to B-17s as a gunner. Then, fate took one of its interesting turns.

While in Denver and on pass I met a guy at a bar who told me he was doing some top-secret work. Of course, his comments made me want to find out what he was doing. He told me there was a B-29 parked in a remote section of the airfield and it was covered by a tarp with armed guards around it. This stranger told me he was in central fire control, whatever that was. I didn't know anything about it but as I listened he told me more. Later I found out that some of what he said was true and the rest wasn't. But the idea of flying in a completely pressurized aircraft intrigued me enough that I went over to headquarters the next day and told the officer in charge that I wanted to transfer to become a central fire control gunner on a B-29. He put my papers in. I interviewed for the job and was given the opportunity.

The B-29 was awesome. I just couldn't get over how big it was. Flying in it was like flying in a commercial airliner. Crewmembers normally didn't have to wear oxygen masks and it was quiet in flight. It was plush compared to all the other combat planes.

The central fire control system was one of the more complex units on a B-29. Essentially, it was a computerized remote firing system. We gunners were stationed in Plexiglas blisters with our gun sights and controls and were linked electronically to remote turrets where the guns were located. All kinds of circuitry and switches enabled any gunner to control any of the turrets that could be aimed properly.

As the CFC gunner, I was located in the top blister. I would sit in a chair like a barber's chair and my head would be in the blister. It was pretty comfortable. The seats were padded and my feet rested on a pedestal. I could turn 365 degrees when I activated my guns. I would look through a gun sight and wherever the gun sight went the guns went. My actual guns were 23 feet in front of me. Others were two feet behind me.

For most of our missions we flew *Red Hot Rider* and I think her name accurately reflected the action we found. We took part in some of the first night fire raids as well as the unforgettable April 7, 1945, daytime clash just outside Tokyo. The flak was horrible and one of our engines was hit. The plane was shaking and vibrating all over the sky. There were holes in the plane structure but we had a very good pilot, Don Bowry, who could do things other pilots couldn't do. Bowry feathered the engine and we made it back on three engines.

Many enemy planes were shot down by B-29 gunners and P-51 fighters during the time we were approaching and over the target. I believe this was the first time we had fighter escort and so the sky was full of planes, small and large, flying everywhere with every kind of speed and direction. The flak over Tokyo sounded like a barking dog just outside the plane. Explosions were everywhere.

Our fire raids would usually take us down to 5,000 feet. I remember looking down and seeing much of Tokyo ablaze. Fire was everywhere. We carried bombs containing gasoline jelly, or napalm. That jelly would stick to everything it hit and create fires that would envelop and destroy the many thousands of wooden structures on the ground.

We were aware of all the damage and carnage down below. There were mixed feelings about it all but we also did a lot of praying for each other during those flights. The turbulence from the fire-induced winds was terrible and as we looked down at the destruction we thought of it as hell on earth. I thought long and hard about the people dying down below but we all knew if we had to invade Japan many, many American deaths would occur.

All of our missions were extra long and mainly over water. We took

John Cunningham (courtesy John Cunningham)

extra gas on some of them by using auxiliary tanks, one of which was in the back bomb bay. On one mission, when the bombardier released the bombs, he punched a button and somehow the gas tank was jettisoned. The tank didn't go out entirely, it just dangled down and swung in the bay. We gunners could look out a window and see the thing dangling there. To solve this problem, our radar operator, a Brooklyn boy named Art Masonheimer, grabbed a fire axe and rushed to the bomb bay. He simply chopped the fuel tank loose, striking metal on metal, until the gas tank fell free. His was a very courageous act.

We ended up with 504 combat hours and all of our crew returned home safely. At the beginning of our tour we moved into our Quonset hut on Saipan as the "new guys." Thirty-nine missions later we were the oldest crew in that hut.

43

Major John Kolemba

DOB: September 16, 1920
Where: Mount Tom, Massachusetts
Air Force: 15th
Bomb Group: 454th
Squadron: 738th
Station: Cerignola, Italy
Decorations include: Distinguished Flying Cross, Air Medal with clusters. Having failed his physical with the navy, John passed the army's test with no problem and soon entered the flying program. Thus began a lifelong love affair with the B-24. He flew 35 sorties in the European theater as a pilot, was credited with 63 combat missions, mostly aboard *Mr. Lucky,* and earned the DFC for nursing a badly damaged craft back to base. In civilian life, John worked in commercial glass sales and management.

Not Even a Scratch

It would seem that my service career was full of close calls. Looking back, it's amazing that I made it through 35 credited combat missions as a B-24 pilot with the 15th Air Force without a scratch.

November 5, 1944, was the day of our fifth mission, this one to Vienna, Austria. Flak was always extremely heavy in that area and it was no different on this day. There were big, black clouds of explosions all around us. "Oh God, please bring us through this," I remember thinking. We were flying in the number six position and I was busy looking for the group leader to drop his bombs when the plane in front of us took a direct hit in the wing at the gas tanks. The plane, which was no more than 20 feet from us, burst into flames. The explosion threw the plane up and right back over the top of us. I remember the searing heat for just an instant as it disappeared behind our plane. Our missions up to that point had been fairly tame but that's when I realized that what we were doing wasn't going to be easy. From that point on, every time we made it back from a mission I just wanted to forget about it and concentrate on living.

We flew a mission on Christmas Day to a marshalling yard at Wels, Austria. On return to our field at San Giovanni, the entire area was fogged in. We had flown some practice missions earlier during which we picked up a river coming off the Adriatic by flying in a certain direction, turning at a precise time, then making another turn at another precise time. If we did all that correctly we would find ourselves lined up on the runway. We had done this a number of times and each time it worked. This time, returning from our mission, we missed the runway by about 150 feet and had to go back up. We were running low on fuel and started our plans to abandon ship by parachuting out when the tower directed us to another field about 40 or 50 miles south where a big hole in the fog had opened up. We and the rest of the group managed to land there but then the hole closed again. The group stationed at the field had already eaten and had sent their Christmas dinner remnants to the residents of the nearby town. No matter, we were just glad to get down

John Kolemba (courtesy John Kolemba)

on the ground. Who would have imagined that a hole would open for us at that crucial point and would then so quickly close back up after we landed? The Lord was looking after us that day.

On a mission to Regensburg, we had just got up into the Alps when the number four engine died. Then, just a few minutes later, the entire electrical system went out. We were crippled at about 20,000 feet and I had no radio to call anyone. The number three engine started losing power about the time the number four engine unfeathered, causing additional drag. At that point, I knew it was time to head back so we turned around and headed for home. We had to throw everything out to keep from losing too much altitude but we kept dropping. Our engineer tried to start the auxiliary power unit but it wouldn't start. We finally got back to friendly territory and I brought our ship in to a little fighter field run by the British. They weren't very sympathetic and told us to get our plane out of there. It wouldn't have been possible to take off on two engines. Our group sent a truck to pick us up and return us to our base. That old plane was just battle weary. I don't think anyone ever flew it again. It had been named *Mechanic's Nightmare*.

On one mission, we flew a plane that had been shot up previously while over the Ploesti oil fields. After that mission it had landed on one main wheel, tearing up a wing. When we took off, our gear came up to about 45 degrees and stopped. We were unable to locate any leak in the hydraulic system although we found out later we had lost a lot of hydraulic fluid while still on the ground. We were told to just fly around for a while, use up as much fuel as possible and drop our bombs in the Adriatic before coming back. The B-24 was equipped with a manual hand crank for lowering the wheels but it was inoperative on this plane. Despite all our best efforts the wheels wouldn't budge so I tried something different. We climbed up to get some altitude, probably around 10 or 12 thousand feet, put the plane in a dive and tried

Vienna, Austria, spread out before U.S. bombers of the 459th Bomb Group. (Courtesy John Kolemba)

to snap the wheels into place using the principle of centrifugal force. After several tries the landing gear finally locked and we landed without incident. To this day I believe our situation was caused either by sabotage or somebody wanting a valve for their homemade tent stove because after landing we discovered that a shutoff valve for the tail skid had been removed.

On another long mission we were flying a battle weary plane when high fuel consumption forced us to land at a field some distance from our home base to refuel. It took quite awhile to get a fuel truck to gas us up and since it was getting late we decided to stay overnight. They couldn't feed us nor give us any sleeping quarters and it was too cold to sleep in the plane so we decided to change plans and fly back home. This night had a high overcast and

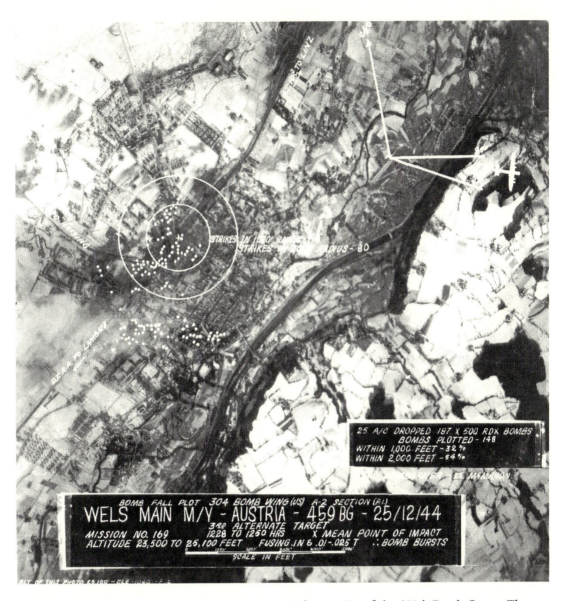

Bomb fall plot for the Christmas Day mission to Wels, Austria, of the 459th Bomb Group. The circles represent the boundaries for bombs dropped within 1,000 and 2,000 feet of the target, a marshalling yard. (Courtesy John Kolemba)

no moon. Italy at night had no lights anywhere and we were having trouble locating our field. Remembering that there was a searchlight at our field, I asked the tower to have it turned on. They did, but about 15 or 20 searchlights came on. There was no way of telling which one was ours. Finally, I thought of a solution. I asked the tower to fire signal flares. With that help we were able to land safely. There would be no more night flights for us!

On another mission, we lost two engines on the right side and managed to return to our field far behind the other planes. We encountered 55 mph crosswinds from our right side so to compensate for wind drift we made our approach at approximately a 45-degree angle to the runway. With all engines functioning, it would have been possible to drop a wing into

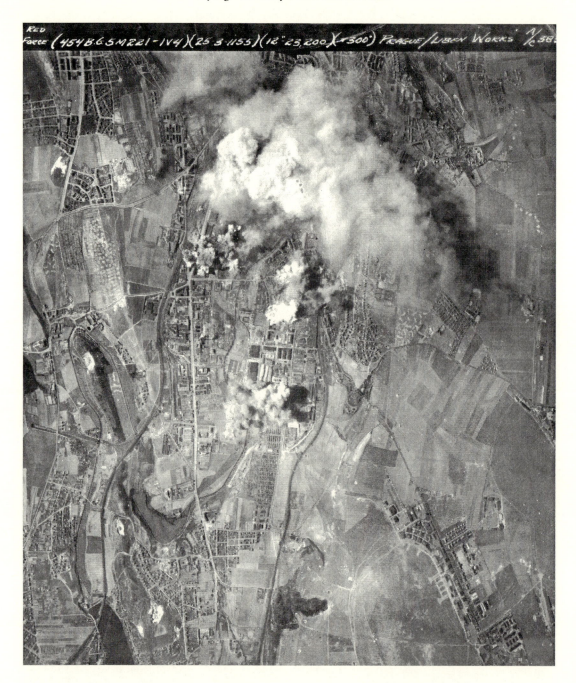

Bomb bursts mark the target, a factory near Prague, hit by B-24s of the 459th Bomb Group on March 25, 1945 (Courtesy John Kolemba)

the wind to compensate for the drift but without engine power it would have been almost impossible to pull the wing back to level. Just prior to touchdown we turned the plane to line up with the runway but before we could touch down the wind blew us off the runway. I had made our approach at a higher speed than normal and that enabled us to hold our altitude to go around for another attempt. At the normal landing speed we would not have made

Aerial photo showing the bombing of a train yard at Alessandria, Italy, on the river Tanaro roughly 55 miles south of Turin. The date was April 5, 1945. It was John Kolemba's final mission. (Courtesy John Kolemba)

it. On our next attempt, we lined up about 50 to 60 feet to the windward side and successfully landed. We zig-zagged down the runway, the wind catching our rudder and blowing the ship sideways. With no power to compensate for the drift, I was only able to use the brake on one side to try to stay on the runway. When we finally stopped near the end of the run-

way, our plane was completely turned into the wind. We were unable to taxi to our hardstand and had to be towed.

My entire crew was saddened on the day we bombed a railroad bridge in the Brenner Pass. A B-24 in the lead squadron took a direct flak hit in the waist and broke in two. There were no survivors. The navigator on that plane had been a member of my crew and was transferred to another squadron because he was trained in radar. My original navigator and bombardier were also killed in action while flying with other crews. None of the other members of my crew was ever injured, although a pilot flying his first mission with us in the copilot's seat had his helmet gashed by a piece of flak that flew through the windshield. Perhaps all this could be explained by the fact that for most of our missions the plane we flew was named *Mr. Lucky.*

Opposite, top: Flak bursts encountered by U.S. planes over target in the European theater. (Courtesy John Kolemba). *Opposite, bottom:* B-24s dropping bombs over target while encountering the predictable and often deadly flak bursts. (Courtesy John Kolemba)

44

Major Cooper Schley

DOB: March 11, 1919
Where: Savannah, Georgia
Air Force: 8th
Bomb Group: 97th
Squadron: 414th
Station: Morocco

Decorations include: Distinguished Flying Cross, Air Medal with clusters. On May 25, 1943, Cooper led 26 planes of his group to bomb the ferry slips at Messina, Sicily. Ninety minutes from the target his formation was attacked by at least 30 Me 109s. After repeated attacks and severe damage to his ship, Cooper accomplished his bomb run, helping to demolish two of the ferry slips and severely damaging a third. He nursed his ship back to base with a wounded crewmember while landing on only one working engine. He was awarded the DFC for his actions. In all, Cooper flew 50 combat missions, all but one as pilot of the B-17 *STINKY JR*. His business career was spent in mechanical engineering and chemical sales.

Diary Entries

1942

July 7: Left Presque Isle, Maine, en route the U.K. Held up at Goose Bay, Labrador, for 7 days because of bad weather.

July 14: Took off for Bluey West 8, Greenland, to pick up "Tom Cat Yellow," Lt. Starbuck's P-38 which needed a new tail assembly. Col. Hank Stovall (World War I pilot from Stovall, Miss.) kept us in Greenland for 10 days until the P-38 was repaired.

July 24: With Hank as passenger, we led Starbuck and Teague over the ice cap to Indigo (Reykjavik, Iceland) where we met the rest of the 414th taking off for U.K. Col. Chambers had us have an engine change before proceeding. We encountered a German sub shortly before we arrived at Iceland and Starbuck dove on it from 10,000 feet and made it crash dive.

Cooper Schley (courtesy Cooper Schley)

July 31: Lt. Dick Murfitt, an unassigned pilot, joined us for our flight to U.K. I let him fly *Stinky* to Prestwick, Scotland.

August 1: After a pleasant evening in Prestwick with our first WAAF's, we left for the final destination, Grafton Underwood aerodrome. Saw most of the squadron for the first time in months. Also the end of per diem!

August 17: We missed out on the first raid on Rouen, but were content with the second mission on Abbeyville aerodrome to lose our virginity. This was *STINKY*'s one and only. *STINKY JR.* (B-17F), which came from the 92nd Bomb Group, made the rest.

Sept. 8: We moved permanently to Polebrook much to our chagrin.

Oct. 9: First American 100 bomber raid. We went to Lille on Coulter's wing but messed up over the target and had to jettison bombs in the Channel on the way home.

Dec. 6: We moved up the line to Blida with our bomb load. I misjudged our weight and landed short of the runway, cutting a tire bad. The ground crew was able to change the tire with a pocketknife and makeshift tools. I flew to our base at Biskra after a sloppy, wet 8 days.

Dec. 18: Target Bizerte and it's getting rough. Dallas (Fred) went down.

Dec. 22: Bizerte again. Nick went down. We had a "target of opportunity" and sunk an Italian cruiser.

Dec. 26: Bizerte! Borders blew up (behind *STINKY JR.*) on the bomb run knocking Larry out and almost got Thacker.

1943

Jan. 4: Bizerte!! The "Bizerta Deserter Yo Yo" club is started. We had engine trouble and turned back.

Feb. 17: Finally got to lead an element on Cagliari, Sardinia. Mission OK

Feb. 22: Led again on snafu raid on Kasserine Pass. We didn't drop but the other flight accidentally (SH!) hit a town.

Mar. 10: Eighty Fortresses and 40 P-38s on Tunis aerodrome. Flew on Teague's wing for a poor show of formation. Lots of fighters — scared to death.

Apr. 6: My thirtieth mission and probably the roughest! Convoy off Bizerte. No escort, lousy bombing, running fight with Me's for ¾ hour.

Apr. 12: The weather fine — the bombing stunk. Led 2nd element with John Kelso as copilot. Smartt led the Group. No fighters but plenty of flack. On yeah, it was Bizerte docks.

Apr. 13: Led squadron on aerodrome at Milo, Sicily. Bombing good. Flak bad and several fighters. 2 planes from 342nd went down. I made my 2nd, 3-engine landing in one week. April 6 was the first.

Apr. 17: Supposed to lead squadron but had to turn back because ball turret forgot to bring his suit extension cord. Tried to catch formation but couldn't.

Apr. 23: Led squadron on cargo vessel 20 miles off Trapani, Sicily. Poor system of bombing but we set the boat on fire. She was later sunk. Bad weather on the way back compelled us to land at Bone where we were weathered in till Easter morning (Apr. 25).

Apr. 29: Saunders and I led Group on shipping at Bizerte. Weather was bad over target so we brought the bombs back. My first day as Capt. of *STINKY JR.*!

May 9: Mothers Day! I led the squadron on the town of Polermo, Sicily, and about the roughest yet. The bombing wasn't too hot and we had a running fight with 109s, 190s, 110s and 210s for 30 minutes. The formation got all screwed up and we got a lot of holes. Paine chewed Holmes' tail off and he had to crash land back at base. I flew next to him for cover all the way home.

May 11: I led 2nd element behind Thacker on a wine warehouse at Massala, Sicily. Beautiful day, a little flak, no fighters, good bombing. On way back we passed 118 B-26s, B-25s and P-38s heading for Sicily. Flew over Bizerte at 5,000 feet. All American show! Our first taste of Victory.

May 14: Holmes, Kelso and I took #423 to Bone, picked up Engle and crew and flew over to Sidi Ahmad aerodrome at Bizerte (unauthorized!) The boys there informed us that we were the first Allied combat plane to land there since taken. We spent 2 hours there seeing the town and looking over the planes. What a mess the town is and what marvelous workmanship those Nazi planes have!

May 18: I led squadron in #473 destined for Messina, Sicily. The weather was stinko so we bombed Trapani instead. The bombing wasn't bad. We didn't see much action but the P-38s shot down 6 Me's and lost 2 themselves.

May 22: Led 2nd element behind Smartt on another aerodrome. The flak was below us but about 25 Me 109s met us in turn off target. Holmes, flying on my right wing, was shot up again but made it back OK. Our attack was coordinated with large P-38 strafing attack.

May 24: Led squadron on shipping at La Maddalena, Sardinia. The bombing was God-awful — the Group lead stunk. Very inaccurate flak and no fighters. Gen. Partridge, A-3 Bomber Command, was passenger on *STINKY JR.*

May 25: Col. Donovan and I led the Group on the ferry slips at Messina, Sicily. We were intercepted by about 25 Me 109s an hour and ½ from the target and had a running fight for 20 minutes at 10,000 feet. The 341st Squadron had 2 ships shot up and turned back and half of the 342nd the same. We were met at the IP by more fighters (109s). The flak was most accurate yet, peppering *STINKY JR.* and hitting all 4 engines and #2 gas tank. I feathered #2 engine 30 minutes off target and had to feather #3 in traffic pattern as it ran out of gas. Made my first 2-engine landing. The bombing was excellent! This was Lee's fiftieth mission and my absolute roughest. (Resulted in my DFC)

May 28: Thacker led squadron and I led 2nd element on marshalling yards at Naples, Italy. Thacker tried AFCE [automatic flight control] bombing and the bombardier couldn't see target (head up ass!) consequently bombs went everywhere but the right place. Little flak on us and we were attacked by 3 fighters. One Me 110 dove head on thru the Group but his rounds were short.

June 1: "Dear Diary" What a day! Briefing was held at a nice, conservative 10:30 A.M. Winston Churchill, Anthony Eden, Gen. George Marshall, Air Marshall Tedder, Gen. Spaatz, Gen. Doolittle and a raft of other British and American big shots attended the briefing (to see me off on my last mission). The P.M. said a few words commending our work and telling us the importance of the target which was Pantelleria Island. No flak, no fighters and my element scored the only hits (thanks to Casey's skill by not dropping on the lead bombardier's drop). Thacker led the 20 planes in the Group and I led the 2nd element. P-38s dive-bombed with 1,000 pounders as soon as ours hit. Well, that's it — 50 missions and better than 250 hours and the Group's 116th mission. Now let's go home!

June 20: We finally got transportation on the *SS Mariposa* and set sail 5:30 P.M. on the 27th. The trip was fairly pleasant. We got good grub and played a lot of cards (Hearts).

The gathering of some of World War II's leading figures — all under one tent — for Cooper Schley's final mission briefing. From far left, standing, Marshal of the Royal Air Force Arthur Tedder, U.S. Air Force General Jimmy Doolittle (behind Tedder), U.S. Air Commander General Carl "Tooey" Spaatz, and British General Harold Alexander. Seated toward the right wall of the tent are British Chief of the Imperial General Staff Alan Brooke, U.S. Army Chief of Staff General George Marshall, British Foreign Secretary Anthony Eden, British Prime Minister Winston Churchill, and U.S. Air Force General Joe Atkinson, commander of the 5th Bomb Wing (Courtesy Cooper Schley).

July 4: Docked in the fair city of Boston at 9 A.M.. What a wonderful feeling! Wasted no time catching train for NYC.

What a Send-off!

My fiftieth and final mission in the B-17 *STINKY JR.* was to an island called Pantellaria. Apparently it was important to the higher ups because we were preparing to cut off the Germans from Italy. We had a visit during our mission briefing from notables: Air Marshall Arthur Tedder, Deputy Supreme Commander; General Jimmy Doolittle, 12th Air Force Commander; General Tooey Spaatz, U.S. Strategic Air Force Commander in Europe; General Harold Alexander, Allied Ground Forces Commander; General Alan Brooke, British Chief of Staff; General George Marshall, U.S. Chief of Staff; Anthony Eden, British Foreign Secretary; and Winston Churchill, British Prime Minister.

I felt great that day. It looked like it was going to be a fairly easy mission. We were also going to have some P-38s flying along with us. Our target was some naval facilities off this island. It was certainly impressive having those big shots there and apparently they felt it was important for them to be there since preparations were underway for the invasion of Italy. Churchill had actually been there for a day or so. I had walked right by him the day before. Imagine walking in to the tent where all the other briefings had occurred and suddenly finding yourself among such power! I remember Churchill speaking to us and underlining how important our mission was.

All along, I sort of thought this was all set up for me, that they were determined to give me the biggest and best send off on my final mission. I wouldn't have known George Marshall if I had run into him. Jimmy Doolittle I knew because just before another briefing I was standing just a few feet away from him early one morning. There was complete cloud cover overhead. We were standing there waiting for someone to tell us to go in when all of a sudden we heard this airplane above the clouds and then we heard the unmistakable sound of automatic machine gun fire. All of us hit the deck and as I looked up I saw the only one standing was Jimmy Doolittle.

Turned out the plane was a P-38 practicing over an adjoining field. I never forgot that. I was always impressed with Doolittle's suave manner. There had to be at least 150 people of all ranks that hit the ground that day. He just stood there looking up at the clouds. I was just swept up with the rest of them thinking I ought to fall down and get out of the way of that machine gun.

Not long after my final mission I had the choice of taking a ship or plane back to the states. I was told there would be lots of nurses, 50 or so, on the ship so I chose the ship. I was tired of flying so I expected my return trip to be one big party. As it turned out there were only five nurses on board and all of them were pregnant. I don't think I even saw them the whole trip. On the other hand there were 1,500 prisoners. They smelled to high heaven, having been in the desert so long. We had to queue up for meals together. It gave us kind of a funny feeling knowing they were our enemy. We had been dropping bombs on them for so long and now here we were 50 feet away from them just killing time. They didn't look very impressive.

We were unescorted coming back from Casablanca and since this was the middle of 1943 we zigzagged all the way back to Boston. None of us wanted to go to Boston; we wanted to go to New York. So as soon as we landed we caught a train to New York and the first thing I did was to order a beer. It had been over a year since I had one.

Captain Cooper Schley, right, stands with other crew officers celebrating 50 missions completed, all but one aboard STINKY JR (Courtesy Cooper Schley).

45

LIEUTENANT JACK DOWNEY

DOB: July 21, 1918
Where: Chattanooga, Tennessee
Air Force: 8th
Bomb Group: 491st
Station: Metfield, England
Decorations include: Purple Heart, Air Medal, POW Medal. Jack hardly had time to settle in at his base before his B-24, with him as navigator, was shot down while bombing a German buzz bomb base on the northern coast of France. It was his seventh combat mission. Suffering from serious injuries, Jack spent the next nine months as a POW in *Stalag Luft 3* and *Stalag 7A*. After the war he was an attorney with the Veterans Administration before entering into private practice and real estate development.

Upside-down Chute

We took off in the afternoon from our base at Metfield, England, on what we thought would be a milk run just across the Channel to a buzz bomb base at Villers l'Hopital on the French coast. I was so unconcerned about this mission that I wore my parachute harness loosely rather than as tightly as possible, something that was drilled into us time and again during training. I wanted to be as comfortable as possible but my comfort level soon hit a new low.

We had had our share of dangerous missions where the sky was black with anti aircraft fire and targets were well defended but there wasn't much of that this time. As the navigator on our B-24 with a seat up front in the nose, I could clearly see the sky ahead and except for a small puff of black smoke in the distance, everything appeared smooth. Soon that puff was followed by another puff a little closer but still no need to worry. The third puff, though, hit very close to our ship, giving us a bump and knocking out the plane's controls.

The pilot was helpless and soon enough our plane went into a flat spin. Even though it sounds bad, a flat spin, at least initially, is better than a tight spin. In a tight spin the centrifugal force keeps you from being able to move, much less jump out of the plane. Fliers who would otherwise be able to leave their planes and perhaps survive were lost because they were trapped that way in their falling planes. With a flat spin there is time to jump, at least at first.

We kept going around and around and everyone was anxious to get out. To this day the bombardier insists I put my foot to his back and pushed him out the front escape hatch even though he barely had his chute on. When I saw him sitting in the hatch I thought he was frozen. I grabbed my own chute but was in such a hurry that I put it on upside down. I remember looking down while still spinning and seeing the words, "this side down." Not exactly encouraging words for someone facing such uncertainty.

Because my chute wasn't on right, I chose to pull the cord as soon as I fell free of the plane rather than waiting and counting to ten. That meant the Germans had a better bead on me but I figured I had a better chance of surviving, especially if I needed to open the chute manually and pull it out. Remember that loose harness? It came back to haunt me when I jumped because I suffered a broken pelvis when the chute opened violently. With all the excitement and confusion I didn't feel it at the time but it caused me some real problems later.

Jack Downey (courtesy Jackson Downey)

As for the rest of the crew, most of them jumped at roughly the same time and were captured quickly by the Germans. The pilot and engineer jumped later because they were trying to set up the autopilot. They ended up in the woods and were rescued by the French partisans. One of the gunners, a 19-year old kid named Tommy, died when his chute didn't open soon enough. That was a real tragedy. Tommy was a nice young man from New England who never even drank his post mission whiskey shots. He always gave them to me and I always gladly accepted.

I ended up being alone when I landed in a tree. Training called for me to cross my legs and fold my arms but instinct demands that you grab for a limb and that's what I did. Soon enough I fell to the ground and was knocked out. When I came to, a bunch of French civilians were hovering around me and planning to carry me off. I still didn't feel much pain from the broken pelvis. I was so eager to get out of there and probably still in shock that I was able to walk just a little with my arms around these strangers. I believe they were taking me to the hospital instead of to a hiding place, at least that's what they told the German soldiers who jumped us with machine guns drawn. My days of freedom were past and my time in captivity was just beginning.

I spent nine months in the hospital, at times in a cast from my chin to my toes, and at first was treated by a group of captured English doctors. That was at Lille, France, after being moved there by train and where, if I had stayed two weeks longer, I would have been liberated. But the Germans had other ideas so they went to all the trouble of putting me on a train again and sending me farther behind the lines. Eventually I ended up at *Stalag Luft 3* and then, along with thousands of other prisoners of many nationalities, marched and transported by railcar in the bitter, biting cold and snow of winter to *Stalag* 7-A.

That wasn't pleasant but I can't say I was terribly mistreated by the Germans while in captivity. I only weighed 145 pounds while in the service and even though our food wasn't very good I lost only about five pounds. We did stage our own protest at *Stalag* 7-A when we gathered outside the barracks and demanded that our captors fumigate our beds because they were infested with fleas and bed bugs. We were soon facing the business end of a machine gun and were told if we didn't go back in we would be shot. *Stalag* 7-A was a bad camp and overrun with prisoners. The Germans knew they were losing the war so they crowded the camp with prisoners from other facilities.

In April 1945, after several months at *Stalag* 7-A, we heard the booming guns of the Allied forces and knew that our liberation was coming. We were told to stay in our barracks but we could see out the doors and windows as our troops came in the front gate, including General Patton riding on one of the tanks. It seemed like we waited forever to get out of that place. A friend assigned me to a war crimes team. He gave me a jeep and told me to take statements from troops who had been prisoners. I had the choice of staying and working on that project or going home. Which choice do you think I made?

Today I think about my experiences during the war. Our crew never got back together, even at reunions.

46

SERGEANT ROBERT HOWELL, JR.

DOB: October 7, 1925
Where: Mount Juliet, Tennessee
Air Force: 15th
Bomb Group: 301st
Squadron: 32nd
Station: Foggia, Italy
Decorations include: Air Medal with clusters. Barely 19 years old, Bob found himself in the ball turret of a B-17, flying 21 combat missions before the war ended. As a gunner, he encountered some of the German jets introduced in the last stages of the war. Once the war ended Bob spent 28 years as a teacher before retiring and entering business for himself as a home designer.

Life as a Gunner

Combat training for us overseas-bound gunners included simulated fighter attacks by Bell King Cobra fighters. We "fired" at the fighters with cameras on our guns to record our scores. This was good practice for us gunners and for the pilots who trained flying in high-altitude, tight formation. During one of the simulated attacks we were flying in a big formation of bombers when a fighter hit a B-17 right behind the cockpit. The B-17 did a wing over and down into a spin. We thought all aboard were killed but when we got back to base we discovered that the copilot managed to get the big plane under control and back to base. The fighter pilot, who was a veteran of the Pacific campaign, was not hurt. His fighter disintegrated, throwing him clear.

Our crew arrived in Lincoln, Nebraska, to pick up a brand new B-17 for our flight overseas. We took her up for equipment tests and returned to base around dusk without incident. As I was coming back from chow I heard my name announced over the base PA system. I was directed to report to a particular barracks because my parents were there to visit me. That was the shock of my life. I grabbed my pilot and radio operator and we hurried over to see my mother and daddy. They had taken the train to Lincoln from Nashville, Tennessee. Since all trains around that time were crowded with troops, both of them had to stand up a great deal of the time. A young sailor gave up his seat for my mother during part of the trip. I remember daddy telling my pilot, "Here's my son, bring him back." Fifty-six years later when I saw the pilot again he remembered our meeting and those words as well as the Bible my mother brought me. There were lots of hugs and long goodbyes since we had to leave the next morning before daylight but I have always remembered the special, unexpected time I had with my parents.

We landed at Marrakesh, North Africa, on our way overseas and stayed in a little hotel away from base. Our orders restricted us from going into town but four of us decided we would go anyway. We crept through a hole in the city's walls and came face to waist with the biggest, tallest armed Arab we had every seen. We quickly moved around him and soon arrived at what looked like an athletic field. In the distance we saw a jeep kicking up a cloud of dust headed toward us. A captain, the provost marshal, jumped out and arrested us, exclaiming, "I've a good mind to put you on permanent KP! We don't have room to hold you overnight so report to a hearing at 0800 tomorrow morning. Be there! Dismissed!" By 0700 the next morning we were rolling down the runway to get out of that place, a little worried about MP's waiting for us at Tunis, our next stop.

Ground crews never got the credit they deserved. They worked day and night, eyes bloodshot, hands cracked and greasy, clothes rumpled, and eternally dirty. They worked so many hours they were sleepy most of the time. Our crew chief was a real salty dog. He was in his 30's and always had an unlit cigar sticking out of his mouth I suppose because he worked around gasoline all the time. "Don't you mess up my airplane today," he would say about our plane. "You may get some holes in it but take care of it." I would wake up during the night and hear the engines being run up on the planes for testing purposes. All kinds of specialists would work all night long to keep our planes in the air. When one finished his job he would move over and help his buddy finish his task. There was always an important job to be accomplished with the ultimate goal of keeping each ship airworthy.

After 15 missions, I was sent on rest leave to the Isle of Capri for 10 days. I stayed at a small hotel and had a great time. Years later, I found the same hotel. My wife and I walked in and immediately spotted a short, grey-haired fellow, the manager. I told him I had been in the very same place during World War II. He told me he was there as well. As a little boy he had hung around the hotel to earn a little money or food carrying the duffel bags of troops staying there.

There were relief tubes positioned at several points in our B-17 for those who needed to relieve themselves during missions. I had such a tube in the ball turret but it was useless since it always froze during flight. A gunner who had almost finished his tour gave me some good advice early into my time overseas. "Drink

Robert Howell, Jr. (courtesy Robert Howell, Jr.)

your water at night," he said. "Don't drink any water the morning of a mission, just a few sips of coffee if you need it." From then on, my normal pre-mission breakfast included a slice of bread with orange marmalade and a few sips of coffee.

I didn't go into town to get drunk like many of my fellow fliers did. Instead, I enjoyed going down the flight line, observing B-17s and learning all I could about them. Even though I was a gunner, I ended up with 15 hours of instrument flying in the base link trainer as well as 10 hours of radio range work. I tried to learn all I could during my time overseas. I was about the only one of my crew who loved to fly.

I remember very fondly the work of the Red Cross at our Foggia, Italy, base. After each mission its mobile unit would greet us with steaming hot coffee in mugs and some doughnuts. Nothing tasted better. It was a pretty sight for a crew coming back from a tough mission. "How did it go today?" the girls asked us. "You look like you could fly another mission." They didn't probe too much. They knew exactly what to ask and how to ask it, providing us with some very important positive reinforcement.

90, 95, 100?

My closest call occurred in February 1945, on takeoff. I remember it as a dry day at our Foggia, Italy, base. Each engine on our B-17 had reached maximum power of 2,550 revolutions per minute. They checked out perfectly. We taxied out and lined up for takeoff. When the plane in front of us got to the end of the runway, our plane with its full bomb load slowly came to life and started rolling. "Seventy, 75, 80," the engineer called out our air speed in five-mile increments. We knew this was one of the most dangerous times of any mission.

I sat in the radio room behind the bomb bay watching the control cables moving as we rumbled over the steel mat runway, quickly gaining speed. "Eighty-five, 90, 95" the engineer intoned with what sounded like concern. We kept rolling and rolling and rolling. None of us could see what was going on but we all felt something wasn't right. We were approaching the end of the runway and still hadn't hit the minimum speed of 110 miles per hour for takeoff. The plane lurched upward as the pilot tried desperately to pull it up. But I could feel the plane sinking and cold, hard fear suddenly hit me.

We knew we were going in. We had seen a plane do the same thing a month earlier and it wasn't pretty. Normally at this point the copilot flipped a switch and the landing gear retracted but this time the pilot, Jim Stynes, gave a thumbs down for the gear to remain down. He bounced that plane hard on the ground and all of us thought the gear would collapse but somehow it didn't. Our ship bounced off the field beyond the runway, back up in the air, and that was when the miracle happened.

The manifold pressure and the rpm on the number three engine returned to normal. After bouncing off the ground with a load of twelve, 500-pound bombs and 2,780 gallons of 100-octane fuel and having our landing gear withstand such a jolt, we finally lumbered into the air. The pilot, Stynes, later told me he thought we were gone. That didn't make me feel any better. Stynes was a veteran pilot, having completed a tour in the Pacific flying B-24s before coming over to Europe to fly B-17s.

The engine ran perfectly throughout the rest of our mission to and from Brux, Germany. Something strange and inexplicable happened when we bounced hard off the ground. Instead of the landing gear and wings folding up and us dying in a gigantic ball of flame, we lived to fly another day. Other pilots who saw all this happen and the people in the tower thought we were all gone. "You don't know how lucky you are," they told us reassuringly. After the mission I shook like a dog passing peach seeds.

A Drunk Major

"At the convenience of the government, you gentlemen will become gunners." With those words, all chances and hopes of me going to flight school went out the window. It seems that at the time Uncle Sam needed gunners more than pilots. So I went to Kingman, Arizona, for gunnery training and even though I was never a hunter and didn't have much experience firing guns, I had fun. Six of us students would get into the back of a pickup truck with an instructor and travel around a perimeter track at about 40 miles per hour all the while shooting our 12 gauge shotguns at clay targets. I did other things to prepare for my eventual job as a ball turret gunner on a B-17 but this helped me to discover some good natural instincts that I never knew I had.

We were all nervous on our first mission as we gathered around our plane before daylight. It promised to be a long day: an eight-hour mission to Brux, where we expected to encounter some heavy flak. As we were getting ready to board and just before start engine time, a jeep suddenly skidded to a stop nearby. As soon as the jeep stopped, a heavy-set major, drunk as he could be and red-faced, staggered out, bragging about his flying abilities and his prowess with women. He really thought he was putting on a show. He walked around the nose of the airplane and proudly announced to all of us, "Time to board."

Well, the major, who was our operations officer and also a check pilot, couldn't pull himself into the nose hatch so the pilot had to boost him up. After he finally got him in his cockpit seat, the pilot put an oxygen mask on the major to help sober him up. The pilot, who sat in the copilot's seat for this mission, was pretty nervous throughout the whole ordeal but managed to help get the plane taxied out. I remember sitting in the radio room just behind the bomb bay and watching the control cables for the plane's rudder. The major had that plane moving all over the runway on takeoff but the ship managed to stagger off and up in the air.

Before we got to the target, the major was fairly sober. I heard later that he often volunteered his own crew for night missions and that they never got a scratch through it all.

47

SERGEANT ROBERT SHEEHAN

DOB: January 3, 1923
Where: Eufaula, Alabama
Air Force: 8th
Bomb Group: 445th
Squadron: 700th
Station: Tibenham, England
Decorations include: Air Medal with clusters, POW Medal. On September 27, 1944, Bob was flying his thirteenth combat mission as a B-24 radio operator/top turret gunner when his plane was shot down. He was captured and remained a POW until April 25, 1945. While claiming not to be a hero, his story is one of courage and survival. Following the war Bob worked for 36 years with Bell South. He became an avid runner, participating in many marathons.

Bloody Kassel

I was a radio operator on a B-24 bomber named *Little Audrey*. We left Norfolk, Virginia, and flew to England the first week of July 1944. Our destination was the airbase at Ipswich, north of London. There, we were assigned to the 8th Air Force, 2nd Air Division, 445th Bomb Group. After practice missions, we started bombing missions over Germany in late July until our fateful thirteenth mission on September 27, 1944.

Our target was the railroad yards at Kassel, Germany. After breakfast, briefing, and prayer with the chaplain, we boarded our planes for our mission. There were about 1,000 bombers that flew over England that day and I still can't understand how that many planes flying that close didn't collide.

Let me say here that I grew up in a Christian home and, as a young person, accepted Christ. During my time in combat I felt the Lord was with me and that things would work out. We were young and inexperienced. Although I hadn't been anywhere or done anything I felt like I would come away okay. I was always optimistic. I also felt that if things didn't work out, I'd go to a better place. At 21, I wasn't ready to go but I also knew it wasn't my call.

When our planes were assembling into formation, it was amazing. I'd look out in every direction — up, down, sideways — airplanes were everywhere. Several hundred fighters (P-38s and P-51s) flew ahead of us to strafe the flak batteries in the target area and to escort us into the target. As we turned on the initial point toward our target, the crew threw out some chaff (aluminum foil) to disrupt the enemy radar. On earlier missions we had some problems with the bomb bay doors closing prematurely so my job was to sit on the flight deck, three feet above the bomb bay, and hold my foot on the manual lever.

Now get this picture: I'm looking down 25,000 feet and all my life I have been afraid of heights. In fact, anything over five feet and my wife, Betty, has to hold the ladder. This was not my favorite assignment. Since there was no radio contact during a bomb run I didn't have anything else to do unless I replaced the top turret gunner. So I was chosen to sit in the bomb bay. I sat up on the flight deck with the bomb bay door handle to my left and held my foot on the handle to keep it open. The bombardier would say "Bombs Away!" and then my job was to confirm that all the bombs had dropped. If not, I had to kick the bombs out. I never had to do that, thank goodness.

I was wearing a flight suit with oxygen mask and a flight helmet but no parachute; my chest chute was in my seat. The plane was rocking around and the wind was whistling and I was really shook up. I didn't dwell on my bomb bay job, I just had to do it. I looked down and watched the German gunners shooting up at us and saw the puffs of flak gradually coming toward us. The shells from three anti-aircraft guns in a four-gun battery of 88s burst below us. The last burst was 500 feet below us and the next blast would have hit us but it didn't fire.

As we neared the target area, our group made a navigational error. Instead of bombing the railroad yards at Kassel, we bombed a target 45 miles southeast of Kassel. We were separated from the main strike force because of our error so we didn't have fighter protection. Over the years, there has been lots of speculation about why the mistake was made. I know that it was heavily overcast and we couldn't see the other planes.

We ended up bombing a target just outside Gottingen. As we turned to head for England, behind the others that had hit Kassel as planned, our world changed completely. We were attacked by waves of Fw 190s and Me 109s. According to mission reports, we lost 25 of our 35 planes in five minutes. The German fighters were coming at us from underneath because they knew we didn't have our ball turret guns; they had been removed to give us stability in flying at altitude and to reduce weight. It was reported that our losses were the heaviest for any 8th Air Force group in the war. In spite of the losses, our group bombed the same target with fewer planes the next day.

I was on the flight deck when we got hit. Within minutes, I looked out and the number two engine was completely blown away. The number three engine on the other side was blown out. We were flying on two engines. The tail gunner position suffered a direct hit, shattering the glass

Robert Sheehan (courtesy Steve Sheehan)

47. Sergeant Bob Sheehan

and cutting the gunner's face. The nose gunner was hurt and one of the waist gunners was badly injured. The pilot had me go to the waist of the plane to see what I could do to help. When I got back there, the tail gunner was bleeding and the waist gunner was dying. I did what I could to stop the bleeding.

We were dropping down to tree top level and throwing everything overboard. The other waist gunner kept firing at the attacking planes. The lower we got, the more small arms fire we took. I started back toward the flight deck through the bomb bay. When I got there the engineer, Jim Engleman, grabbed me and pushed me down. We were about to crash but I hadn't heard the crash alarm. We quickly assumed the crash landing position: my back to the pilot, facing each other, our feet together and holding hands. I had just barely got into that position when our plane belly-landed on the side of a hill.

Upon impact, the propeller from the number one engine sheared off and cut the fuselage overhead like a can opener. Had I been sitting straight up, my head would have been taken off. Surprisingly, the B-24 didn't catch fire even though we saw sparks and smelled gasoline. I found myself looking into the open air but my foot was caught on the backrest of the bench near me. "Jim!" I yelled, "Do whatever it takes, break it if necessary." He was able to twist my foot free and we climbed out of the hole cut by the propeller. I quickly made it back

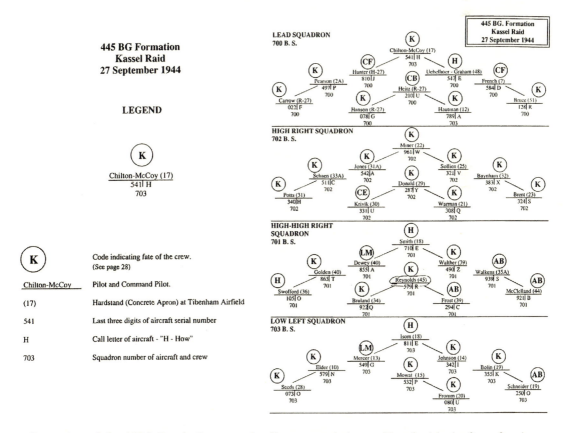

Formation of the 445th Bomb Group on its disastrous mission to Kassel with the fate of each crew. Bob Sheehan flew as a gunner on the Reynolds crew, 701st squadron. He served the rest of the war as a POW. The legend is K: shot down over Germany; CF: crashed, France; CB: crashed, Belgium; CE: crashed, England; H: back safely to Tibenham; LM: landed, Manston; AB: aborted. (Courtesy Steve Sheehan)

to the waist of the plane and saw that two of the guys were dead. Then I heard the navigator screaming that his head was caught between the fuselage and the top turret. He lived but I don't know how. Without question, Jim Engleman saved my life.

We had crashed somewhere near Eisenach. Of our 236 crewmen missing in action from the Kassel trip, 112 were killed including one of our crew who died in the hospital after bleeding to death. He was a hemophiliac and we didn't know it. The Germans quickly arrived with their guns pointing at us and told us to get out. I will always remember September 27, 1944, and our thirteenth mission. On that day I began an odyssey that led me through so many hair-raising experiences I couldn't begin to imagine any of them happening to me.

The Death March

Of a crew of nine on my B-24, six of us walked away from a crash landing after the terrible mission to Kassel. Somehow we had made a navigational error and bombed the wrong target. Fighters jumped us and we were one of 25 planes from our group to go down. Our group suffered the greatest number of losses of any mission flown by the 8th Air Force.

We were immediately surrounded by German soldiers, loaded on a truck, and carried to local Luftwaffe headquarters for interrogation. Besides name, rank, and serial number they wanted to know the plane we were in and the name of our base. They tried to fool us into believing they knew everything but all I provided was name, rank, and serial number. We were taken to a *Dulag Luft*, a temporary holding facility, at Frankfurt on Main for further questioning. Then the Germans took us by streetcar to a former school converted into a prison. The cell I entered was about 8 × 10, housing 20 to 25 men, most sitting on benches.

When I walked in, they stopped talking and looked at me with obvious suspicion even though I was still wearing my flight jacket. After a while they asked me how the war was going. "Ya'll don't have anything to worry about," I said, "the Germans can't hold out much longer." They laughed and knew I wasn't a German posing as a POW because no German could say "y'all" with such a southern accent. I was in that cell one day before being moved by rail to my permanent POW camp, *Stalag* IV, in Pomerania, northeast of Berlin. God spared me again en route because the Berlin rail yards took a ferocious beating from Allied bombers the night I was being moved. The earth shook and bombs hit fairly close but my boxcar wasn't hit.

At *Stalag IV*, the gates opened and the guards greeted us with guns drawn. The camp had four compounds with 10 barracks and 200 men in each barrack. Food was scarce, mainly sour red cabbage, kohlrabi (like a big turnip) and some small amount of meat we were afraid to identify. We loved the kohlrabi even thought it was a common food fed to cattle.

I think the Germans were undecided about how to treat us since the Russians were getting closer. Since noncoms didn't have to work, life for us was the same each day. When the sun came up, the windows were opened and we were left on our own. That meant walking around the compound, visiting with friends, sometimes playing a supervised game of baseball, and, especially around Christmas, playing music on the few instruments sent to us by the Red Cross. We spent lots of time trying to take care of ourselves; we dealt with the constant problem of lice and other pests.

Our leaders, chosen by the prisoners, brought us word from the Germans and, in addition, each compound had designated radio men who would surreptitiously listen to the Armed Forces Network and the BBC. Lookouts were posted to alert us when the Germans approached.

47. Sergeant Bob Sheehan

We also had to report to roll call every morning and be counted. One of the guards we would regularly see we nicknamed "Stoop" because he was so tall, about 6'6". He was a mean guy with a stooped over body that made him look even more intimidating.

We didn't get much to eat, but we survived. It helped not to be physically beaten, although I heard of such things going on elsewhere in the camp. There was always the threat of such action but we simply adjusted the best we could.

On February 7, 1945, after four months, we left camp. Our departure turned into an 86-day march covering 600 miles in the coldest part of winter. The purpose was to escape the oncoming Russians. This has become known as "the death march" to historians and those familiar with our plight. After covering 20 miles the first day, I felt like I couldn't go on, but there was no escape and we certainly had no weapons. Our march took us through northern Germany near the Baltic Sea, past the Nazi sub base at Swinemunde. We headed west toward the Allied lines, trying to avoid the Russians.

One day we were walking through beautiful farm country when we spotted a stand by the road with a 50-gallon milk container on it. Farmers had put their milk there to be picked up and sold in town. It was hot and we didn't have anything to drink so a few of us jumped up on the stand and used our battered tin cups to dip into the milk. The mouth of the container was just bigger than my cup. All of a sudden, everyone jumped down from the stand and I'm left standing there by myself when I looked up and saw a German guard with his gun pointed at me. He quickly and forcefully ordered me down. Why he didn't shoot me I'll never know.

We had little to eat on the march except what we could "liberate." We didn't consider our actions to be stealing since this was a matter of survival. One night 200 of us stayed at a huge farm with a large manor house and several small laborer houses. While my partner got us a place to sleep in the barn, I left to find us some food. All the guards were in a meeting elsewhere, getting their assignments. I knocked on the door of a laborer's house and when no one answered I walked in. I saw a lady standing at a stove. Neither of us could understand the other but when I held up my cup and indicated I was hungry she filled it with rabbit stew. Just as I started to leave there was a knock on the door. I looked out and there standing was a German soldier. I hid behind the door not knowing whether she would tell the soldier about me. I couldn't understand what they said but I was very grateful she kept my secret. When the solider left I thanked the lady for her generosity. We found out later she was one of the slave laborers from a conquered country. That night my partner and I were the only ones to dine on rabbit stew.

On another day we stopped walking early and word came around that the Germans couldn't get anyone to peel the potatoes they were giving us for soup. I went to one of the leaders and asked him if those who peeled potatoes could be first in the chow line. I got people peeling potatoes and, sure enough, we got to go first. The soup was like something from heaven. They kept filling my can and I thought later how selfish I was for taking as much of it as I did. So the next time I decided I'd wait until everyone got his soup before taking mine. Wouldn't you know it, the soup ran out before it got to me. I remember thinking how stupid I was.

I wasn't raised on a farm but I slipped away from our group one day and into a barn to milk a cow. I couldn't get anything to come out. Not one drop from a cow that obviously had plenty to give. I just didn't have the right touch. The farmer walked in on me and wasn't pleased when he saw what I was doing. I got out of there as quickly as I could.

We made our way back to north of Berlin and were put on trains with 100 men to each car. We got on the train on Good Friday 1945, and got off the train on Easter Sunday in

Magdeburg. While there, we slept in huge tents, about 1,000 men per tent. It was so crowded we couldn't turn over so we had to sleep in the same position all night.

We were liberated on April 25, 1945. The Germans just let us go so we walked across a bridge over the Elbe River and into the American line. As we crossed, we threw our lice-infected things into the river. I remember gawking at some of the American soldiers who must have weighed 165 pounds and thinking how big they were. My weight was down to about 115 pounds.

After liberation, our military didn't know what to do with us. We stayed close to a big mess hall in a headquarters area. I still had not gotten any good clothes; I wore an English jacket, GI pants, British flying boots, and some kind of cap. I saw guys coming out of the mess hall and noticed they were raking their leftovers into a garbage can. I went over with my cup and asked if they would rake their leftovers into it. One of them said, "Who are you?" I told him and he said, "Come on in here and get you some food." After delousing we were given GI clothes.

We were flown to Rheims, France, and were there when the Germans officially surrendered. Then it was on to Camp Lucky Strike at Le Havre.

Ike

After our liberation from POW camp, we were flown to Camp Lucky Strike at LeHavre, France. Because of being in a prison camp we were restricted to what and how much we could eat, just so our bodies could get used to eating decent food again. I was in the chow line one day when I looked up and saw a lot of "brass," generals and colonels, standing close to the serving line. This was a huge area; you walked through a serving line and into big tents nearby.

I walked through the chow line with my tray and one of the servers asked, "Would you like another steak?" This generosity occurred on down the line with other types of food. I thought I'd died and gone to heaven. So I entered one of the tents and sat down at a table with some other guys. There was a lieutenant sitting across from me when this civilian came through. It turned out to be U.S. Senator Tom Connally from Texas. The senator went up to the lieutenant, put his hand on his shoulder, and asked how everything was going. "I just wish I could get away from here," replied the officer. "They promised us we could leave." Connally replied, "Hold that thought."

The next thing I know Senator Connally is back and he has with him none other than the Supreme Allied Commander, General Eisenhower himself. Ike put his hand on the lieutenant's shoulder and the lieutenant almost turned the table over trying to get up. "I understand you're having some troubles trying to get home." Ike then turned around and spoke to all the men in the tent. "I want you boys to know how much I appreciate what you did, what you have been through, and I want you to know that you will either be home or on your way within a few weeks." What welcome words those were! We all gave him a round of applause.

Well, I was so excited I didn't finish my food. I just got up and started following General Eisenhower. I walked behind him to see people's reactions as they discovered our Supreme Commander in their midst. His visit raised morale more than anything. I was aware of how big he was but he seemed even bigger to me, since I had lost so much weight as a POW. He had broad shoulders and his Ike jacket looked great on him. I still remember the incredulous looks people had when they spotted him. They almost broke their arms saluting as he walked by.

Throughout my experiences — being shot down on our thirteenth mission, time in prison camp, the death march — I felt God's presence. I thought all along I would make it but there was always the assurance of my salvation and I knew that God was in control.

48

LIEUTENANT BOB CARTWRIGHT

DOB: August 19, 1923
Where: Gallatin, Tennessee
Air Force: 8th
Bomb Group: 379th
Squadron: 527th
Station: Kimbolton, England
Decorations include: Air Medal with clusters. Maybe it was the carrots he was told to go home and eat but Bob finally passed the color test portion of the eye chart exam all pilots took. Trained as a B-24 pilot, he and his crew were told they would fly B-17s once they arrived in England. The transition was smoothly made. Bob ended up with 35 combat missions, some flown in a plane named for a famous English actress, *Lady Anna*. Once the war ended, he worked in footwear engineering for 36 years.

Hits and Misses

Basic training while staying in a luxury hotel at Miami Beach sounds nice but it was a lot of mopping and scrubbing. We were all scared of a particular sergeant. Maybe it was because one day he wanted everybody who could type. Those guys who stepped forward got the job of carrying mattresses up four or five floors. That's when we learned to never volunteer for anything.

During training at Maxwell Field, I was impressed with the drum outs. We were called out in the middle of the night with sudden banging on our doors and told we had only a few minutes to form up wearing our Class A uniforms. We marched to a certain point to be met by an officer holding a scroll. By flashlight, the officer read a name and said that person had been caught cheating. As a result, his name would never be mentioned again at Maxwell Field. Scared us to death.

Every now and then while flying an AT-10 during training at Stuttgart, Arkansas, my instructor would take over and say, "Let's go down for a ride." He would reach down and pick up some gravel off the ground before we took off and put it in his pocket. Once in the air he reached in that pocket and threw it out onto the tin roof of his girlfriend's house. She would come out and excitedly wave at us. I got my wings at Stuttgart, the most exciting thing that ever happened to me.

One instructor I had in basic training nearly washed me out. Even though four of us were supposed to solo after ten hours, none had. We got up to 14 hours without a solo and we all had the same opinion of this guy. He would take us up, sit in the rear of the plane, and proceed to tell us that the plane would fly a whole lot better by itself. "Hold the stick as if you were holding an egg, just nice and easy." Then he would disregard everything he just said and jerk the stick back and forth, bruising our knees. Eventually we were taken away from him and soloed quickly. He was one of those instructors who was dying to go overseas but couldn't.

I picked up my crew at Lincoln, Nebraska. Then we went to Tucson for combat training. I never had a problem with my crew except one who was a smart aleck. Those of us still around get together when we can.

December 1944, found us heading overseas on the *SS Manhattan*. I discovered a friend from Goodlettsville, Tennessee, down on the very bottom deck. He was on the top bunk of a four-bunk stack hanging his head over the side puking into a two-gallon bucket. The smell and the heat were just awful. He told me he would never leave Goodlettsville if he ever got back home.

We arrived at Liverpool and were transported to our base at Kimbolton, a B-17 base. I said there must be some mistake, we're a B-24 crew. We really didn't mind switching to the B-17. To me, it had a better wing but poorer engines. The big problem for us was converting from one type of landing gear to another. We had 20 days to learn how to handle the plane, most of it practice landings. From a pilot standpoint, the 17 was far easier to fly.

We had a 19-year old navigator who would always lay his cap on his desk during bomb runs and start counting off the seconds beginning with 120, all of this over the intercom. It just about drove us crazy. On a mission to Berlin, a piece of flak flew through his cap, hitting an orange he had in it. Seeds and juice went everywhere and the orange disappeared. That was the last time he counted.

Our thirty-third mission took us to Oranienburg. We had just turned off the target when Walter Howard, on our right wing in the high element, failed to anticipate the loss of his position because he had farther to go to catch up with the rest of us. Basically, he fell asleep at the switch and lost formation. He was picked off by a Me 262 which was then picked off by our top turret gunner. Walter became a POW and our engineer, Chris Yeakos, got credit for a kill.

My copilot invariably had to urinate within an hour after takeoff. At that point he

Bob Cartwright (courtesy Mary Cartwright)

would be on oxygen. It was not practical to get a portable oxygen bottle to enable him to get up and go to the relief tube. So a large grapefruit juice can was kept handy to help him with his dilemma. This same copilot never learned to keep close check on his oxygen supply. There was an indicator on the instrument panel with two lips which opened each time a breath of oxygen was inhaled. When they stopped opening, it was an indication that the tube to the mask had frozen. He would sit there in a partial coma until the engineer reached over and squeezed the tube, breaking up the ice clog.

We spent one of the coldest winters in England's history on base. The coal truck delivered coal to the barracks during the day so if you were flying you got no coal. The pot-bellied stoves at either end of the barracks did a meager job of heating the place even when there was coal. Our practice was to go down to the barbed wire–enclosed coal yard at night. We'd hoist somebody over the fence to fill our tow sacks and then drag the sacks of coal back to our barracks where we'd stow them under our beds. Inspections were rare so we were never caught.

On Saturday night, there would be a dance at the officers' club. Trucks fanned out to the neighboring towns and picked up the girls for the dance. The girls were first interested in getting a good meal since their daily rations weren't much. While they ate buffet style, the men drank and then came to the dance. Afterwards, the girls were loaded on the trucks and taken home. No men were allowed on the trucks but my friend made a valiant try at it every Saturday night.

In the wee hours of the morning, I was never sleeping so deeply that I didn't hear the creak of the door being opened and then feel the gentle nudge of the orderly as he stated the time of the breakfast and the briefing. In the briefing room there was never any horseplay. Momentarily the target would be known, either a milk run or one of the killers, long or short. With a dramatic flair, the curtain was pulled and a red ribbon stretched across the map to the target, sometimes with accompanying groans and sighs.

Of the four crews who came over from Tucson, two were lost; one by a flak hit, the other from an enemy fighter. So upon reaching the North Sea and beginning our descent, we maintained a vigilant eye for marauders. As we reached 10,000 feet and removed our oxygen masks, someone broke out the Hershey bars and the cigarettes. After five or six hours on oxygen, nothing could have been more satisfying. We knew we were close to home.

Lady Anna

On April 9 our crew "stood down," or was relieved of duty for the day. The noted British actress Anna Neagle and her movie director husband, Herbert Wilcox, were at our base to christen a fairly new B-17 which had just arrived and had been assigned to us. We were all treated to a steak dinner at the MP mess hall. Mr. Wilcox was very entertaining, enthralling us with stories about his World War I experiences as a bombardier in an open-cockpit, two seat plane. He told us how he sat in the back seat with a box between his legs and, every time a target presented itself, would reach into the box, grab a 25-pound bomb, hold it over the cowl, aim by his eye, and let go. He certainly had a great flair for story telling.

After dinner, we all went out to the new plane and had a picture taking session. Mrs. Neagle christened the plane *Lady Anna* as another bottle of champagne went down the drain. She and her husband invited our crew to dinner in London on some convenient night. Though none of the rest of the crew saw fit to accept the invitation, I joined the famous couple in the dining room at the famous, swank Claridge Hotel on April 22. I do not remember what we

Lt. Bob Cartwright and his crew with British actress Anna Neagle in front of the B-17 named in her honor, *Lady Anna*. While it was proclaimed a new plane, it was not, having seen combat action and the death of at least one crewmember. Cartwright stands over the left shoulder of Ms. Neagle (Courtesy Bob Cartwright).

ate but I do recall that one waiter was assigned to each of us at our table for three. It was a very elegant dining room with the sound muffled somewhat, probably due to the heavy carpet and drapes. I was not accustomed to such service which, I suppose, was given titled persons or people who had distinguished themselves in their professions. The waiter made me somewhat uncomfortable by placing my napkin in my lap and replacing every swallow of water drunk from my glass.

I am inclined to think that in their busy lives my two hosts were probably glad to fulfill their obligation and move on. They could not have been nicer and my recollection more memorable.

The thing we didn't know when we got *Lady Anna* was that it wasn't a new plane. It had already flown several missions, including one during which the navigator had been killed. I didn't know that until 1992 when my friend in England, who had become an authority on the 379th Bomb Group, told me. He was in the first grade at a nearby school and whenever our planes took off his whole class would jump up and run to the windows to watch.

I flew *Lady Anna* until I finished my missions. Then it flew three more during the war before being transferred to the 91st Bomb Group at Bassingbourn for the return flight to the U.S. She arrived at Bradley Field, Connecticut, and was earmarked for storage at Plains, North Dakota. Ultimately, *Lady Anna* was declared excess property and was transferred to the famous desert storage facility at Kingman, Arizona, in December 1945. She languished there until she was eventually melted down.

Finding Our Way Home

Mid-February 1945, and we were on a mission to Dresden, one of our longer trips to target. Flak and fighters were not a problem at the target but, as we passed over enemy lines upon our return, we encountered heavy AA fire. Our squadron lost one crew, my plane's Gee Box, a navigational device, was knocked out, and we were low on fuel. Formation flying increases gas consumption so we decided to drop out of the formation, throttle back, and go it alone, stragglers in the vastness of the enemy's sky. Easy pickings for the *Luftwaffe*!

Soon a couple of fighters appeared as specks in the distance. We expected them to be Germans but, as they flew nearer, we were happy to see our own P-51 Mustangs. By waggling their wings, they indicated their intention to help. They lowered their wing flaps so that they could get enough lift to fly at our slower speed and positioned themselves on either side of our plane. They lead us to a recently liberated fighter strip at Liege, Belgium, an area of countless bomb craters and general destruction. Bulldozers had been feverishly working to create some kind of landing surface and workers had just placed a steel mat down to meet the need. We landed and gassed up but could not get our Gee Box repaired.

For security's sake, different sections of the English coast were designated daily as places to enter the country from the Channel. Crossing the English coast from any other spot was definitely not recommended since the English had a reputation for having no mercy. Any intruder was shot down.

Each plane carried a Very pistol which was used to fire flares for identification. Each day, a different set of three colors was designated the colors of the day. If the need for identification arose, these colored flares were to be fired in the correct order. Our engineer had been warned that if placed in such a situation to make certain the flares were fired properly. Darkness had already fallen when we crossed the coast. All of a sudden, in the inky blackness of night, we found ourselves in the crossfire of several searchlights. Our engineer lost his cool and, in his excitement, began firing flares one after another with no regard for color. The scene looked like the fireworks on closing night at the state fair. I will never know why we were allowed to continue unscathed.

Safe now, at least inside the country, there was the problem of finding our home base. The English had devised a very clever system for helping us. The entire country was divided into areas of 10 miles in size. In each area, there was a radio with only a 10-mile range, and all on the same frequency. An aircraft could tune in to this frequency and from the station below request a heading to such and such a place. For those planes that had lost radio reception, the station below would turn on a searchlight and, from a straight up position, lay the beam to horizontal, indicating the heading for your request. As the aircraft passed from one 10-mile area to another, the whole procedure would be duplicated until the plane eventually arrived at its destination. This system of lighting the way back home obviously could not be monitored by a listening enemy and, at least in our case, proved to be critical for a successful return to base.

49

LIEUTENANT JERRY NEAL

DOB: April 7, 1921
Where: Kansas City, Missouri
Air Force: 8th
Bomb Group: 490th
Squadron: 849th
Station: Eye, England
Decorations include: Distinguished Flying Cross, Air Medal with clusters. During the war Jerry piloted the B-17 but most of his 35 combat missions were flown inside the B-24. He was awarded the DFC for accumulated deep penetration flights into Germany. Several members of his crew were lost in the crash landing of their B-24 on D-Day. Jerry remained in the air force reserve, serving in administrative positions. He retired after 20 years as a captain. His professional career included sales and marketing positions with Honeywell and owning a distribution business.

Going Down on D-Day

We were told about our mission at the morning briefing and learned that it was in support of the beginning of the invasion of Europe. Our group was to destroy roads going into and out of Caen, France. Some of those roads lead directly to the beaches so by destroying them we could block the German Panzers from getting to the fight.

We left our base in East Anglia for a short distance mission, flying at a low altitude of about 12,000 to 15,000 feet because we would have to visually identify the target. The day was hazy, Caen was in from the beaches a few miles, and we didn't know where our troops would be by then. We had to be sure that we were not bombing our own men. When we reached the target we could not see the ground through the haze so we circled and circled. Finally we had to return to base because we were running out of fuel.

My plane was flying the "tail end Charlie" position thus we ran out of fuel because we had to fly farther. With no fuel, the engines stopped. Seven of our crew bailed out, leaving the navigator, the other pilot, and me in the plane. The glide pattern of the B-24 with the

Davis wing design and its low lift properties and with heavy bombs still on board meant we weren't going far.

We saw a rock/sandbar in our glide path and I started trying to land on that when I remembered the bombs! I pulled the salvo lever in the plane and dropped the bombs in the English Channel. Fortunately, we were so low that the bombs didn't fall far enough to arm themselves. We started sliding. We hit a shack and then clipped telephone poles, damaging our wings. The bomb bay door, which had remained open, acted like a big shovel and we collected dirt and rocks which tore off the rear half of the fuselage and then all four engines including the mounting brackets in the wings.

The nose tore off when we hit the shack and it ground off the front fuselage all the way to the flight deck. When we finally stopped, we had some wing structure and the flight deck but nothing else. The strong wing saved us. None of the crew had any broken bones but we were very sore that next day.

Jerry Neal (courtesy Jerry Neal)

Incredibly, we three walked out of the plane and, within an hour or two, were picked up by the English. We went to the headquarters of the military in that area, reported in to our base and asked that an ambulance be sent in case our crewmembers who had parachuted were in need of assistance. We searched all the medical units looking for them and found three. We spent five or six days searching for the others but four of our crew were lost. All other planes in our group got back to base, reloaded, and went back to the target.

There are stories of other missions — planes limping home on one engine, planes so damaged by flak that they were put in the scrap heap, crewmembers shot and killed inside their planes — yet we continued our missions. I was not particularly religious at the time but you can't fly combat without realizing that there is a God with a master plan. Psychologically, you adopt an attitude of almost fatalism. If you don't expect to come back and don't make plans for afterwards, you don't have to worry if you will make it. You just execute your professional training to the best of your ability to get your job done and your people back to base safely.

I completed my required 35 missions and got back to the U.S. at Christmas 1944. I expected to be retrained to go to the Pacific so, after a 30-day Christmas leave, I was deployed to a base in California where I was tested physically and psychologically to determine my next assignment. For the first time, I was asked what I wanted to do. I told them I would like to be a multi–engine bomber pilot instructor. I was told I'd get my orders in ten days. When the orders arrived, I was assigned to instructor school for single engine fighter pilots. I wasn't a fighter pilot but a bomber pilot. Typical army!

50

LIEUTENANT BOB ELLIOTT

DOB: August 16, 1924
Where: Chattanooga, Tennessee
Air Force: 8th
Bomb Group: 389th
Squadron: 566th
Station: Hethel, England
Decorations include: Air Medal with clusters. Of Bob's 18 combat missions as a B-24 pilot one of the most exciting was his fifth mission, a Berlin run, in April 1945. Two engines were damaged by flak and his bomb load landed in a lake before he nursed his B-24 back to a fighter base, landing in the grass at Koblenz, Germany. For over 50 years after the war Bob worked in the insurance business, eventually owning two agencies.

Galloping Katy

One of the toughest missions we had as a crew was aboard *Galloping Katy*, a B-24 with, as it turned out, a short future. We flew out of Hethel Air Base, Norwich, England, as part of the 8th Air Force, 389th Bomb Group, headed for Berlin. I believe it was my ninth or tenth mission as copilot. Berlin was always heavily defended but on this day it seemed doubly so.

The flak exploded all around us on our bomb run when all of a sudden the plane seemed to just lift straight up. Hits to our plane had rendered numbers two and three engines inoperative. The only ones we had left were the two outside engines, one and four. Number three engine operated the hydraulic system so we had to do some quick figuring.

I still don't understand how we avoided catching fire. The plane was shaking all over as we tried to feather both dead engines. Thank God we had an engineer who remained calm throughout the ordeal. He was a big guy who had played football at Michigan State. While the bombardier had control of the plane on the bomb run, I yelled for the engineer to crank the bomb bay doors open. We dropped our load short of the target. I believe the bombs ended up in a lake. Then we had our work cut out for us trying to keep up with the rest of the formation.

50. Lieutenant Bob Elliott

Bob Elliott (courtesy Bob Elliott)

We had a young nose gunner from Clearwater, Florida, who panicked during all the turmoil. He wanted to bail out. We had a hard time trying to get him settled down. Finally, the navigator hog-tied him and sat on him to keep him in the plane. I know strange things happen in combat but I guess I never thought I would see that. Trying to catch up with our group on two engines wasn't possible because we were too slow and were losing altitude at the same time. We were lucky not to be hit by the *Luftwaffe*.

At about 10,000 feet we thought we saw some friendly planes. It was a fighter base near Koblenz, Germany. They were busy flying P-47 sorties off a wire mat runway so we landed in the grass nearby. The Germans repaid our friendly visit to Berlin by flying over that night and riddling *Galloping Katy*. That ended her combat career.

The British got us to Brussels and the American Red Cross where we chowed down on hot food and finally scraped off our filthy flight suits. I believe I had the best shower I ever had.

The war made me grow up, so I suppose that's why I'm in favor of every 18-year old serving time in a branch of the armed services. My service experiences helped me deal with some serious challenges later in my life.

The Train Station

All our missions up to this point had been aimed at damaging or destroying military targets but this mission to Munich in early 1945 would haunt me for a long time. I was a copilot on a B-24 as part of the 8th Air Force. We couldn't hit our primary target because of bad weather, so we moved on to our secondary target which, on this day, happened to be different from past targets.

We had hit dumps, rail yards, factories, and the typical military or military-related sites but this was the first time we were to hit a railway passenger station and it was to be Munich's. Thanks to the incredible Norden bombsight, we pounded the station, which was probably full of German troops coming in and heading out. It was also probably full of civilians. We couldn't help but kill a lot of people on that raid.

I'm sure Bert Parsons, the pilot, felt the same way I did. In fact, we talked about what had happened and, frankly, didn't feel very good about it. We knew we had a job to do and we did it to the best of our ability but that didn't stop us from thinking about what happened or how many non-military folks were at the station when our bombs hit.

During my 18 combat missions I took the attitude that "I'm here today but might be gone tomorrow." A lot of the guys lost it while over there. You simply had to be emotionally stable to cope with the tensions and pressures. I felt at times like I was losing it. I believe anyone who says they weren't afraid is lying. We were all afraid.

After the war ended we felt like the ground crews needed a little reward for their round the clock work to keep our planes flying. So we took them over Germany to show them the damage caused by our bombing. I remember flying up the Rhine River so low that the water was splashing on the props. Those "trolley missions" involved flying our crew plus ten over cities like Frankfurt where we flew around the few smokestacks standing to let them see all the damage up close.

I've toured Germany since the war ended, including three nights in Frankfurt. The people there treated me well.

51

Lieutenant Eino Latvala

DOB: March 10, 1922
Where: Sebeka, Minnesota
Air Force: 9th
Bomb Group: 387th
Squadron: 559th
Station: England and France
Decorations include: Distinguished Flying Cross, Air Medal with clusters. Eino flew as a bombardier/navigator on 48 combat missions aboard the Martin B-26. A graduate of the University of Minnesota, he spent his professional career in engineering, including a stint at the Arnold Engineering Development Center near Tullahoma, Tennessee. Eino was recalled during the Korean War, serving with the 5th Air Force in a civil engineering squadron. He retired from the air force reserve as a lieutenant colonel.

A Horrendously Black Friday

Over the winter of 1944–45, the 559th Bomb Squadron along with three other squadrons of the 387th Bomb Group was stationed at air base A-71, near Saint-Quentin, France. On the morning of Friday, December 9, 1944, 36 B-26s from the 387th Bomb Group took off as scheduled to bomb a German supply depot. Each aircraft was loaded with 16, 250-pound demolition bombs. On the way to the target the aircraft were recalled to the base because of severe weather conditions. All of the aircraft were instructed to land with their bombs aboard.

A plane piloted by Lieutenant J.L. Allman of the 559th Bomb Squadron, attempting to land, got caught in the prop wash of the plane ahead of him, overturned, and crashed in a field about 200 feet from the end of the runway. Firefighters, medics, and others rushed to the crash sight. Shortly after crashing, the gas tanks of the aircraft caught fire and the bombs aboard detonated, killing the six crewmen and all those who had rushed to the scene.

The total number killed was reported to be 39, including Major Robert L. Murphy, CO of the 559th Bomb Squadron, Lieutenant Mac Fritch, 559th Bomb Squadron Communications

Officer, and Captain Lyle Walters, 556th Bomb Squadron Flight Surgeon. Unfortunately, the actual number killed and their names have been lost or were not properly recorded at the time of the accident. Historical documents prepared after World War II at Maxwell Air Base indicate 26 deaths which I believe is incorrect. I believe the figure of 39 people reported killed at the time of the accident is correct. It was by far one of the darkest days in the history of the organization and particularly sad because a full accounting by name of those who lost their lives does not exist in any historical records.

The tragic accident and the loss of so many lives was an especially sad event for the 387th Bomb Group and its four squadrons. Everyone who witnessed the accident and/or felt the explosion had vivid memories of that day. I was on an aircraft that had already landed. I had just exited the plane when the bomb explosions occurred. Although I was some 1,000 to 1,200 feet from the explosion site, I was knocked off my feet by the blast. Several who rushed to the crash site were killed, even several who were at the end of the runway about 200 feet from the crash site. In one case, a lieutenant from group headquarters was killed by the blast while a lieutenant standing next to him was unhurt.

Besides the grief of losing friends and comrades, grim reminders of the accident continued for days and even weeks after the accident. While going to the latrine the next day I saw two mangy dogs chewing on a human hand. Similar gruesome incidents were witnessed and reported by others.

A ghastly incident occurred at the 387th Bomb Group headquarters a week or 10 days after the accident. Several staff members reported seeing Captain Walters enter the headquarters building one morning. Unknown to the staff was the fact that Captain Walters had an identical twin brother, also stationed in France, who had come to the 387th Group headquarters to learn of the circumstances of his brother's death. It was a traumatic experience for the staff until they learned that the man they saw was Captain Walters' twin.

Eino Latvala (courtesy Eino Latvala)

There are relatives of those killed who continue to seek more information about the accident. I have recently been contacted by two sons whose fathers were killed. Upon learning of the location of his father's death, one of the sons visited the now abandoned air base in France.

The Marvelous Gee Box

During World War II I was a bombardier-navigator serving with the 559th Bomb Squadron of the 387th Bomb Group in Europe. The 387th was one of six B-26 medium bomber groups based in France after August 1944.

Sometime in October or November 1944, the Gee Box equipment was introduced and installed in several of the 387th Group aircraft. The Gee Box was a British navigational device for determining aircraft location or position. Its introduction was met with some skepticism, especially by pilots who preferred visual verification of the airplane they were piloting.

I do not recall any formal introduction or training with the Gee Box equipment. Instead, I recall being given a pamphlet called a technical order and told to acquaint myself with its possible use. The Gee Box turned out to be a great navigational device during the closing months of the war. It was occasionally used to drop bombs on enemy targets when cloud cover prevented visual target location and bomb release using the Norden bombsight.

Although the Gee Box equipment required much mental and ambidextrous skill for successful aircraft location, the principle of operation was rather simple. Ground stations transmitted electromagnetic signals the strength of which diminished with distance. The Gee Box in the aircraft accepted the signals that appeared on an oscilloscope-type screen. Intersection of signals from two ground stations determined the location of the aircraft. How this was accomplished by the Gee Box is technically complex but, in simple terms, the signal from a station appeared as a moving blip on the oscilloscope screen and the height of the blip was an indication of signal strength previously calibrated as distance from a particular ground station. These signal strengths were shown on special maps as numbered lines. The trick for the Gee Box operator/navigator was to simultaneously interpret the signals from two ground stations in order to determine the exact location of the aircraft. The major problem was in determining what was a true ground station signal as opposed to false signals. Once the true ground stations were found, it became necessary to continuously keep the valid ground signals in view. This was accomplished by a number of adjustment knobs. Taking your eyes off the scope would generally result in losing the correct ground signal. Simultaneously, it was necessary to plot the aircraft location on the special line/strength position map.

An experienced operator could determine aircraft location or position very accurately. On February 8, 1945, during a mission to a rail yard at Matterborn, Germany, dense cloud cover prevented visual location of the target. The group of 36 aircraft dropped their bombs on the Gee Box signals determined from the lead aircraft where I was the Gee Box operator/navigator. Reconnaissance flights the next day showed complete destruction of the intended target for which I was awarded the Distinguished Flying Cross.

A Forgotten Tragedy

I was not one to dwell on or keep personal records of my combat mission experiences during World War II. So in writing about my time overseas I must depend on my memory or on official orders, flight logs, and award citations that I have kept in my files throughout these many years. Also, because of my particular flight specialty, I flew in lead aircraft and with many different crews whose names I have mostly forgotten except for the 1st pilots whose names and great skills I will never forget.

A mission that I vividly recall was on February 9, 1945, to bomb a rail bridge at Neuwald, Germany. We encountered heavy anti-aircraft fire on the mission; so much so that the aircraft piloted by Lieutenant Adkins, in which I was the navigator, suffered severe damage. Fortunately, the two engines of our B-26 were not damaged and we thought that all was well. But after leaving Germany and crossing into France, Lieutenant Adkins reported that we were running short of fuel. Almost immediately the two engines conked out. The aircraft's fuel tanks had been hit by flak.

We were about to bail out when Lieutenant Adkins shouted over the intercom that what appeared to be an airstrip was in sight and that he would attempt a landing. Without power, we rapidly lost altitude. There was no way to lower the landing gear as well. Almost instantly we belly-landed, crashing through a stone hedgerow.

When we finally came to a stop, I discovered that I was unhurt but felt sure that the bombardier in the nose of the aircraft had been killed. When I climbed out of the wreckage, I saw that the two pilots and most of the rest of the crew appeared to be okay. But the bombardier was lying on the ground in great pain and the tail gunner was unconscious in the rear of the aircraft. In time, which seemed like hours, two ambulances showed up and the bombardier and tail gunner were taken to a nearby U.S. army hospital. Although not officially or otherwise reported, I later learned that the bombardier died from his injuries. As far as I know the tail gunner survived.

Apparently, it was a policy that combat and accident deaths would not be reported to survivors back in the squadrons. In this case, as well as with others where crewmembers did not return from combat missions, we never received any official notification of what may have happened. In most instances we witnessed what happened, especially when a plane was shot down by enemy aircraft or by anti-aircraft fire.

52

SERGEANT GEORGE SHREEVE

DOB: June 20, 1924
Where: Nashville, Tennessee
Air Force: 15th
Bomb Group: 301st
Squadron: 85th Depot Repair
Station: Bari, Italy
Decorations include: Purple Heart. George flew a total of 41 sorties during the war, a combination of supply and combat missions. During hostilities he was a top turret gunner (flight engineer) on B-17s and was wounded over Austria. After the war he graduated from Peabody College, taught school for a short time, and eventually became a builder and Realtor.

The Bombing of Bari

I was in North Africa for a short time and then Sicily before arriving at Bari, Italy, in November 1943. My team was assigned to make preparations for the squadron moving up from North Africa, including finding a place to pitch tents. During those days the 15th Air Force was just getting organized under General Jimmy Doolittle. We ended up choosing a good location in a beautiful olive orchard.

The orchard was near the Bari airport, a primitive flying field with a single runway and a few old buildings. There was a rock quarry at one end and a railroad track running through the airfield itself. Not the best of conditions for our planes but soon it would become very busy with Allied aircraft moving in and out. Our location was directly across from Bari and its harbor, a busy and important spot for Allied ships to unload supplies and troops during the Italian campaign. Clearly, the Germans thought it was an important port as well because what they did the night of December 2, 1943, was nothing short of a disaster for our forces.

The Bari docks operated 24 hours around the clock during those days. Even so, there were lots of ships in the harbor waiting to be unloaded. One, the *John Harvey*, contained a very special and top-secret cargo. We had just finished eating that early evening, anticipating a night of playing cards. Since dark came early that time of year we had set up a tiny generator connected to an extension cord to supply just enough juice for a single light bulb in our tent.

But before we had a chance to settle in, the nerve-wracking wail of air raid sirens filled the air. We quickly turned the light off and ran as fast as we could for our foxholes. About the time we jumped in them we heard and saw German planes flying very low over the airfield, probably no more than 150 feet up. Their target wasn't our location, but the harbor with its ships fully loaded with fuel, ammunition, and supplies. When those bombers roared by there seemed to be hundreds of them swarming the skies.

I hunkered down in the front of our two-man foxhole, covered with the logs we had placed above us for added protection, and listened to the many explosions, the anti-aircraft fire, and even the German strafing runs. The night was very dark except for the bright flashes of guns and explosions when suddenly the whole sky blossomed into bright orange. I thought just for a moment that the Germans had dropped a bomb right on top of us. As I foolishly stuck my head above the rim of the foxhole it was violently pushed back by the concussion from the tremendous blast aboard one of the ships at anchor, the ammunition ship *John L. Motley*. Five thousand tons of ammo went up in an ugly-looking flaming orange ball that could be seen for miles. My nose and ear started bleeding but I couldn't seek help because everyone was tied up trying to save the lives of those poor folks down at the docks and in the water. However bad I felt I remember thanking the good Lord I wasn't down there where many people were suffering violent and excruciating deaths.

George Shreeve (courtesy George Shreeve)

We did the best we could to make it through that night but the explosions, fires, and general pandemonium went on for days. Seventeen Allied ships were sunk in the raid and there were thousands of military and civilian casualties. Many died days later after briefly experiencing mysterious pain and blisters. For days medical personnel couldn't identify the reason for the deaths so they couldn't treat the injuries properly. Finally some doctors were sent to the scene from elsewhere and quickly diagnosed the problem.

The following morning I remember smelling something very strange, like an aroma of rotten eggs. We weren't otherwise affected by the smell but we found later that it came from the secret cargo carried by the *John Harvey*. Mustard gas. The kind of gas used during the awful trench warfare in World War I. That explained the mysterious ailments, the blisters, and the burns that killed so many people following the raid. President Roosevelt and British Prime Minister Churchill were concerned that the Germans were going to start using mustard gas so approval was given for the special shipment to be used by our forces, if necessary.

The rest of the world had a hard time finding out what happened at Bari. Military censors did their job well and the higher-ups refused to talk about it. But for those of us who were there — the ones who saw the vivid destruction, the bodies and parts of ships flying high in the air, the dark evening bursting into artificial sunlight, and who experienced the strange smell of a deadly chemical — that evening will always be remembered as a terrible tragedy. In addition to the widespread damage and the many deaths, the bombing of Bari shut down port operations for months, affecting our supply capabilities and hampering further Allied advances across Italy.

Secret Mission to the "Mickey" Ship

I flew 41 sorties out of North Africa and Italy as a gunner on B-17s. Over half were training and supply missions so most were uneventful. The trip on February 22, 1944, was not. It was a bombing mission to Weiner Neustadt, Austria. We were catching a lot of flak and I was sitting on a small sling seat near the top turret I manned. We knew the German fighters wouldn't venture into their own flak so I tried to make as small a target as possible to wait out the ground fire. Unfortunately, some flak found its way inside our ship, ripped through my flight suit, and grazed my leg. I didn't know it until the copilot happened to turn around, looked down, and yelled, "What's wrong with your leg?" I looked down and noticed that my leg was red from the blood. That's when the wound starting hurting real bad.

After landing I was sent to a British hospital run by New Zealanders at Bari, Italy. I wasn't hurt seriously but it was enough to get me out of combat. I thought I would be there for a week or so but the second day they came to my ward and told me, "You've got to get out. We need your bed. There's a trainload of wounded coming in from the Italian front." So they put me on crutches and I returned to the nearby air base where I had initially landed.

By that time a lot of bomb groups had moved in. The base had also turned into a home for four depot repair squadrons. I was assigned to one of them with the idea that as soon as I recovered from my wound I would be sent to a replacement depot for reassignment. Before long I met a captain who had graduated from the University of Alabama. We became pretty good friends, good enough for him to know I wasn't real excited about returning to combat. One day he told me, "I'll try to keep you here as long as I can but I can only do so much." True to his word, he gave me little jobs here and there. "Can you learn to drive a tractor, a V-8?" he wondered. "Sure, I can do that," I quickly responded. This tractor had a 60-foot boom on it. The guy who ran it was hospitalized for something and would be gone for a couple of weeks.

I had never driven a tractor but I learned how in half a day. We used the tractor to clear the runway at the base. If a plane was on fire or had crashed we hooked it to the tractor and swung it off the runway so other planes could land. That was a scary experience because some of the planes blew up before we could do anything with them.

When that job ran out after a couple of weeks my friend the captain approached me with another opportunity. "We've got a crew going over to the island of Vis, right off the coast of Yugoslavia near Split." So we flew over there. At first we were going to spend only about two weeks repairing a couple of B-24s that had landed there. We ended up staying 30 days. That's because planes kept coming in and crashing. The strip was a small one bordered by mountains so it was a tough one to approach and make a successful landing, especially when it was an emergency. One day, planes were coming in and people were bailing out all over the place. I remember one swooping in about 60 feet off the ground when suddenly the waist gunner jumped right out of his window. He was actually moving his legs as if he was running in the air. I didn't think he had a chance of surviving such a fall. He hit the ground, got up, and kept running. His plane crashed and burned, killing the entire crew.

When we got back to Italy my friend the captain wasn't so sure I could stay much longer. A day or two later I got called to a meeting in the orderly room. There was a brigadier general, a colonel, and six men: a 2nd lieutenant and five enlisted men. "We've got a mission we're going to send you on," we were told. "You are going into Yugoslavia. We have a "mickey" ship (a plane equipped with radar) that's down. It has some advanced radar on it. It's on a mountain there and we want to get the radar out of it." We were given a curious warning about not telling anything to anyone about our religion. We later learned that if we practiced the wrong religion we might get our throats cut.

Initially we were going to make a jump even though we didn't have any experience doing that. So we loaded up a C-47 and flew to Yugoslavia. Our destination was located around eight or nine thousand feet high but the mountains surrounding it ran on up to 15 or 16 thousand feet. The wind blew very hard up and around the sheer bluffs. So the colonel decided that we couldn't jump given those conditions. As he put it, it would be suicide for us to try. Back we went to Italy.

Very early the next morning we went up to the Cape of Manfredonia, the little spur that sticks out of the back of the boot of Italy. There, we got on an LCT (Landing Craft Tank). We had a six by six truck with an attached trailer and a jeep. The British ran the American-made boat. They took us across the Adriatic Sea to Vis, where I was earlier, and we stayed in the harbor until dark. We were then taken over to the mainland of Yugoslavia. We sat right up against the shore and were told to be very quiet: no lights, no smoking, absolutely nothing to give the enemy the smallest hint of our presence. We didn't know why we were sitting there until we heard a high-pitched sound about a quarter of a mile away. "That's a German E-boat, same thing as our PT boats," someone whispered. The German craft passed us presumably headed for Split, about 15 miles down the coast. We sat there and waited and after about an hour it came back. That whole experience was a little scary since we had some 40mm guns aimed at the E-boat. I heard one guy say, "If he turns in, blow him out of the water." Luckily we weren't discovered.

Soon we were underway again. Very quietly we made our way to what looked like a rocky road, a little gravel road that came down to the water. It looked sort of like a boat ramp. The gate was dropped and we got off in the middle of the night and set foot onto no man's land. Hours later we were joined by two Yugoslav partisans, one an attractive female 2nd lieutenant who looked to be about 25. Her name was Maria. The other woman was a sergeant in her thirties who spoke a little English. Maria, by the way, spoke perfect English. In fact, she had been reared in England so she had a British accent. She was to be our guide.

We took off in the direction of Sarajevo, up in the middle of Yugoslavia. The partisans held the mountains in that area and the British were with them. There was a British artillery battery that fired 25-pounders nearby in support of the partisans. We rode at night and hid in the daytime because the Germans traveled the roads during the day. We ended up at a base where elements of the British 8th Army were located. We got some rations from them since all we had were K rations. If you've ever had a steady diet of those you know they keep you alive but are not very appetizing.

We spent a day or two there, just enough time for a strange incident to occur. We were following a road going up a mountain and were about half a mile from the top. This road was very narrow with a drop off on one side, maybe 400 feet deep. On the other side of the road was a little vineyard. The mountains rose even higher from there. Quite a few Yugoslav partisans were in the area. We went into a little cook tent on the side of the road the British had set up. The cook, a Scotsman, called everybody "Jacque." He would say, "Jacque, I got something good to eat this morning." "What's that?" I answered. "I got you some mush." We took our mess kits out and he loaded them up with mush. As another guy and I walked up the road I took a bite or two of that mush. It tasted like wallpaper paste and I'm not sure but that it was exactly that.

Our complaints about the mush quickly took a backseat to what happened next. Two German 210s suddenly appeared from behind the mountains, firing their guns straight down the road. We threw our mess kits over the side of mountain and dived into the vineyard. I'll never forget what I saw next. Standing in the middle of the road was a big Yugoslav woman wearing a British uniform and handling a big six-shooter. She was taking direct aim at those incoming planes and blazing away with her gun. It's amazing that she didn't get hit. Bullets were striking all around her and when I looked over at the mess tent it was torn all to pieces. The guy next to me said, "I hope they killed that cook." After the planes disappeared we walked to what remained of the tent and discovered that the cook had hidden behind his iron stove. He wasn't hurt at all. The shells sprayed from the planes had ripped the tent all around him. He couldn't speak he was so scared and we were, too.

We continued up and over that mountain with our guides, all the while pulling away from the British. There were still a few partisans with us. That was a good thing because we had a few close calls. One time we stopped at a tiny village just before daybreak to get some water. The well was located in the middle of two roads that bisected the village. While we filled our water cans, a Yugoslav sergeant stood on the top of our truck armed with a .50 caliber machine gun. Before long some people ran out to us and started yelling that the Germans were coming. Soon enough a motorcycle came roaring down through the middle of town with what appeared to be a German courier. The sergeant swung that machine gun around as the German sped right past us on the other side of the road headed out of the village and up the far road. That's when the sergeant cut loose with a burst of fire that sent the German right over the bluff, motorcycle and all. We never saw him again.

We started back on our mission and finally found the plane that was down. It was a B-24 that had slid in on top of the mountain and had burned underneath. Everything on top — the wings, the fuselage — looked like it was intact. When we finally got to the crash site we were nearly eight or nine thousand feet up. We were exhausted. We discovered that all the crew had died. There were five on board and we buried what remains were left, mostly ashes. We retrieved their dog tags, found that the radar unit was destroyed, and decided to move on.

In a day or two we found our way to another little village, a place with about 12 houses or buildings. Maria told us we would spend the night in a hotel. That sounded great to us so we stuck the truck in between two buildings out of sight and also hid the jeep. We went up the back steps to the top floor of a very small, three-story building where we occupied two little rooms. We were very tired so we stretched out on the floor and tried to go to sleep, guarded by the Yugoslav sergeant who sat at the top of the stairs with a machine gun.

Meanwhile, people were going in and out downstairs. We were listening to all the hubbub when Marie came in and told us we were going to stay there all day because there was too much activity going on and no one knew what it was. Later, about 9 o'clock, we heard noise outside. We looked out a small window and had a view that stretched down the road that went right in front of the hotel. All the noise we heard happened to be a German column of troops with tanks, trucks, and other vehicles. I remember that some of the trucks were charcoal burners. The German army was on the move directly toward us, it seemed. We didn't know what was happening so we just sat tight.

Some of the Germans entered our little building trying to get some wine but they didn't come up the steps. About 4 o'clock in the afternoon the last of the troops passed by. Behind them came a group of Yugoslav partisans. Marie came back and announced, "The Allies have invaded France today." It was June 6, 1944. In a few days, we moved out of the village to a place about 20 miles away where a C-47 flew in and picked us up. We left our truck and jeep there. I still wonder what happened to them.

53

LIEUTENANT MARK OSBORNE

DOB: February 8, 1922
Where: Pulaski, Tennessee
Air Force: 8th
Bomb Group: 489th
Squadron: 847th
Station: Halesworth, England
Decorations include: Air Medal with clusters. August 6, 1944, began with Mark as the pilot of a B-24 on a mission to Hamburg, Germany. By the end of the day, after flying his twenty-sixth combat mission, Mark was a prisoner of war, his plane shot down by flak. That was only part of an experience that would consume most of his life. Mark spent his professional career in the food brokerage business.

An Explosive Landing

I remember vividly the time from June 6 to 10, 1944. We were on a combat mission shortly after D-Day, June 6. We had flown two missions, one on June 6 and the second a day or two later. Our third mission was a support mission for our invasion troops who were having a tough go trying to break out of the beachhead.

We were given a low level mission, around 6,000 feet, carrying 100, 60-pound fragmentation bombs in our B-24. That meant we had to drop visually so as not hit our own troops. But the weather was partly cloudy and we were not able to visually drop those bombs.

The anti–aircraft fire from the big ground guns produced shells bursts that looked like the size of boxcars. When they hit a plane it simply disappeared. I know because I saw that happen to a plane near us. We experienced some minor damage ourselves, nothing serious.

During our return to base I failed to command that we drop our load of bombs over the Channel. Being a replacement crew and inexperienced, we were never briefed, to my knowledge, on having a mission aborted.

The weather was bad as we made our return and we were not sure where we were so I chose to land at the first airstrip that we found on our return to England. We were in the traffic pattern but were going the wrong way so we made a circle and came back and landed.

I had never landed a plane with a 6,000-pound load. My copilot and I had our feet on the brakes when we realized that we could not slow the plane enough. One of the tires, the one on the right, gave way and we had a blow out. The plane skidded into a ground loop and we parked that plane lined up beside the runway, at a 90-degree angle, just as though it was our intention.

It was only after we were down that the bombardier informed us that our bombs were fully armed and ready to explode. He had already pulled the pins, arming them to be dropped. We were fortunate that we did not become a casualty of our own mistakes.

Our experience was a fairly common one where inexperience resulted in severe circumstances that cost the lives of many young men. As for us, once the plane stopped in its incredible position we simply got out and walked away. No one was hurt, no one said anything to us about having three tons of armed bombs aboard, and before long we caught a ride back to our own base.

Gratitude Long Overdue

I was the pilot of a B-24 Liberator bomber flying my twenty-fifth or twenty-sixth mission on August 6, 1944. Our ship was *Cover Girl*, named for the 1944 musical starring Rita Hayworth. It was a beautiful Sunday afternoon when our group, the 489th Bomb Group of the 2nd Air Division, arrived over Hamburg, Germany. Altitude was about 20,000 feet and there was not a cloud in the sky. The flight had been uneventful until we were nearing the target.

Suddenly we were in the midst of an intense anti aircraft barrage. The puffs of smoke looked close enough to walk on and the flak seemed to rain on our aircraft. I felt a sudden jolt or thud but did not think too much about it at the time since I was concentrating on the bomb run. Then, bombs away! We veered, trying to get away from the flak.

Suddenly our tail gunner, Bill Wooten, a North Carolina boy, shouted, "I see fire behind the tail!" Our engineer, Tom McGory, who was also our top turret gunner, quickly appeared beside me. "Lieutenant," he said, "we have fire in the number two engine." That's the engine closest to me on the left side. Immediately, our copilot, Jack Kennedy (a 19-year-old from Maryland and not the future president) and I started trying to follow emergency procedures. We set the controls on autopilot and feathered the number two engine. We found out that the bomb bay doors

Mark Osborne (courtesy Mark Osborne)

were still open. Perhaps, thankfully, they had failed to close. That was the escape route we had to take.

McGory the engineer soon returned to the cockpit and this time I noticed he had a hole in his flak helmet. Almost half of it appeared to be gone. Then I found out that the upper gun turret had been blown away. If he had not been a big boy he would have gone out with it. He told me in a very matter of fact way, "Lieutenant, I think that we better get out of here before the plane blows apart."

Needing no further encouragement, I gave the abandon ship command and tried to push my armored canopy seat back to get myself out of the cockpit. The pilot and copilot sat on their chutes in the cockpit. I certainly couldn't leave without that! But I found my seat jammed and I couldn't move it to get out. In times like this, you don't really know what you're thinking. I found myself saying, "Lord, help me. Let's get out of here." McGory, the big, strong flight engineer from New York state, had thankfully stayed long enough to see my predicament. He unfastened the jammed seat and I finally made it out. God bless that country boy from Ithaca, New York.

The plane was very unsteady as we moved toward the bomb bay, careful not to get hung up before jumping. Then, out we went. I was impressed by the quiet after all the clamor in the plane. I passed others while keeping my arms and feet crossed and falling straight down. I saw the ground coming up quickly so I pulled the cord to open the chute. Eventually, all ten of our crew were able to leave the aircraft and survive the parachute jump.

I landed in a wheat field in the midst of several farm workers who were harvesting their crop. Thinking quickly, I gave my chute to a farmer and his son nearby and told them to give the silk to the farmer's wife. They probably didn't understand. Soon the workers started gathering and it's safe to say there were several after my head. I didn't have a sidearm so I couldn't defend myself that way. I remember that one of the workers hit me in the jaw but at the time I didn't feel it because I was in shock. A couple of elderly men, wearing a kind of uniform that made them appear to be members of the Home Guard, walked up. They escorted me away from the field, one walking in front of me and one walking behind, and took me to a nearby stable.

That's where I was held for officers to come and pick me up. After about half an hour, a truck with a wood-burning steam engine pulled up, the door opened, and this tall Prussian-type uniformed officer wearing a high-spiked helmet walked in. "Lieutenant," he said, "for you the war is over!" I was there only for about half an hour before I was picked up and taken to Frankfurt am Main. There I remember seeing captured Americans arriving after bombing raids. During my interrogation, the Germans told me about the group to which I belonged and how many planes had been shot down on my raid. In fact, I quickly discovered they knew more about me than I knew about myself. There was verbal intimidation but no physical abuse despite the fact that I simply gave them my name, rank, and serial number.

I spent the next nine months as a prisoner of the *Luftwaffe*, primarily in *Stalag* 17B south of Berlin. I remember it being a big camp located in the midst of thick, tall pine forests. It had a walking track around it with layers of barbed wire and many guard towers separating us from freedom. The American camp was full at the time of my arrival so I was placed with the British, Canadian, Australian, and New Zealander prisoners many of whom had been imprisoned since the beginning of the war. I remember meeting a Royal Marine pilot who was flying patrol duty when a sub surfaced and shot him down. Thankfully, they accepted me and I still correspond and visit with one of them who lives in Toronto and Palm Beach.

Eight of us were crowded into one room of our barracks. We had regular roll calls each morning and evening. Food provided by the Germans was limited primarily to soup, potatoes, and something like cabbage. It would have been really tough without the Red Cross parcels we got once a week which included two cans of meat, a concentrated chocolate bar, and 5 packs of cigarettes. We bartered them for whatever we needed: raisins, prunes, and other fruit, margarine, and milk.

The British had been in *Stalag* 17B so long that they had set up a school. I took Spanish lessons from a man from Argentina and I took shorthand lessons as well. Hard to believe but plays and musicals were staged by the prisoners. Always in the audience, with a reserved seat of honor, was the camp commandant. Little did he know that directly under his seat was the entrance to a tunnel that had been dug out by prisoners. As for news from the outside world, we inmates were very much aware of what was going on since some fellows technically inclined had built their own little crystal sets. We could even pick up the BBC.

The Russians were advancing into Germany from the east, so our captors began moving us in February 1945. During the next three months we were marched around the country and rode on forty and eight-style boxcars, occasionally hearing bombs falling nearby. Each time we moved the conditions were less hospitable. We were often billeted in old barracks that had been abandoned. They were cramped and cold and there wasn't much food. In fact, I saw my ribs for the first time during these forced marches. I remember seeing parts of planes falling out of the sky during bombing raids. It wasn't unusual to see wings and landing gears dropping near us. The Germans knew they had lost the war. Nevertheless they were doing the best they could to adhere to the Geneva Convention while handling POWs.

I woke up one morning at our last stop and the Germans were gone. It was April 1945. Soon the liberating American forces entered our camp with General Patton in all his splendor riding into view within minutes after the first U.S. soldiers arrived. He was dressed like he had just come for a general inspection with his neat, well-pressed uniform, shiny boots and, those famous revolvers on each hip. We were all cheering him and he was obviously enjoying every minute of it. It was a great day for thousands of us POWs.

Many years passed and I was a happy, married man. God had blessed me in various ways: good health, a loving wife, three children, six grandchildren, and four great-grandchildren. I had a comfortable home and an extended family that were real blessings. Then, I remembered the man who had been my benefactor, Tom McGory, and how I had done nothing to thank him for the service he had rendered on my behalf. This began to bother me. Years and years passed and I still did nothing of a rewarding nature for the man who had saved my life.

This finally became such a burden for me that I realized I had to try and do something for Tom's contribution to the blessings of life that I enjoyed. After talking it over with two retired army friends who encouraged me to undertake the project, I decided to make the effort and an interesting saga began.

I wrote a letter to Senator Bill Frist's office and explained what had taken place and asked if he would help me and pass my request to the proper authority. It was a request that the Distinguished Flying Cross be considered as an award to the man who saved my life. No answer came. After about six weeks, I called and asked them about my letter. They didn't know anything about it. The office manager asked me to write again and call it to his attention and he would follow through. I did and he did. I received a letter from Senator Frist stating that he had turned the matter over to the air force liaison to the U.S. Senate.

After several weeks, I wrote the liaison officer asking him what action had been taken on my correspondence. No reply was forthcoming. Time passed and the infamous day of 9/11 took place. I just assumed that my request got lost in the Pentagon disaster. I wrote Senator Frist a third time and nothing came back. I was ready to give up until the Senator's office sent a reply from the Deputy Chief of the Congressional Division, Office of the Legislative Liaison. It informed me that the statute of limitations for such a commendation had run out two years after such action had taken place.

Congress had waived this timeline on February 10, 1996. Again the "but" followed the good news. Officials were unable to locate any Tom McGory. He didn't exist. There was another "but" after that. If I could follow all the requirements set out in the letter, providing all the information the office needed, my request would be considered. These instructions were listed and I sought to follow them. First, I learned a fire in St. Louis had destroyed most of the records of army air force veterans in World War II. With the help and encouragement of friends and other extraordinary people, we were able to put together a history of Tom McGory's service record and once again I sent my letter and once again a "but."

A letter from the office of the Air Force Secretary said they had no additional information other than the information I had collected and sent. They would have to rule on what they had in hand. Once again I asked for special consideration, describing my plight and asking that my sergeant not be penalized for my mistakes. Soon I received an invitation to be in Ithaca, New York, along with our copilot on July 5, 2003, for the award of the Distinguished Flying Cross to Staff Sergeant Tom McGory. Tom was 87 years old and one of the few surviving members of our crew. A lot of effort went into the project but I did learn that if you follow the rulebook and go through proper channels, those responsible officials will see that justice is done. Ironically, in my high school yearbook my favorite saying was listed as "Yes, but..."

54

LIEUTENANT W.C. GIBSON

DOB: February 12, 1924
Where: Nashville, Tennessee
Air Force: 8th
Bomb Group: 486th
Squadron: 833rd
Station: Sudbury, England
Decorations include: Distinguished Flying Cross, Air Medal with clusters. Late in the war W.C. flew 19 combat missions, earning the Distinguished Flying Cross for his actions as a squadron leader on several raids including those to Frankfurt and Hamburg. In civilian life, he was an engineer and cost analyst with E.I. duPont for 32 years.

Squealing Tires, No Cigar, and a Big Coincidence

About halfway through basic training I thought I was doing just fine. I had had no problems with my instructors and check pilots until one day, at the training field near Bainbridge, Georgia, I was unfortunate enough to draw a guy who had a reputation for being mean. I was already nervous when he asked me to do two or three things while in the air. Predictably, he didn't like the way I did them and he yelled at me. The more he yelled, the more I got upset.

By the time I got back to the field, I was convinced he was going to wash me out. He told me to land the twin-engine trainer we were in and just as the wheels touched the runway he yelled at me again for some reason. It startled me so that I involuntarily touched the brake pedals and made the tires squeal. I released the brakes almost immediately but the incident really infuriated him. I was a basket case at that point.

The next day my instructor asked me what in the world happened and then told me the guy wanted to wash me out. Thankfully, the instructor convinced him otherwise and I went on to pilot B-17s in combat. I still don't understand what happened that day but my instructor was responsible for keeping me on flying status.

Before I flew B-17s I was a copilot on a B-24. We were scheduled for a night training flight out of Chatham Field near Savannah when, for some reason, this captain said he wanted

54. Lieutenant W.C. Gibson

to go up with us. There was a place for him to sit behind the copilot's seat so he made himself at home there, stuck a big cigar in his mouth and, with his Zippo lighter in his hand, seemed seriously intent on lighting it.

Right after we took off, one of the crew started screaming over the intercom that something was wrong. I couldn't understand what he was saying until finally I heard something about gasoline fumes in the plane. It turns out that the fellows in the back of the plane smelled gasoline. I looked out my window and saw a stream of gasoline flying across the wing and entering the plane through the back window. Not knowing all this, the captain started to light his stogie. That's when I yelled at him to stop right there; don't light up! We circled the field and landed as quickly as we could only to find out that someone had not replaced the gas cap properly on one of the right side tanks after refueling.

Most of my crew stayed together for our 19 combat missions. After our eleventh trip, my pilot was promoted to command pilot and I moved over to the left seat as first pilot. While I was still copilot, though, our crew was designated as a lead crew. That meant I had to vacate the copilot's seat and let a command pilot sit there. Standard practice when that occurred was for the copilot to move into the tail gunner's position in the rear of the plane and become what was known as a squadron observer. If anything happened to the planes in our squadron, I was supposed to make a note of it and report it back at base.

W.C. Gibson (courtesy W.C. Gibson)

Being a little over six feet, one inch tall, the tail gunner position was not for me. I was all cramped up but occasionally I managed to get on my knees. I hated it. The whole rear on our B-17 was Plexiglas so I could see from one side all the way over to the other side, a field of vision of 180 degrees. I never saw so much flak in my life. When I was on the flight deck, I looked at the instruments most of the time. As pilot on the bomb run, I had to concentrate on air speed and elevation (altimeter) so I missed seeing a lot of flak. But in the tail gunner's position I saw it all. I was in that position when we flew over Berlin where there were more anti-aircraft guns than anywhere. I was petrified because those bursts were hitting very close to the plane. In fact, I was convinced we were going to get hit that day so I put my chute on and prepared for the worst. By some miracle, our plane escaped damage. My job as a squadron observer/tail gunner lasted for four missions and during that time I never fired my guns in combat and never saw an enemy plane.

I was in England about seven months. During that time I made about four trips to London. One of those trips resulted in a big "coincidence" which I'll explain later. In the meantime, let me tell you about my relationship with my cousin, Tom Gibson.

To say that Tom and I grew up together would be an understatement. We were born on the same day—February 12, 1924—in the same house, our grandmother's residence. I never knew why our parents chose to have us born there but they did. Tom and I grew up in the same neighborhood and, from the seventh grade on, went to the same schools, eventually graduating from Central High in the same class.

I decided to attend the University of Tennessee while Tom went to Vanderbilt. Both of us intended to study engineering. Both of us, independently and without each other's knowledge, entered the army air force at the same time, enlisting in the reserves while freshmen. In April 1943, both of us were told to report for active duty — on the same day!

We stayed together all the way through pilot training, from April 1943, till June 1944. After that, we were finally separated with Tom heading to B-17s and me to B-24s. We were sent to England where I soon switched to B-17s. When I arrived, I don't believe I knew that Tom was there but I soon found out. His airfield was not too far from mine, maybe 20 to 30 miles, so one time I got a one day pass and took the train to see him. Other than that, the only other time I saw him overseas was when we bumped into each other while in London. Imagine the odds! We might have been at a Red Cross-operated hotel, I'm not sure, and I don't remember our reactions when we saw each other, but I'm still amazed that we found each other by accident.

Tom and I flew B-17s during combat and returned unscathed, thankfully. One other coincidence: after the war, Tom and I studied engineering at Vanderbilt, graduating in 1948. Then, we both went to work for DuPont until the day we retired. Tom was in film sales for about 35 years, living in different places, while I worked as an engineer, mostly at the Old Hickory, Tennessee, plant for 29 years. Virtually from our births, through the years growing up, then through training and at times during the war and finally after the war our lives were intertwined through hardly any planning at all. It makes me want to believe that there were more than just "coincidences" involved.

The Buncher

Most of my concerns in combat didn't include the missions themselves as much what happened *before* the missions. There was a whole science dedicated to the midair ballet of forming up hundreds, if not a thousand B-17s safely and moving them off to their selected targets. Gaining altitude and reaching formation had their own demands, challenges, near misses, and even collisions resulting in deaths.

Often our B-17s would take off from our base near Sudberry, England, in the dark of the morning. Usually there were three squadrons of 12 planes each, totaling between 36 and 40 aircraft overall. Each squadron had a lead plane with a designated takeoff time. Once those lead planes were in the air, the tail gunner would flash his Aldis lamp, a bright light shining through the Plexiglas, and each squadron would form up on its designated color.

Eventually, after 30 or 45 minutes, sometimes longer, of circling the field counter-clockwise, the planes began their long trip to the targets. There was a good reason for doing a tight circle over our field: there were many fields just like ours spread around the eastern part of England, each with its own group of aircraft. All of them had their running lights on, creating a huge Christmas tree effect all over the sky. It was pretty traumatic being up there leading a group of planes and trying to figure out where the other fields' planes were going, especially when the consistently poor English weather moved in.

From the eighth mission on, our plane was a squadron leader, one of the first to take off. After leaving the ground, we headed for a predetermined altitude, usually from 6,000 feet to 20,000 feet, depending on the weather. All of us, though, depended on the buncher.

Every airfield had its own buncher which emitted a particular radio signal. Each plane had a radio compass so that when we flew toward the buncher, the compass would go straight up. When we flew over the buncher, it would point straight down. When circling the buncher, the needle would point to the left and that's where we would try to keep it so our flight path wouldn't overlap the flight paths of the planes from the neighboring fields. Daytime missions were a lot less stressful since you could actually see those other planes either moving toward you or away from you.

One particular mission stands out because of the bad weather, so bad in fact that we had to reach formation over the continent, rather than our base in England. The overcast was very thick and as it turned out our assembly point over our designated buncher was not more than 500 feet above the clouds. Our planes were leaving contrails as we circled while waiting on the other planes to join us. The contrails got larger and larger till we were flying through clouds of contrails. Throughout that entire mission, eight hours, we never saw the ground, flying instead over heavy overcast.

I was doing all the flying up to that point when I realized something was wrong either with the instruments or with me. The altimeter said we were losing altitude but I didn't believe it. Finally, I asked the command pilot to take control of the plane for a while. Looking back, I was obviously suffering from vertigo. After about 20 minutes, I was okay and resumed my duty as pilot.

Visibility was very poor for the entire mission. In fact, about all we could see were the lights of the group in front of us which were very close. We were keeping our eyes on those lights when suddenly out of the mist rose a B-17 directly in front of us, probably no more than 200 feet away. It was climbing and was so close to us that its prop wash made our plane rock like crazy. I was fighting the controls to keep our ship from moving too much one way or the other. Whoever it was kept climbing and went out of sight into the clouds. He was clearly lost and didn't appear to be trying to hook up with a formation nearby. Why, I still don't know.

Then, about five minutes later, the same plane came back down directly in front of us and kept going down, disappearing again from our sight. Believe me, I had a few choice words for that guy.

55

Major Calvin Fite

DOB: March 25, 1920
Where: Memphis, Tennessee
Air Force: 15th
Bomb Group: 485th
Squadron: 828th
Station: Venosa, Italy
Decorations include: Distinguished Flying Cross, Air Medal with clusters. Cal Fite joined the Army Air Corps on September 9, 1940, becoming a squadron commander and flying 30 combat missions as a B-24 pilot. Among his many duties was to write letters to the families of those who died in the line of duty. His postwar career as an air force officer included active service in the Strategic Air Command where he primarily flew the B-47 Stratojet. After his retirement Cal graduated from Vanderbilt Law School and entered the banking profession. He invested in real estate and once owned/managed a golf driving range and par 3 course.

Missions to Remember

An early mission I remember was to Salonika, a small town in Greece. We were to bomb a marshalling yard and port facility. The Germans had quite a bit of activity going through that port. I was flying the number 3 position in the lead box of the group, left of the leader. In such a position, I had a good view of the number 2 plane just off the leader's right. The number 2 plane received a direct hit. In all my years of flying I have never seen anything like it. You could see the plane get hit and the dust and debris flying. It was the shock of seeing such a thing. Then a flame erupted almost immediately. It started at the fuselage and went out to the tips of the wings. That plane literally melted in the center because those wings just folded right up. God almighty, it got your attention. The group went on and bombed the target. Nobody got out of that plane.

In November 1944, as squadron operations officer I got to fly with our squadron commander, Ed Nett. Ed was an outstanding man and a fine fellow in addition to being a great

Calvin Fite (courtesy Calvin Fite)

pilot. I was flying deputy lead to him and was on his right side in the number two slot. The target on this day was Blechhammer in east Germany, north of Czechoslovakia, not too far from the Polish border. It was a benzol plant. The Germans didn't have too many petroleum supplies. Constant bombing of such supply areas meant they lost much of their production capability. But the Germans were technically brilliant. They built these benzol plants mostly over coal mines. Benzol was a type of fuel that didn't produce the high octane that regular petroleum did but it was used as a substitute.

This plant was apparently over a huge underground coal mine. The refinery was built right over the coal supply. We bombed it several times and it was always very heavily defended. It was a huge target, miles long. Part way to the target the commander had mechanical trouble and turned back. I took over the mission and eventually received the DFC for my actions. As I said, the flak over this target was always heavy. We got some hits, actually lots of holes, but fortunately we made it through. We did lose two planes on that bomb run; one was hit directly and another was hit bad enough that the crew had to leave it after they got off the target. My main concern at the time was not leading the squadron but that my crew would do a good job because in that kind of formation everybody would follow our lead. The navigator had to navigate properly and the bombardier had to do a good job since all the others dropped their bombs on his action. Fortunately, both were first rate.

The most interesting mission I ever had — and the most stressful — occurred on December 24, 1944. We were members of the 15th Air Force, part of the 55th Bomb Wing. The wing had four groups in it at the time. Our high command called a stand down for Christmas day and the day after. At the time, we had a new group commander, Doug Cairns, a very fine officer. He had been a professor at West Point. He had an excellent education but not much operational experience. Still, he was a superior group commander.

Christmas night all the squadrons had their parties. Some way or another there was a big supply of alcohol available. We had a big party at the squadron's officers club and I guess I went back to my quarters around midnight. I had quite a bit to drink; I wasn't staggering but I was feeling good. Cairns drove up in his jeep just as I was getting off my German motorcycle. "The 55th Wing called and said we've got a mission in the morning and I'm flying with you," he said. "The target is Blechhammer. You will brief the mission." That meant getting up in front of all the assembled crews flying on that mission and providing them with the information they needed for a successful effort.

It also meant getting there at 5 A.M. to provide target and route information and any special instructions. I got about three hours sleep, drank lots of coffee, and made it. I told the guys that when they saw me start my engines, they better start theirs because I didn't fool around on that parking ramp for long. Shortly after getting all four engines running OK, I always began to taxi out.

I was flying left seat and Doug was in the right seat as copilot. This was one of his early missions. We proceeded toward Blechhammer with no difficulty but as we approached the pre IP, something on the ground that can be readily identifiable to help the navigator, I noticed that there was a group on my right flying a converging course with me. I could tell Doug was nervous. To compound matters, just at that time we ran into an atmospheric condition that caused our windows to frost up. I called the navigator to see if we were on the right course. "Yes, sir, just like we ought to be." "Well," I said, "there's a group on the right that keeps edging toward us."

So I just held my own. There was no way to communicate with them since all of us had to practice radio silence. The other group kept coming and coming and finally they gave up and eased off to the right. We went on to bomb the target and lost three airplanes to flak. As we routed off the target I remember thinking it was the worst day of flying in my life. I was hurting all the way and I was worried about the colonel. That other group was very close to us when they broke off. They were probably cussing me the whole way. I thought I didn't rip it with Doug on that mission. A few months later I was promoted to lieutenant colonel.

On December 16, 1944, I was leading the group to Pilsen, Czechoslovakia. The target was a synthetic oil refinery. We were somewhere over Austria when my plane's oxygen system malfunctioned. We were above 20,000 feet and there was nothing I could do to stay with the formation. I had to turn the lead over to the deputy lead and head back to Italy. I dropped down to a lower altitude, not quite 14,000 feet. The crew was young so we could stay above that a little. We were flying south near Munich when here came two or three Me 109s. They got our attention. Our odds at that time were not looking great. All of sudden, we saw at about the same time two P-51s, their markings showing they were part of the Tuskegee airmen. "Big brother, you need any help?" one of them called out. "We sure do," I said with some relief. "You see those bogeys?" "Yea, we see them." Because of the P-51s, the Germans didn't bother us. It was just happenstance that those Tuskegee airmen showed up when they did.

The Sad Letters

Our squadron had a flight crewmember I will call "John Doe" who had gone through training with us in the States. I'll call him "John" because, even after all these years, I would rather none of his family find out how he really died. While we were based in Italy, "John" badly wanted to go to Rome. As it happened, we had a plane going to that ancient city. It was a B-24 stripped of armament that was used to fly re-supply trips. This time it was heading to Rome to pick up something, I don't remember what. "John" asked if he could go with them and I told him he could. The plane had a regular crew on it plus some passengers including "John." I'm sure he was looking forward to a good time.

The plane took off and just as it broke ground it lost an engine. I'm not blaming the pilot but he just didn't handle the situation right. He should have feathered the engine and flown straight ahead to get his speed up. Then, whether it took five or so miles, just fly straight and level and then start a gentle turn, flying carefully back to the field. This pilot made the mistake of turning too soon and dropping his wing. It hit the ground, causing the plane to cartwheel and burn. Sadly, I had to go out there and identify the bodies.

That accident was so bad for many reasons but especially because it was needless. It didn't accomplish anything. It was not in combat, but was designed to be a simple overnight trip. "John" just wanted to see Rome. Now, because he was not married, I had to write his parents. That was a tough thing to do. I didn't tell them he was going to Rome to have fun on a trip that was designed just for the heck of it.

Writing letters to parents or wives was very, very tough for me. When I became a squadron commander I spent a lot of time doing that. You just did the best you could. I hated to see guys get killed. I just never got used to tragic things like that happening.

Index

Admiralty Islands 39
Adriatic Sea 36, 150, 152, 193, 236
Air Force Reserve 10, 25, 90, 126, 150, 153, 175, 180, 224, 229
Air-Sea Rescue (British) 84
Alaska 171, 173
Alessandria, Italy 197
Alexander, General Harold 203–204
Alexander, Kenneth 45
Allman, Lieutenant J.L. 229
Alps 35, 107, 130, 144, 150, 193
Alto Airfield, Corsica 27
Amarillo, Texas 133
Amendola, Italy 85
Anzio, Italy 49, 61
Appian Way 164
Armstrong, Clyde 35
Army Air Corps 5, 10, 19, 23, 30, 72, 124, 133, 246
Arnold, General H.H. "Hap" 88, 165, 173–174
Ascension Island 24
Atkinson, General Joe 203–204
Aviso Viaduct 34–35

Bachus, Joe 111
Bakersfield, California 20, 24
Balchen, Colonel Bernt 155
Balikpapan, Philippines 14
Baltic Sea 217
Bangkok, Thailand 181
Bari, Italy 33, 144, 233, 235
Barksdale Field, Louisiana 26
Barton, David vii
Bassingbourn, England 223
Bastogne, Belgium 28
Battle of the Bulge 64, 97, 146
Baylor University 39
BBC 7, 96, 109, 146, 216, 242
Beahan, Captain Kermit 173
Becker, Captain Bill ix, 77–78
Bedford, Ohio 162
Beech AT-10 Wichita trainer 219
Behrens, Captain Arthur 133, 135
Behrens' Brood 132

Belgium 65–66
Benefield, England 114
Benson, Captain R.M. ix, 5–9
Beppu Bay, Japan 81
Bering Sea 172
Berlin, Germany 48, 54–55, 57, 68–69, 114, 217, 226
Beselare, Belgium 102–104
Bess, Michael vii, 3–4
Biersteker, Lieutenant Joe 166
Bilbrey, Captain Beecher ix, 25–29
Biskra, Algeria 201
Bizerte, Tunisia 201–202
Blanchard, Colonel William 171
Blechhammer, Germany 249–250
Blida, Algeria 201
Bloody Hundredth 126
Bloom, Sergeant Zane 167, 169
Blumenkranz, Howard 93
Bode, Gordon 107
Boeing B-17 Flying Fortress 7, 54–56, 63–66, 82–83, 110–113, 160–161, 209, 245–247
Boeing B-17 Flying Fortress (modified) 70–71
Boeing B-29 Superfortress 99–100, 132–135, 136–141, 165–174
Boeing PT-17 Stearman 12, 143
Boise, Idaho 17
Booby Trap 73
the Boomerangs 59
Borders, Lieutenant Earl 179
Borneo 10, 14, 41
Boston, Massachusetts 105, 109, 204
Boston College 105
Bowry, Don 190
Bradbury, Gerald 187
Bremen, Germany 83, 101
Brenner Pass 27, 34, 38, 144–145, 199
Bressanone railroad bridge 144
Brice, B.B. 99
Brindisi, Italy 152
Brooke, General Alan 203–204
Brooklyn, New York 142

Brown, Joe E. 91
Brown, Captain Stacy 186
Brunei 15
Brussels, Belgium 92, 103, 227
Brux, Germany 211–212
Buck, Lieutenant Roy ix, 82–84
Budapest, Hungary 34, 36, 50
buncher 63, 246–247
Bungay, England 102–103
Burma 19–20, 181–183

C-61 Fairchild 183
Caen, France 224
Cagliari, Sardinia 201
Cairns, Doug 249–250
Cairo, Illinois 113
Calcutta, India 183–184
Calhoun, Lieutenant Eugene 157
Camp Lucky Strike 109, 218
Camp Patrick Henry, Virginia 144
Campbell, Wayne vii
Canton Island 18
Cape Girardeau, Missouri 123
Cape of Manfredonia, Italy 236
Capua, Italy 164
Carnevale, John 155
Carpetbaggers 153–159
Cartwright, Lieutenant Bob x, 219–223
Casablanca, Morocco 204
Cassino, Italy 87
Cerignola, Italy 30–31, 129, 185, 187, 192
Chambers, Lieutenant Bob x, 180–184
Chatham Field, Georgia 44, 46–47, 244
Chattanooga, Tennessee 27, 206, 226
Chetniks 32
Chicago, Illinois 173
Chickasha Field, Oklahoma 44
Chieti, Italy 164
Chin Hills 24
China-Burma-India Theater 21, 75, 180

253

Index

Churchill, Prime Minister Winston vi, 3, 203–204, 234
Cincinnati, Ohio 77
City of Osceola 132–136
Civil Air Patrol 5
Claridge Hotel 221
Clark Field, Philippines 121
Clarksville, Tennessee 99, 101
Clovis, New Mexico 99
Colby, Major William 155, 157–159
Cole, Captain Bush ix, 48–53
Cologne, Germany 57
Connally, U.S. Senator Tom 218
Conrad, Cliff 61
Consolidated B-24 Liberator 12, 14, 36, 102–104, 129–131, 148–149, 153–159, 175–176, 178–179, 192–196, 198–199, 206, 213–216, 239–241
Consolidated B-24 Liberator ("mickey" ship) 237
Cooper, Lonnie 32
Corliss, Loren 77
Corning, New York 32
Corpus Christi, Texas 48
Corsica 60, 105–106
Cover Girl 240
Croatia, Yugoslavia 36
Cross, Barry vii
Cunningham, Sergeant John x, 189–191
Curtiss C-46 Commando 13
Cypress, Lieutenant Mandel ix, 16–18

Dakar, West Africa 185
Dallinger, Al 81
Daruba, Morotai 13
Davis wing 225
Davis-Monthan Field, Arizona 180
D-Day 70–71, 95, 224, 239
DDT 33, 109, 112
Decimomannu, Sardinia 59, 106
Deene, Major General John 119
Deenethorpe, England 114
DeMontbreun, Sergeant Jim ix, 44–47
Denmark 154
Denver, Colorado 44, 189
the Depression 19
Dessau, Germany 110
Detroit, Michigan 54
DeVac, George 71
Dijon, France 25, 27
DiMaggio, Joe 143
Doolittle, General Jimmy 203–204, 233
Dorr Field, Florida 143
Douglas C-47 Skytrain 14, 36, 236
Douglas DC-4, 33
Douglas SBD Dauntless 184
Downey, Lieutenant Jack x, 206–208
Dresden, Germany 33, 57, 223
Driscoll, Lieutenant Art x, 110–113
Duke University 142
Dulag Luft 216
Dunbar, Dick 108
Dunkirk, France 111

Dutch East Indies 13
Dyersburg Field, Tennessee 88

Eastland, Sergeant Bill x, 175–179
Eden, Anthony 203–204
Eighth Army (British) 236
Eisenach, Germany 92, 216
Eisenhower, General Dwight 218
Elliott, Lieutenant Bob x, 226–228
Elmhurst, New York 34
Engleman, Sergeant Jim 215–216
English Channel 6, 9, 63, 69–71, 82, 111, 201, 206, 223, 225, 239
Epps, Alabama 90
Ernst, Lieutenant Ben x, 162–164
Eufaula, Alabama 213
Evans, Major Clarence 90–98
Evans, Kaye vii
Evans, Winston vii
Eye, England 148–149, 224

Fairchild C-119 Flying Boxcar 10
Fairchild PT-19 Cornell 82
Feni, India 19–20, 73
Ferrara, Italy 87
Fesmire, Captain Robert x, 153–159
Feudin' Wagon 175, 178–179
Finder, Captain Theodore 173
fire raids (Japan) 165–170, 189–191
Fisher, Frank 164
Fite, Major Calvin x, 248–251
Flame McGoon 37
Floto, Eugene 61
Focke-Wulf Fw 190 34, 36, 214
Foggia, Italy 85, 87, 151–152, 209–210
Ford, "Tennessee" Ernie 16
Fourteenth Armored Division 28–29
Fourteenth Army (British) 75
France, Captain Robert 157, 159
Frankfurt, Germany 107–108, 228, 244
Frankfurt am Main 216, 241
French, Lieutenant Thomas ix, 39–43
Fresno, California 144
Frist, Senator Bill 242–243
Fritch, Lieutenant Mac 229
Funafuti, Tuvalu 18

Gallatin, Tennessee 219
Galloping Katy 226–227
Gardner, Dick vii
Gee Box 111, 223, 230–231
George, Lieutenant Pete 157
George Field, Illinois 26
Gibson, Tom vii, 245
Gibson, Lieutenant W.C. x, 244–247
Giessen, Germany 64
Giles, Lieutenant General Barney 171–174
Goodlettsville, Tennessee 220
Goose Bay, Labrador 200
Gotha, Germany 92–93
Gottingen, Germany 214
Grable, Betty 52
Grafton Underwood, England 201

Grand Island, Nebraska 5
Graves, Lieutenant Tom ix, 72–76
Great Ashfield, England 54, 110–113
Great Yarmouth, England 84
Greenland 200
Greenville, Mississippi 25
Greenville, Tennessee 79
Greenwood, Mississippi 132
Gregg, Captain Bob ix, 59–61
Grimes, Major Corwin 188
Grizzell, Captain J.O. x, 150–152
Grossostheim airfield 57
ground crew 23, 179
Guadalcanal 13, 39
Guam 132, 170–171
Gunga Din 60
Gustrow, Germany 57

Halesworth, England 239
Hall, Austria 146
Hall, Steve vii
Halmahera Island 13
Hamburg, Germany 57, 97, 239–240, 244
Hamilton Field, California 144
Hanover, Germany 69
Harlingen Field, Texas 12
Harriman, Averell 118–119
Harrington, England 153
Harris, Sandra vii
Harvard Law School 90
Harvey, Robb vii
Haskell, Texas 39
Hawes, Lt. Colonel Ed 81
Hawks, Tom 107
Haymes, Dick 52
Hayworth, Rita 53, 240
Heavenly Body 82–83
Heidelberg, Germany 29
Hermann Goering Tank Works 186
Hethel, England 226
Hildegarde 173
Hill, Grabel 161
Himalayas 20
Hiroshima, Japan 121
Hokkaido, Japan 171–172
Holland 69, 103
Holzapple, Colonel Joseph 106
Holzwickede, Germany 57
Hong Kong 121
Horton, Steve vii
Howard, Lieutenant Walter 220
Howe, Billy 75
Howell, Sergeant Robert, Jr. x, 209–212
Hume-Fogg High School 16
the Hump 24, 180
Hunter Field, Georgia 46
Hynes, Samuel vii

IFF (Identification Friend or Foe) 134, 138–139
IJmuiden, Holland 69
India 181
Innsbruck, Austria 107, 146–147
Inverness, Scotland 157–158
IP (initial point) 5, 9, 35–36, 92, 202
Ipswich, England 213
Irrawaddy, Burma 74–75

Isle of Capri 210
Iwo Jima 133–134, 136–137, 140, 167–170

Jackson, Lieutenant Charles ix, 19–24
Jankousky, Lieutenant C.K. 152
Japan 99–100, 165, 170–174, 190
Jefman Island 123
Jensen, L.E. 74
Jernigan, Lieutenant Bill ix, 10–15
Jesselton, Borneo 40
John Harvey 233–234
John L. Motley 234
Johnson, A.W. 34–35
Jones, Sergeant Bill x, 160–161
Jones, Sergeant Don 169
Jones, Tisdal 170
The Judge 148–149
Jungle Air Force 14
Junkers Ju 88, 36

Kaiserslautern, Germany 57, 102, 110
Kaiyo 81
Kansas City, Missouri 224
Kassel, Germany 213–216
Kasserine Pass, Africa 201
Katz, Carl Otto 100–101
Katz, Sergeant John ix, 99–101
Kawanishi N1K2 "George" fighter 167
Keeley, Jack 155
Keesler Field, Mississippi 30
Kelly, Sergeant George 167
Kelso, John 201
Kennedy, Jack (future president John Kennedy) 109
Kennedy, Lieutenant Jack 240
Kennedy, Jim 32–33
Khartoum, Sudan 20
Kiel, Germany 57, 176
Kiev, Ukraine 117
Kimbolton, England 219–220
King, Lieutenant Myron x, 114–119
Kingman, Arizona 160, 212, 223
Kingsbury, Lieutenant Colonel Bill 170, 172
Kirtland, Lieutenant Jim x, 185–188
Kirtland Air Base, New Mexico 143
Kobe, Japan 166
Koblenz, Germany 56, 227
Kolemba, Major John x, 192–199
Korea 48
Korean War 25, 89, 229
Kremlin 118
Kuflevo, Poland 116–117

La Maddalena, Sardinia 202
La Spezia, Italy 48–50
Lady Anna 219, 221–223
Lady Winifred 68, 70
Lake Chad 20
Lake Como, Italy 106
Lancaster, John 155–157
Lancaster, Ohio 59
Larsen, Don 142
Las Vegas, Nevada 23
Latvala, Lieutenant Eino x, 229–232

Lavochkin La-5FN fighter (Russian) 116
Leavenworth Federal Penitentiary 136
Lechleiter, Lieutenant John x, 126–128
Ledo Road 74, 180
LeMay, Colonel Curtis 23
LeMay, General Curtis 137, 165, 170–174
Lexington, Tennessee 153
Liberandos 1, 146
Lida, Belorussia 116–117
Liège, Belgium 223
Lille, France 201, 208
Lincoln, Nebraska 209, 220
Lindbergh, Charles 42
Linz, Austria 112, 186
Little Audrey 213
Liverpool, England 220
Livingston, Texas 48
Lockheed C-130 Hercules 10, 13
Lockheed P-38 Lightning 36–37, 112, 124, 183–184, 201–202, 214
Logerot, Lieutenant John 135
Loose, Frank vii
Lowe, Lieutenant Richard 118
Lublin, Poland 116

MacArthur, General Douglas 13, 121
Macon, Georgia 62
Magdeburg, Germany 8
Maiden U.S.A. 114–119
Mandalay, Burma 20, 75, 181–182
Manfredonia, Italy 152
SS Manhattan 220
Mantua, Italy 105–106, 108
Manziana railroad bridge 60
March Field, California 12, 120–121, 144
SS Mariposa 203
Marrakesh, Morocco 210
Marschke, Frank 60
Marshall, General George 203–204
Martin B-26 Marauder 25–26, 59–61, 105–106, 229–232
Masonheimer, Art 191
Massey, Myrel 165, 167, 169–170
Maxwell Field, Alabama 11, 17, 143, 219, 230
Mayer, John 53
Mayo Clinic 17
McCluney, Joe vii
McCluney, Margaret vii
McGehan, Lieutenant James 186
McGonagle, Lieutenant John x, 105–109
McGory, Sergeant Tom 240–243
McGovern, George 120
McGregor, Captain Carter 166
McGuire, Captain Charles 157–158
McWilliams, Ernie 35
Mechanic's Nightmare 193
Meiningen, Germany 95–96
Memphis, Tennessee 248
Menzel, George vii
Merrill's Marauders 74
Merseburg, Germany 5, 56–57, 127
Merville, France 111
Messerschmitt 210 36

Messerschmitt 262 36, 56, 149, 220
Messerschmitt Bf 109 34, 36, 65, 105–106, 200, 202, 214
Messerschmitt Bf 110 36, 202
Messina, Sicily 163, 200, 202
Metfield, England 155–156, 206
Metz, Germany 57
Miami Beach 10, 219
Michigan State University 226
Middle Tennessee State Teachers College 11
Midland, Texas 82
MiDNiTE MiSS 134, 136
Midway Island 16–18
Mifflinburg, Pennsylvania 180
Mika, Sergeant Leonard vi, ix, 54–58
Milo, Sicily 202
Milspaugh's Milk Runners 160–161
Mindanao, Philippines 44
Minneapolis, Minnesota 173
Mission to Moscow 119
Mississippi River 113
Mr. Lucky 192, 199
Mitsubishi G4M "Betty" bomber 124
Moder River 28
Monte Cassino, Italy 61, 150
Moore, Sergeant Dick 165, 167–168, 170
Moosbierbaum, Austria 187
Moosbierbaum oil refinery 35
Moosburg, Germany 97
Morocco, Africa 200
Morotai Island 10, 13–15, 77
Morotai Strait 13
Morse code 11, 30, 79
Moscow 118
Mt. Etna, Sicily 163
Mount Juliet, Tennessee 209
Mount Tom, Massachusetts 192
Mountbatten, Lord Louis 180
Mumford, Cathy vii
Munich, Germany 6, 9, 146, 176, 227, 250
Murata, Japan 166
Murfitt, Lieutenant Dick 201
Murphy, Major Robert 229
mustard gas 234–235
Myitkyina, Burma 73–74

Nadzab, New Guinea 13, 79–80, 125
Nagasaki, Japan 173
napalm 190
Naples, Italy 151, 164, 202
Naru Island 18
Nashville, Tennessee (as home) 1, 10, 18–19, 25, 44, 68, 82, 102, 126, 129, 160, 189, 233, 244
Nashville, Tennessee (classification center) 143
Natal, Brazil 185
National Airport 173
National Geographic 20
Neagle, Anna 221
Neal, Lieutenant Jerry x, 224–225
Nett, Ed 248
Neuhause, Lieutenant Bill 182

Index

New Guinea 123
New Orleans, Louisiana 30
New York Times 173
Ngazun, Burma 75
Nichols, Lieutenant Jack 130
Nimitz, Admiral Chester 18
Nis, Yugoslavia 37
Nolensville, Tennessee 154
Norden bombsight 78, 143, 227
Norfolk, Virginia 213
Norris, Sergeant A.J. 145
North Africa 233, 235
North American B-25 Mitchell 19, 21–22, 72–76, 123–125, 162
North American P-51 Mustang 133, 149, 183, 190, 214, 223, 250
North Pickenham, England 175
North Sea 57, 68, 83, 92, 103, 127, 155, 158, 221
Northern Lights 172, 173
Northrop P-61 Black Widow 134, 136, 139
Norway 157–159
Norwich, England 103

Oahu, Hawaii 16
Oak Ridge, Tennessee 21
Oak Ridge Gaseous Diffusion Plant (K-25) 21
Oakland, California 182
O'Donnell, Brigadier General Emmett 171–174
Okinawa 10, 13, 81, 172
Oklahoma Baptist University 113
Oldashi, Sergeant David ix, 79–81
One Hundred First Airborne 28
Orangeburg, South Carolina 12, 180
Oranienburg, Germany 220
Osaka, Japan 132
Osaka Bay, Japan 166
Osborne, Lieutenant Mark x, 239–243
OSS (Office of Strategic Services) 79–80, 154–155, 157–158
Ozark, Alabama 148

Palawan Island 78
Palermo, Sicily 162–163
Pandaveswar, India 180
Pantelleria Island 203–204
Paris, France 128
Parks, Lieutenant Robert 154–156
Parsons, Lieutenant Bert 227
Patchogue, Long Island 142
Patton, General George 97–98, 163, 242
Pavlas, Sergeant Ernest 118
Peabody College 233
Pearl Harbor, Hawaii 17, 48, 72–73, 142
Peterson, Lieutenant Don x, 120–122
Petrus, Sergeant Richard 103–104
Philippines 14, 39–40, 77
Phipps, Sergeant North 103
Pilsen, Czechoslovakia 149, 250
Pinckney, Michigan 185
Ploesti, Rumania 36, 88, 146, 150–151
Po River 106–107

Poddington, England 62, 64–65
Poggi, John 39–41
Polebrook, England 201
Polk, LeAnn vii
Poltava, Ukraine 116, 118
Pomerania 216
Porto San Stefano, Italy 50
Potts, Captain J. Ivan, Jr. vii, x, 165–174
Poughkeepsie, New York 85
Prague, Czechoslovakia 196
Presque Isle, Maine 200
Pulaski, Tennessee 239

QDM's (distress signals) 8
Quantico, Virginia 80

Rackheath, England 175
Raft, George 52–53
Rangoon, Burma 20, 74, 180–181
Rankless Wreck 165–170
Raser, Sergeant Paul 152
Red Cross 95, 109, 210, 216, 227
Red Hot Rider 190–191
Reeder, Captain Bill ix, 68–71
Reeder, Sergeant Bud ix, 85–89
Reeder, Charlie 85–87
Regensburg, Germany 150, 193
relief tube 7, 12
Renville, Minnesota 120
Republic F-84 Thunderjet 25
Republic P-47 Thunderbolt 7, 84, 124, 227
Reykjavik, Iceland 200
Rheims, France 218
Rhine River 228
Richmond, Virginia 72
Rickman, Lieutenant Bill x, 102–104
Ridley, Tom vii
Ritchie, General William L. 119
Roberts, Sergeant Bill vii, x, 1, 142–147
Rogers, Ginger 52
Rogers, Jerry 61
Rogers, Roy 16
Rome, Italy 36, 106, 250–251
Rooney, William vii
Roosevelt, President Franklin D. 3, 96, 109, 234
Rourke, Sergeant Bob ix, 30–33
Royal Air Force (RAF) 70, 111–112, 153, 157, 163
Rugged Rosie 146–147
Russell, Ron vii
Ruston, Louisiana 112

Saarlautern, Germany 57
Saigon, South Vietnam 77–78, 136
St. Lô, France 176
St. Valentine Tank Works 144
Saipan 99, 137, 189, 191
Salerno, Italy 164
Salonika, Greece 248
Samate 123
San Giovanni, Italy 187, 193
San Pancrazio, Italy 34, 36, 48, 142, 144–145
Sanderson, Sergeant Bernard x, 129–131

Sangi Island 15
Santa Ana Air Base, California 143
Santa Monica, California 52
Sardinia 105
Sassy Susy 9
Savannah, Georgia 200
Sawyer, Lieutenant Don 144–147
Schade, Paul 133
Schley, Major Cooper x, 200–205
Schmeling, Max 109
Schneider, Helmut 95–97
School, Jerome 170
Schweighausen, Germany 28
Scott Field, Illinois 79
Scruggs, Jonny vii
Sebeka, Minnesota 229
Second Bomb Division 178
Shanghai, China 121
Shaw Field, South Carolina 12
Sheehan, Sergeant Bob x, 213–218
Shelbyville, Tennessee 165
Shepard, Lieutenant Arthur 134–135
Shepherd, Major Arthur 136–141
Sheppard Field, Texas 143
Shikoku Bay, Japan 166
Shore, Dinah 16
Shreeve, Sergeant George x, 233–238
Shulenberger, Lieutenant Arvid x, 134, 136–141
Shulenberger, Eric vii, 134
Sicily 162, 233
Sidate 15
Sioux Falls, South Dakota 30, 144
Slattery, Tom 32
Smart, Colonel Jacob 88–89
Smartt, Lieutenant Bob x, 148–149
Smartt, Tennessee 148
Smith, Larry vii
Smith, Yvonne vii
Smyrna, Tennessee 73
Snetterton Heath, England 5
Sofia, Bulgaria 151
Soldiers Medal 85, 88
Sorong, New Guinea 124
South Vietnam 10
Southampton, Long Island 114
Spaatz, General Carl 174, 203–204
Spanish Civil War 93
Sparks, Sergeant John 145
Sparta, Tennessee 175
Spittal/Drau 107
squint hop 134, 137–141
Stalag IV 216
Stalag 7A 206, 208
Stalag 17B 241–242
Stalag Luft 1 105–109
Stalag Luft 3 206, 208
Stalin, Joseph 3, 118–119
Stendal, Germany 178
Stevenson, Elbert 60
Stewart, Jimmy 90–91
Steyr, Austria 144
Stillwater, Oklahoma 110
STINKY 201
STINKY JR. 200–202, 204–205
Stinson L-1 Vigilant 75
Stinson L-5 Sentinel 75, 184
Stockholm, Sweden 155–156

Stovall, Colonel Hank 200
Stowmarket, England 82
Straits of Messina 164
Stuttgart, Arkansas 219
Stynes, Lieutenant Jim 211
Sudbury, England 244, 246
Suedekum, Captain Al x, 123–125
Sulmona, Italy 164
Sumney, Sergeant Suds 111
Sunday Punch 21–22
Sweden 154
Sweeney, Lieutenant Jack 111–112
Sweeney, Lieutenant William 114, 118
Swinemunde, Germany 217
Szczuczyn, Poland 117

Tarawa 12–13, 18
Targoviste, Rumania 37
Tedder, Air Marshall Arthur 203–204
Texas A&M University 49
Thorpe Abbots, England 126–127
Thurleigh, England 68
Tibenham, England 90, 213, 215
Tinian 137, 165, 168
Tobruk, Libya 107
Togian Islands 15
Tokyo 100, 121, 137
Tokyo Rose 15
Topeka, Kansas 176
Tortorella, Italy 151–152
Toulon, France 50
Townes, Bill 173
Trelon, France 128
Trieste, Italy 150
True magazine 136
Tucker, Ken vii
Tucson, Arizona 220–221
Tulane University 30
Tunisia, North Africa 162
Turin, Italy 197
Turner Field, Georgia 12
Tuscaloosa, Alabama 16
Tyrrhenian Sea 151

U.S. Air Force: Fifth Air Force 79, 81, 120, 123; Sixth Air Force 136; Seventh Air Force 16, 18; Eighth Air Force 5–6, 54, 62, 68, 82, 90, 102, 110, 113–114, 126, 148, 153, 160, 175, 200, 206, 213–214, 219, 224, 226–227, 239, 244; Ninth Air Force 162, 229; Tenth Air Force 19–20, 72, 180; Twelfth Air Force 25, 59, 105; Thirteenth Air Force 10, 39, 43–44, 47, 77; Fifteenth Air Force 30–31, 34–35, 37, 48–49, 85, 129, 142, 146, 150, 152, 185, 187, 192, 209, 233, 248–249; Twentieth Air Force 99, 132, 165, 171, 189
U.S. Air Force Groups: 7th Bomb Group 180; 12th Bomb Group 19–20, 72–74, 162; 22nd Bomb Group 170; 38th Bomb Group 79, 81, 123; 40th Bomb Group 165, 170–171; 42nd Bomb Group 44; 85th Bomb Group 82; 91st Bomb Group 223; 92nd Bomb Group 62, 201; 95th Bomb Group 160–161; 96th Bomb Group 5; 97th Bomb Group 85, 88, 200; 99th Bomb Group 150, 152; 100th Bomb Group 110, 126; 301st Bomb Group 209, 233; 305th Bomb Group 23–24; 306th Bomb Group 68; 307th Bomb Group 10, 15–16, 18, 39, 41–42, 77; 319th Bomb Group 105; 320th Bomb Group 25, 27, 59; 330th Bomb Group 132; 336th Bomb Group 160; 376th Bomb Group 1, 34, 48, 50, 142, 144, 146; 379th Bomb Group 219, 222; 385th Bomb Group 54, 110, 113; 387th Bomb Group 229–230; 389th Bomb Group 226; 401st Bomb Group 114, 119; 445th Bomb Group 90, 92, 213, 215; 446th Bomb Group 102; 454th Bomb Group 129, 185, 187, 192; 467th Bomb Group 175; 484th Bomb Group 30–31; 485th Bomb Group 248; 486th Bomb Group 244; 489th Bomb Group 239; 490th Bomb Group 184, 224; 491st Bomb Group 206; 492nd Bomb Group 153, 175–176; 497th Bomb Group 189; 499th Bomb Group 99; 801st Bomb Group 153
U.S. Air Force Squadrons: 85th Depot Repair 233; 548th Night Fighter 136
U.S. Cemetery, Cambridge 64
U.S. Corps of Engineers 175
U.S. Military Academy 90, 108, 249
U.S. strategic bombing campaign 1
University of Alabama 235
University of Georgia 62
University of Kansas 136
University of Kentucky 79–80
University of Michigan 54, 185
University of Minnesota 229
University of Oklahoma 112
University of Tennessee 246
University of Wisconsin 59

Van Hooser, David vii
Vance, Alabama 32
Vanderbilt University 44, 97, 246
Venosa, Italy 248
Victorville, California 16–17
Vienna, Austria 31, 34–35, 37, 146, 186–187, 192, 194
Vietnam War 121
Villers l-Hôpital, France 206
Vis, Yugoslavia 36, 235–236
Vistula River 115
Vultee BT-13 Valiant 20, 24–26

Wake Island 18
Walters, Captain Lyle 230
Warsaw, Poland 115–116
Washington, D.C. 170–174
Weiner Neustadt, Austria 88, 235
Wels, Austria 193, 195
Wemple, Major Neil 166
Wenzendorf airfield 57
Wescler, Major George 166
Wessington Springs, South Dakota 136
West Palm Beach, Florida 20
Wewak, New Guinea 80
Whaley, Lieutenant Jesse 103–104
Wheeler, Lieutenant J.P. 151–152
White, Lieutenant Jim vi, ix, 34–38
Whitehead, Sergeant Charles x, 132–135
Wilcox, Herbert 221
Williams, Lieutenant Harry, Jr. vii, ix, 62–67
Wilson, Tyler 27
Woliver, Lieutenant Robert 133–135
Woodward, Charlie 83
Woody Woodpecker 15
Wooten, Sergeant Bill 240
World War II Bomber Group of Middle Tennessee 1
Wright-Patterson Air Force Base 150
Wyrick, Ed vii

XXI Bomber Command 132

Yamato 42
Yeakos, Sergeant Chris 220
You Know Me, Al 136
Yugoslavia 32–33, 235–238
Yuma, Arizona 144

the zebra 92
Zuider Zee 69, 92